Optimizing Your Supply-Chain Performance

How to Assess and Improve Your Company's Strategy and Execution Capabilities

T0384029

Optimizing Your Supply-Chain Performance

How to Assess and Improve Your Company's Strategy and Execution Capabilities

By
Raymond Kelly

Routledge
Taylor & Francis Group

A PRODUCTIVITY PRESS BOOK

First edition published in 2020
by Routledge/Productivity Press
52 Vanderbilt Avenue, 11th Floor, New York, NY 10017
2 Park Square, Milton Park, Abingdon, Oxon OX14 4RN, UK

Routledge/Productivity Press is an imprint of Taylor & Francis Group, an Informa business

No claim to original U.S. Government works

Printed on acid-free paper

International Standard Book Number-13: 978-0-3672-0846-2 (Hardback)
International Standard Book Number-13: 978-0-3672-0844-8 (Paperback)
International Standard Book Number-13: 978-0-4292-6372-9 (eBook)

Visit the Taylor & Francis Web site at
http://www.taylorandfrancis.com

Contents

About the Author

Raymond (Ray) Kelly is the proud recipient of a BS degree in Operations Engineering from North Carolina State University.

Raymond is a seasoned Lean Six Sigma practitioner with over 25 years as a hands-on industry practitioner holding senior management positions in the US and Asia. His manufacturing employers have been Eaton Corporation (automotive), Telex Terminal Communications (computer peripherals), Northern Telecom (telecommunications), Cardinal Health (medical devices), and Littelfuse (electronics components). Raymond first became involved in just-in-time (lean) manufacturing in the early 1980s and holds several patents for pioneering work in developing manufacturing processes.

Additionally, Raymond has over 15 years' experience in management consultancy, developing subject matter expertise in lean manufacturing, Six Sigma deployment, and supply-chain optimization. He was employed by a few of the big consultancy firms: Coopers & Lybrand, PricewaterhouseCoopers, and Deloitte Consultancy. He has also owned his own consultancy business and worked as a freelance consultant. Raymond has provided his consultancy expertise to an extensive and diversified range of clients in more than 20 countries. His client list includes Hewlett-Packard, Texas Instruments, Manitowoc/Frymaster, Abbott Laboratories, Panasonic, Toshiba, Suzuki, Siemens, Infineon Technologies, Unilever, Mead-Johnson Nutrition, Royal Dutch Shell, and British Petroleum.

Raymond is a certified Lean Six Sigma Master Black Belt.

Raymond has a passion for leading companies in substantial supply-chain transformation initiatives. He has led over 100 initiatives resulting in annualized cost savings of over $200 million over a 15-year period.

Some of the quantitative results that Raymond has successfully facilitated include:

- 40–67% reduction overall process lead time
- 35–90% reduction in cycle times
- 33–65% reduction in raw material inventories
- 25–70% reduction in finished-goods inventories
- 50–72% reduction in work-in-process inventories
- 24–50% reduction in late deliveries
- 30–50% reduction in labor hours/unit
- 20–58% reduction in scrap rates
- 25–71% reduction in customer complaints
- 30–60% reduction in floor space
- 60–80% improvement in overall quality
- 30–97% reduction in setups/changeovers

The case-in-point examples (40) in this book reflect Raymond's hands-on experiences in leading supply-chain optimization initiatives. He is very proud of his accomplishments in the deployment of Lean Six Sigma tools and methodologies across a very extensive and diversified business landscape. The objective of this book is to share Raymond's successes, and a couple of failures, with you, so that you can optimize your company's supply-chain operations.

Chapter 1

Introduction

This is my second book with the intent of sharing my experiences as a management consultant and as an operational practitioner. The focus of this book is optimizing the end-to-end supply chain with an emphasis on supply management, inventory-management, manufacturing execution, and overall supply-chain optimization. I've also touched on the importance of business continuity, and I've provided some grassroots approaches to identifying risks.

I will be providing insight based on my extensive background of more than 40 years' experience, but I am not telling you what to do; my hope is that I'll be giving you a potentially different perspective, which will allow you to consider your situation (objectives and constraints) and then make decisions that fit your purpose.

And the case-in-point examples provide insight to actual real applications of concepts and methodologies. There are 40 case-in-point examples and more than 300 figures (e.g., pictures, diagrams, tables) included in this book.

I have over 27 years' experience as an industry practitioner and another 13 years as a management consultant. And I think consultants are often perceived in a bad way, but during my days as a consultant, I learned far more about data analytics than I ever did as an industry practitioner. And I take a lot of pride in my direct hands-on manufacturing and supply-chain operations background. But industry practitioners don't always challenge their perceptions, their legacy-barriers, and so on, and companies are often resistant to going for breakthrough changes. And that's where I think that companies fail in optimizing their operations, as it's difficult to break old paradigms because we have a hard time viewing data differently than in very traditional ways.

In this book, I'm going to discuss many analytical tools and methodologies with case-in-point examples for them all. Some may not be new to you, but I suspect that many will be. I have seen many tools and methodologies commonly misapplied, but I think that the case-in-point examples that I have provided will show effective ways to use the tools and methodologies. It should take you from not understanding a tool or methodology to it becoming simple and, basically, common sense for you.

Some of the analytical tools and methodologies that I've included are:

■ A-B-C Stratifications
  – This is a concept that is very often misunderstood and misapplied
■ Lean Building Blocks (many are trying, and many are failing)
  – Value-Added and Non-Value-Added
  – Pure Waste
  – Cellular Manufacturing
■ Routing-by-Walking-Around
  – Spaghetti Diagram
  – Yamazumi Chart
■ Triple-Play
■ Supply Management: Commodity and Spend Analysis
■ Kraljic Matrix
■ Value Stream Mapping
  – Kaizens
  – Benefit and effort
■ Inventory-Management Systems
  – Lean techniques
  – K_{max}-K_{min} Kanban System
  – CONWIP System
  – WIP Cap
■ Manufacturing Execution Strategy
  – Rhythm/Pattern Production
  – Every-Product-Every-Interval (EPEI)
■ Business Continuity
  – SWOT
  – Fishbone
  – FMEA
■ Oliver Wight Business Excellence Checklist

Chapter 2

A-B-C Stratification/ Applications

Introduction: Pareto and Juran

Figure 2.1 displays a couple of the most common applications of A-B-C stratification.

"A-B-C Stratification" is a methodology that I will repeatedly use throughout this book, as it is an important concept that I find necessary to reference across various supply-chain optimization techniques.

"A-B-C Stratification" is a derivative of the Pareto Principle, which originates from the economic analysis by Vilfredo Pareto in Italy during the early 1900s. He made an observation that 80% of the land in Italy was owned by about 20% of the population, and this later was referred to as the Pareto Distribution. And Pareto hypothesized that this distribution (80–20) would be consistent everywhere and across varied applications, but especially with wealth distribution. And it then began to be known as the "80–20 Rule." The "80–20 Rule," basically, means that 80% of the effects come from 20% of the causes.

Some potential examples/applications of the "rule" in supply-chain operations are:

- 20% of a company's stock keeping units (SKUs) account for 80% of the company's inventory (value, days-on-hand, demand, etc.)
- 20% of a company's purchased items (#) equates to 80% of the company's total spend ($)

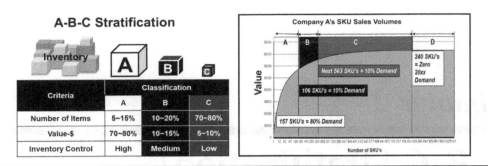

Figure 2.1 A-B-C Stratification.

- 80% of your output is the result of 20% of your actions (inputs)
- 80% of a company's revenue is derived from 20% of the company's product
- 80% of a company's defects are created on 20% of the company's product

In 1937, Dr. Joseph Juran ultimately conceptualized the Pareto Principle based on Vilfredo Pareto's earlier works, and Juran used this as a management principle to get folks to separate the "vital few" from the trivial many." There have been recent movements to officially change the Pareto Principle to the Juran Principle, as Juran, surely, changed the applicability of the principle from an often-misused/misunderstood generalizing principle to a quality or management technique of simply focusing on the vital few, i.e., deciding what has the biggest impact and focusing on that rather than being distracted by the many other things that have a far lesser impact. But as you decide on what's vital, Juran was also a firm believer in making your decisions based on data, not "feelings." Juran has, famously, been cited for having once showed a classroom a dollar bill that has the engraving "In God We Trust" and then informing his students that "yes, in God we trust, but everyone else must bring data."

Figure 2.2 reflects how an 80–20 analysis would be graphed. This example reflects the plotting of SKUs against Demand Volume.

And another of Pareto's namesakes is the Pareto Chart, and this chart has a far stronger alliance with Juran than Pareto. The primary function of a Pareto Chart is to identify the vital few from the trivial many. The basis of the Pareto Chart is that it's a type of chart that contains columns and a line graph, where the columns of individual values are represented in descending order by bars, and the cumulative total is represented by the line. The

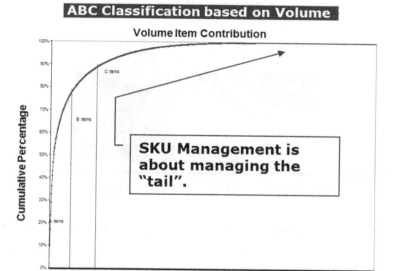

Figure 2.2   Example of 80–20 Graphical Analysis.

purpose of the Pareto Chart is to highlight the most important among a (typically large) set of factors. So, if you're charting the causes of issues such as late shipments, inventory errors, documentation errors, customer complaints, shipment damage, quality defects, etc., then it would seem logical to address the top two or three most frequent causes (reasons), i.e., the vital few.

A-B-C Stratification and Inventory-Management and Procurement Strategies

A couple of the best applications of A-B-C stratification are Inventory Management and Procurement Strategies. In Inventory-Management, you're basically using the Pareto Principle; you can expect that approximately 20% of your SKUs will equal 80% of the demand consumption. So, determine your 20% point and that represents the "vital few," and this is where your focus should be, i.e., the "As." "C"s would be the majority of SKUs, approximately 70% but only about 5–10% of the annual demand; "B"s would be approximately 10% of your SKUs and 5–10% of the annual demand. A-B-C allows you to establish different replenishment strategies, safety-stock calculations, Days-on-Hand (DOH) stocking targets, cycle-count schemes, etc., for each of the A-B-C stratifications (see Figure 2.3).

A-B-C Stratification

Criteria	Classification		
	A	B	C
Number of Items	5~15%	10~20%	70~80%
Value-$	70~80%	10~15%	5~10%
Inventory Control	High	Medium	Low

Figure 2.3   A-B-C Stratification and Inventory-Management.

For Procurement Strategies, your "A"s would be approximately 20% of your SKUs, which should equate to about 80% of your annual spend; again, your vital few. In Procurement, you would want to differentiate your procurement (acquisition) method, inventory targets, replenishment scheme, etc., strategies based on the A-B-C stratification. A key reason for doing this is that typically (traditionally) your acquisition costs will be the same for each SKU or commodity, so a typical scenario could be that a purchase order is costing you $500 to administer, and you'd be spending this for your vital few as well as your trivial many. But common sense tells you that you must reduce your acquisition costs for the trivial many; you must consider a vendor-managed scheme, etc. (see Figure 2.4).

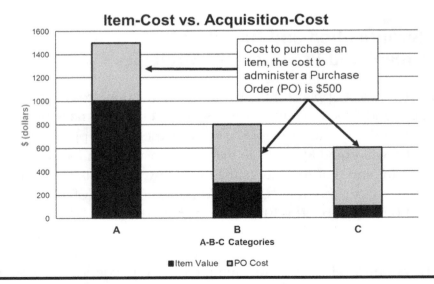

Figure 2.4   A-B-C Stratification and Purchasing Strategies.

Case-in-Point 2.1: Product Portfolio Analysis (A-B-C Analysis)

Company: A Japanese multinational electronics OEM corporation

Background: This was a consultancy client and the stated objective of this Supply Chain Operational Optimization project was "to reduce cost and process lead times within the Manufacturing, Procurement, Planning and Quality areas through the introduction of industry best practices, the simplification and standardization of processes, efficiency improvements, and the reduction in inventory levels."

Scope: The project scope would be limited to an OEM consumer product manufactured at several facilities in the state capital area of Malaysia. The product is manufactured for domestic consumption, although certain models would be exported to a few neighboring Asian countries.

Project Approach: One application of A-B-C Analysis in the assessment phase of a transformation initiative is a Product Portfolio Analysis. Our initial high-level assessment revealed that this site had an amazing thirteen-hundred plus (1,300) finished products SKUs for its residential air-conditioning portfolio. That seems to be an excessive array of air-conditioning products. Maintaining a high variable portfolio of any product comes with high overhead costs, so an initial analysis of a diversified, extensive portfolio such as this is an A-B-C stratification-based annual demand (sales volume) for each SKU.

We created an Excel spreadsheet of all Finished-Goods SKUs versus the sales volume generated by each SKU, and then we sorted the SKUs (in Excel) by sales volume (highest to lowest), and then we added an Excel column that will be the percent of total sales volume that each SKU represents. So now we have a nice baseline: each SKU, its annual sales volume and the percent of total sales volume attributed to each SKU. To start the analysis, we'll create a new Excel column that will represent the accumulative sales volume for the full portfolio of individual SKUs, and then the final spreadsheet development task is to create an accumulative summary of the total sales volume (see Figure 2.5).

No	SKU	Item Description	Sales-Volume	% Sales-Volume	Cumulative Sales-Volume	Cumulative %
1	xxxx-01-10421	Item xxxxxx	2402061	2.83%	2402061	2.8%
2	xxxx-01-01141	Item xxxxxx	2033070	2.40%	4435131	5.2%
3	xxxx-01-00011	Item xxxxxx	1886864	2.23%	6321995	7.5%
4	xxxx-01-10001	Item xxxxxx	1818094	2.14%	8140089	9.6%
5	xxxx-10-00020	Item xxxxxx	1596000	1.88%	9736089	11.5%
6	xxxx-15-10008	Item xxxxxx	1153778	1.36%	10889867	12.8%

Figure 2.5   Excerpt from an Example Excel A-B-C Stratification Analysis.

The results of the sales-based stratification revealed 50% of the company's revenue came from only 56 SKUs (i.e., less than 5% of the active SKUs). The full A-B-C stratification broke the classifications down as follows:

- 157 SKUs were classified as "A"s, which equated to about 15% of the total SKUs that produced about 80% of the historical demand (a.k.a. revenue).
- 106 SKUs were classified as "B"s, which equated to about 10% of the total SKUs that produced about 10% of the demand.
- 563 SKUs were classified as "C"s, which equated to about 53% of the total SKUs that produced about 10% of the demand.
- There were 240 SKUs that are "active" but have no demand over the past 12-months, so we classified these as "D"s, and these 240 SKU accounted for about 22% of the total SKUs but zero demand/revenue.
- We benchmarked a strong regional competitor and found that the competitor obtained approximately 80% of its revenue from only seven models, a vast contrast from our client.

Figure 2.6 is a graphical summary of the product portfolio stratification.

To summarize the A-B-C Analysis, there has been a proliferation of new product SKUs without obsoleting any SKUs. The huge range of SKUs was intended to provide an arrange of options that are perceived to meet the customers' needs.

So the next step was to take a deeper dive into these model options. Figure 2.7 reflects the product tree for the 157 SKUs.

The next step was the most critical to the final resolution. We conducted a Voice-of-Customer (VoC) at several retail locations. We interviewed (and

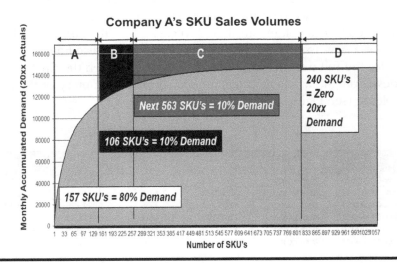

Figure 2.6 Product Portfolio Stratification.

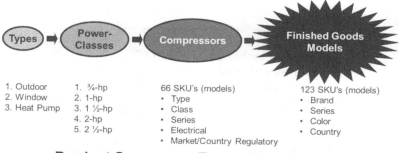

Product Component Tree – 157 "A" SKUS

Figure 2.7 "A" Product Component Tree.

videotaped) potential buyers as they evaluated their potential selections on price, manufacturer, brand, options, etc. And after several days on retail-site interviews, we visited a couple of purchasers of the client's units by searching warranty-registration data.

The overwhelming consensus of our VoC was that existing and potential customers weren't all that enamored by the large selection of units and seemingly unlimited options; they all wanted basic functions (power, quiet, energy-efficient, simple-to-operate, and at a great price). And this information was reinforced as we benchmarked our client against their co-market leader, as their co-market leader only offered seven SKUs of their "A" units versus our client's 157 SKUs.

This data resulted in our client revamping their product platform/portfolio and vastly reducing their product offerings. The 240 SKUs with zero volume would be officially discontinued, and they had a target to reduce the remaining 826 SKUs by 60% minimum. And as a final step, we initiated an assessment of their new product introduction and design processes, and we proposed steps (policies, procedures, and process changes) to standardize their product platform and limit variations to the standard platform. And the revised product platform was based on the VoC findings.

Case-in-Point 2.2: Savings $-Millions from A-B-C Stratification

Company: Japanese FMCG manufacturer
Background: One of the company's Asian manufacturing and distribution networks was performing at a 60% customer-service level. Failing to have the right items at the right quantity at the right time is projected to result in about $20 million in lost sales per year.

The assessment determined that there was no planning and management based on the "vital few" against the "trivial many," and it further revealed that they were clogging their supply chain with too much "A" inventory.

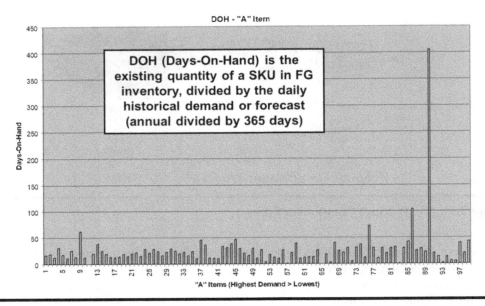

Figure 2.8 "A" Product Inventory: Days-on-Hand.

The amount of inventory being held for "A" items was sporadic, and there were no policies in place to manage it.

Figure 2.8 shows a snapshot of the days-on-hand (DOH) for "A" items; the variance across the SKUs was significant, with a range of zero (i.e., stockout) to more than 400 days.

A policy was developed to established inventory levels based on A-B-C; the new inventory targets were:

■ "A"s = 1 week of inventory held
■ "B"s = 1 month of inventory held
■ "C"s = 3 months of inventory held

Figure 2.9 shows the impact the new policy had on the items, i.e., a bottom-line inventory reduction equivalent to US$5.2 million.

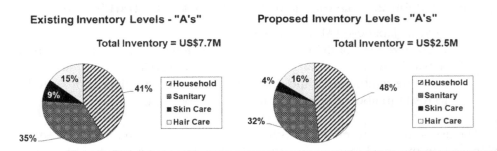

Figure 2.9 "A" Product Inventory Reduction Impact.

Results

Inventory Reduction	~40%
Carrying Cost Savings	US$1.7-million
Inventory Turns	25 from 10
Warehouse Expense Reduction	US$12.2k/month
Obsolete Inventory	US$0.5-million
Carrying Cost	US$0.08-million

Figure 2.10   Summary Results: Inventory-Management Policy for "A"s.

Current Inventory   US$ 11.4-million
Annual Carrying Cost   US$1.7-million

Proposed Concept: Apply "A-B-C" Inventory/Production Strategy

Inventory Levels (Targets)

A	1-week inventory	**Manufacturing focuses efforts on "A's"**
B	1-month inventory	
C	3-month inventory	**Benefits are substantial!**

Inventory-$ As-Is vs. To-Be

	As-Is	To-Be
A	$7.7M	$2.5M
B	$1.97M	$2.04M
C	$1.71M	$2.02M
Total	$11.4M	$6.5M

Figure 2.11   Summary Results: Inventory-Management Policy for "A-B-C"s.

The proposed changes result in a 40% reduction in overall inventory.

Figure 2.10 summarizes the benefits from the new inventory-management policy for "A"s.

Figure 2.11 summarizes the overall strategy for A-B-C inventory target levels.

Case-in-Point 2.3: Pareto Chart Analysis

I want to give a simple example of how to utilize a Pareto Chart.

The scenario for this example is that I was faced with a problem to solve – a problem of excessive process lead time for housing renovations for an oil and gas client. It was currently taking 114 days to turn over housing for its expatriate employees.

So we simply broke the process into activity buckets and then constructed a Pareto Chart of the "buckets" in order to focus improvement efforts on the "vital few."

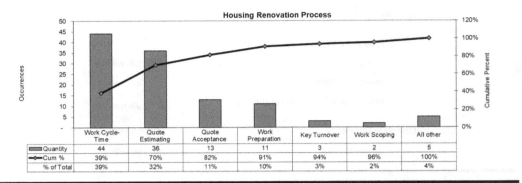

Figure 2.12   Example Pareto Chart - Identifying the Vital Few versus Trivial Many.

From the Pareto, Figure 2.12, the top three contributors to the Process Lead Time were:

1. Renovations Work Lead Time (i.e., time to do actual renovation). A good sign that it was #1. 39% of Total Process Lead Time.
2. Quote Estimating by Contractors 32% of Total Process Lead Time.
3. Quote Acceptance 11% of Total Process Lead Time.

So these three activities were 42% of the process activities and accounted for 82% of the Total Process Lead Time, and after this simple analysis it was very clear where the improvement effort should be concentrated.

Chapter 3

Supply-Chain Management

Supply-Chain Management Introduction

> All we are doing is looking at the timeline, from the moment the
> customer gives us an order to the point when we collect the cash.
> And we are reducing the time line by reducing the non-value
> adding-wastes.

> **– Taiichi Ohno, father of Toyota Production System (TPS)**

The above quote, circa the mid-1980s, was Ohno's answer to a question
regarding "what Toyota was doing." This quote could be construed to
mean that Ohno was strictly referring to the cash to cash cycle; i.e., buying and paying for material, utilizing cash and resources to convert material and labor into a product, and delivering that product to the customer
and receiving payment for it (i.e., closing the cash-loop). But I think that his
quote was looking at the broader picture; i.e., that the end-to-end Order-
Fulfillment Process's lead time can be reduced (i.e., optimized) by eliminating non-value-added activities. And that should be the prime objective of
supply-chain management: to optimize by continuously eliminating non-
value-added activities throughout the supply chain. Eliminating
non-value-added activities from a company's supply chain assists that company in maximizing its customers' value while utilizing minimal resources
(see Figure 3.1).

The performance of a company's supply chain can be a key to a company's success or its failure. A highly efficient and responsive supply chain can
be leveraged as a competitive advantage, whereas a poorly performing supply

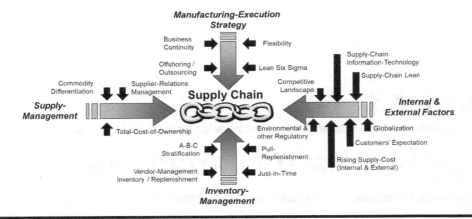

Figure 3.1   Supply-Chain Influencers.

chain can be leveraged against you. Supply-chain development continues to be driven by growing customer expectations, e.g., increased responsiveness to demand fluctuations, shorter lead times, almost perfect delivery reliability, perfect, error-free orders (i.e., defect-free products and documentation).

So how do we manage and improve our supply chain? What comprises supply-chain management?

Supply-Chain Management (SCM) can be described as follows:

- Managing the broad range of activities required to plan, control, and execute a product's flow, from acquiring raw materials and manufacturing execution through distribution to the final customer, in the most streamlined and cost-effective way possible.
- The management of the flow of goods and services involves the movement and storage of raw materials, of work-in-process inventory, and of finished goods from point-of-origin to point-of-consumption.

Additionally, SCM can be further characterized as the design, planning, execution, control, and monitoring of supply-chain activities *with the following objectives*:

- Creating maximum value for its customers while utilizing the minimum amount of resources.
- Developing and sustaining a competitive infrastructure.
- Synchronizing supply with demand across the supply chain.
- Effectively measuring end-to-end supply-chain performance, thus driving continuous improvement.

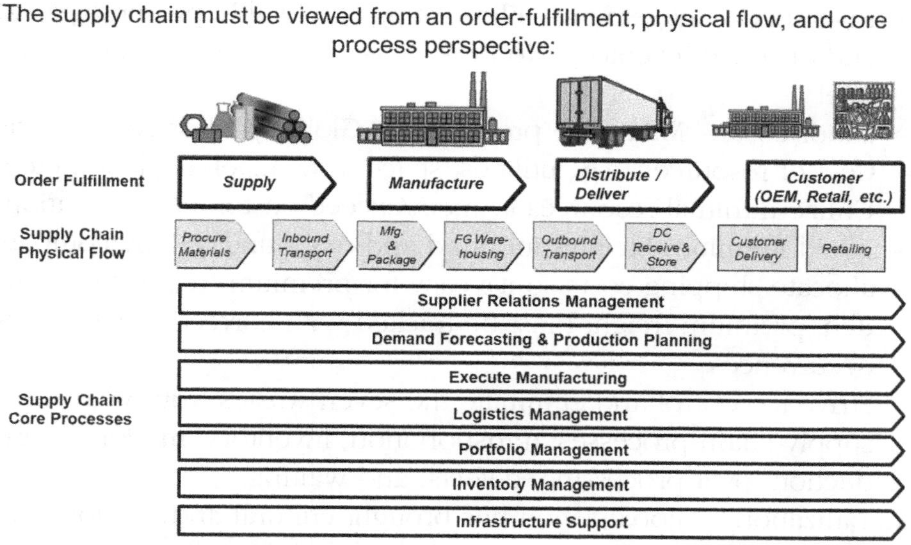

The supply chain must be viewed from an order-fulfillment, physical flow, and core process perspective:

Order Fulfillment	*Supply*	*Manufacture*	*Distribute / Deliver*	*Customer (OEM, Retail, etc.)*

Supply Chain Physical Flow	*Procure Materials*	*Inbound Transport*	*Mfg. & Package*	*FG Warehousing*	*Outbound Transport*	*DC Receive & Store*	*Customer Delivery*	*Retailing*

Supply Chain Core Processes

- Supplier Relations Management
- Demand Forecasting & Production Planning
- Execute Manufacturing
- Logistics Management
- Portfolio Management
- Inventory Management
- Infrastructure Support

Figure 3.2   Supply-Chain Model.

Supply-chain and order fulfillment are often viewed as interchangeable terms; but order fulfillment is best defined as the steps involved in receiving, processing, and delivering orders to end customers; and this covers the administrative activities associated with the order-fulfillment process. The supply chain (see Figure 3.2) encompasses the order-fulfillment process, the physical flow of materials and products, and the core support processes. Order fulfillment is the process required to obtain the necessary material for an "order," manufacture the requirements of the "order" and deliver the "order" to the order's customer. And the order-fulfillment process is not completed until payment is received from the customer for the order received. One of the key objectives of SCM is the synchronization of the supply with the demand throughout every element of the order-fulfillment process.

And in today's SCM environment, we're facing some momentous challenges. Some of the major trends in business right now are low-cost country sourcing, outsourcing, customization, globalization, and even onshoring; all create tremendous complexities and increased-challenges throughout the supply-chain operations. And a company's success is probably dependent on how effective it strategizes to circumvent and/or conquer these challenges. These daunting challenges include:

■ Rising Supply-Chain Costs – It's imperative that companies monitor and manage their supply costs, such as:

- Inventory-management – Eliminating (preferably preventing) excess and obsolete inventory. No just-in-case inventories. Inventory is not free!
- Labor costs – Maximize productivity. Globally labor costs are rising.
- Cost of resources (e.g., utilities, space, raw materials, labor, etc.) – Utilize minimal resources to meet/exceed customer expectations.
- Avoid Premium Freight (inbound and outbound). Many companies allocate shipping costs so it's easy for premium freight to get hidden; premium freight must be tracked with corrective actions for its occurrences.
- Strive to control and eliminate the seven wastes from your supply-chain processes: transportation, inventory, motion, overproduction, over-processing, defects, and waiting.

■ Globalization – Globalization has brought cultural and economic challenges as companies extend their supply chains beyond their national borders and deal with suppliers and customers around the world. Supply chains have become borderless because their processes can span the world. One of the largest challenges of globalization is understanding other nations' *culture*, laws, customs, and business practices. Ignorance can be deadly in business relationships and extremely costly in many ways. I've worked in 23 countries; don't underestimate this challenge. (See *Case-in-Point 3.1.*)

■ Responsiveness to meet customer expectations (increasing demand volatility increases customer need for responsiveness) – Customers are demanding responsiveness and flexibility in accommodating their demand volatility. They are requiring short lead times and even shorter frozen-order constraints. A company's ability to deliver products and services to the market quicker than their competitors has become an advantage, especially in markets where low price and high quality are expected and have ceased to be market differentiators themselves. (See *Case-in-Point 3.2.*)

■ Sustainability – Sustainability refers to a company's processes, products, and services being aligned in a way that is socially, economically, and environmentally responsible. Companies must consider a product's full life cycle; i.e., cradle to grave. Companies must control the inputs, outputs, and technologies used in the manufacturing transformation processes.

- It's no longer optional for a company to actively reduce its carbon footprint; instead, supply-chain organizations must become sustainable and socially responsible if they hope to thrive or even survive. Social responsibility is becoming more and more significant in buyers' considerations when making sourcing/purchasing decisions. A best-in-class supply-chain organization should have a measurable framework of policies and procedures designed to improve the workplace for the greater good of employees, the company, and the community. (See *Case-in-Point 3.3.*)

▪ Collaborative work – Collaboration may be called a challenge, but I see it more as a requirement for being successful throughout your supply chain. Collaboration must include customers, suppliers, and stakeholders throughout your supply chain. Collaborative relationships must replace adversarial relationships

Supply-Chain Lean

So one of the challenges for SCM is the relentless pursuit of removing waste and minimizing non-value-added activities from all supply-chain/order-fulfillment processes.

Identifying waste and non-value-added activities within the order-fulfillment process/supply-chain model begins with defining each waste. Typically, we refer to seven categories of waste and use the acronym TIMWOOD to assist in remembering them. The seven wastes are commonly known as Transportation, Inventory, Motion, Wait, Overproduction, Over-Processing, and Defects (see Figure 3.3).

TIMWOOD as it relates to supply chain functions:

▪ Transportation Waste: The excessive and/or repetitive movement of material within warehouses, within manufacturing, to/from different sites and/or facilities. Optimized facility layouts can help alleviate excessive transportation.

▪ Inventory Waste: Any inventory that's not destined to fill a firm customer demand is a waste. Inventory and Manufacturing must be synchronized with true demand to minimize inventory waste. Inventory waste can lead to longer lead times (more Work-in-Progress [WIP]), obsolete inventory, excessive cost to preserve and store excess inventory, etc. And here's another interesting quote from the father of the Toyota Production System, Taiichi Ohno, *"The more inventory a company has, the less likely they will have what*

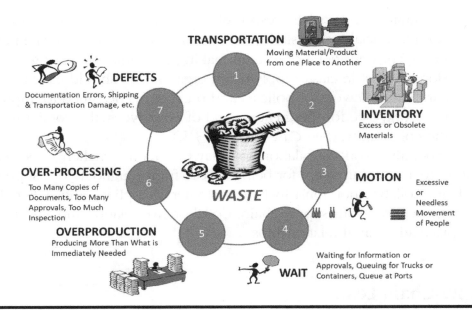

Figure 3.3 TIMWOOD (Seven Wastes).

they need." And my more than 40 years' experience fully supports Ohno's quote.

- Motion Waste: The excessive body movement by a person in completing the required task. This is often a symptom of poor ergonomics, poor workstation/workplace layout, or transferring items from one container to another.
- Wait Waste: The waste of waiting for anything, e.g., equipment queue, WIP (i.e., Little's Law), approvals or signatures, information arrival, inbound/outbound queueing, seaport schedule queueing, any type of queueing, etc.
- Overproduction Waste: Often the result of non-synchronized supply and demand. Overproduction results in excess inventory and other wastes such as transportation (inventory movement), defects (poor inventory preservation), waiting (slow-moving overproduced inventory or queueing for transportation), etc.
- Over-Processing Waste: Doing more than doing the very minimum to successfully execute a task. Over-processing could be the repeating of any activity that was not performed correctly the first time. This classification of over-processing could also be defined as a "defect." Figure 3.4 shows examples of "the Killer Re's" (i.e., repeated activities). Also, Figure 3.5 "The Non-Value-Added Dictionary," shows non-value-adding verbs that may be the result of over-processing activities.

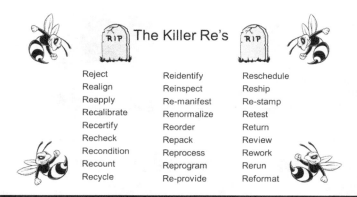

The Killer Re's

Reject	Reidentify	Reschedule
Realign	Reinspect	Reship
Reapply	Re-manifest	Re-stamp
Recalibrate	Renormalize	Retest
Recertify	Reorder	Return
Recheck	Repack	Review
Recondition	Reprocess	Rework
Recount	Reprogram	Rerun
Recycle	Re-provide	Reformat

Figure 3.4   The Killer Re's: Non-Value-Adding Activities.

- Defect Waste: The longer that materials are stored, the higher the risk that the material can be damaged (or even pilfered). Defects can also be caused by damage from transportation which may lead to scrap and/or rework. Defects are also documentation errors, inaccurate part counts, improperly labeled items, etc.

A non-value-added activity is any activity that doesn't add value to the item for the customer. Typically, we'll simply define a non-value-added activity as one that the customer would not be willing to pay for. Another simple definition of a non-value-added activity is an activity that doesn't change the form, fit, or function of an item.

Figure 3.5 shows examples of non-value-added verbs; a verb is a word that means that an action is taking place, but these actions are non-value-adding actions. Also, the prefix "re" typically means doing something again and doing something for a second or multiple times. Figure 3.4 shows "The Killer Re's," all non-value-adding "re's."

The Non-Value-Added Dictionary

Adjusts	Eliminates	Delivers	Selects
Approves	Expedites	Distributes	Set-Up
Assigns	File	Measures	Stage
Changes	Identifies	Monitors	Updates
Collects	Inspects	Moves	Verify
Copies	Issues	Load	Wait-for
Validate	Maintain	Unload	Collates

Figure 3.5   The Non-Value-Added Dictionary.

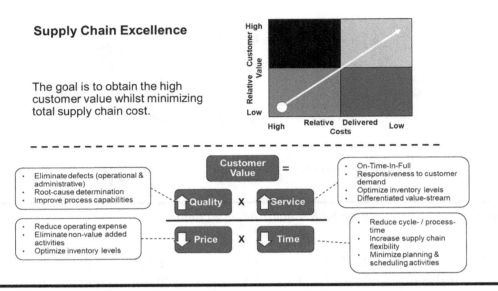

Supply Chain Excellence

The goal is to obtain the high customer value whilst minimizing total supply chain cost.

Figure 3.6 Supply-Chain Excellence.

Additionally, supply-chain management excellence can be measured by the cost required to deliver the highest levels of customer value at the lowest delivered cost. The goal is to deliver the highest value possible at the lowest possible cost. Figure 3.6 highlights aspects of highest customer value at the lowest cost.

In my more than 40 years' experience, I have found that most companies don't put enough effort into defining an overall supply-chain strategy. Companies seem to create bits and pieces of supply-chain strategy but seldom create a robust strategy that will create a competitive advantage by leveraging their supply-chain capabilities. Many companies will create a supply-chain "vision" but don't develop a detailed deployment plan, and most companies will create some supply-chain performance targets around delivery, inventory levels, etc., but seldom include associated staff development plans.

Supply-Chain Management Best Practices

Best practices are methods or techniques that have consistently shown results superior to those achieved with other means. SCM best practices are usually based on safety, quality, time, and money (Safer, Better, Faster, and Cheaper!), such as:

■ *Supply-Chain Council* – One recent "best practice" trend is the establishment of an internal Supply-Chain Council (a.k.a. Supply-Chain Governing Council) within a corporation. The purpose of this governing council is to drive the supply-chain strategy throughout the corporation. Without an internal council of leaders in place, your supply-chain effort may lack a clear strategy for efficiency and functionality; i.e., your efforts may be ineffective and not achieve the overall success of a well-organized governed team. Key activities of the Supply-Chain Council would be:

- Ensure alignment of the supply-chain strategy and the overall corporate strategy/vision and provide direction for deployment of the strategy.
- Establish regular reviews to ensure efficiency and mitigate risk. Risk mitigation in the supply chain must include identifying all elements of risk, evaluating the probability of occurrence, estimating the potential financial impact in the event of an incident, and prioritizing risks for appropriate monitoring and prevention measures.
- Assist in removing any barriers to the deployment of the strategy that may arise.
- Foster internal organizational buy-in that is needed to be an effective supply-chain organization.
- Drive standardization of best practices and performance metrics across the global enterprise.
- Ensure development of supply-chain management skills throughout global supply management organizations.

■ *Increase Inventory Velocity* – Inventory-management is a core element of SCM, but it would be a best practice to focus on inventory velocity. Inventory must move quickly; turns should be high. Inventory should be synchronized to flow from suppliers to manufacturing sites to customers as quickly as possible. Being inventory-rich and cash-poor is not a sound business approach; today, you want to be inventory-lean with the shortest possible cash to cash cycle possible. And this is especially so for "A" items. "A" products and materials sitting in warehouses should be limited as much as possible.

- Inventory velocity impacts operational cost, and all companies obviously desire to reduce costs and improve their bottom line; thus, supply-chain management should consistently look at optimizing its inventory quantities. There are very real costs associated with holding and storing inventory, i.e., inventory carrying-costs. Inventory carrying-cost is, most often, referred to as a percentage of the inventory's value. This percentage would include taxes, associated employee costs (material handling, etc.), depreciation, insurance, and the various costs to keep items in storage (space, security, preservation, etc.). Inventory carrying-costs have traditionally been accepted to be in the 8–12% range; but there are reports that reveals that inventory carrying-costs are more realistically calculated to be 20–25% of the inventory's value. Although in the case of items stored 12 months or more, the true inventory carrying-cost most likely represents up to 60% of the value of an item.

■ *Lean Supply-Chain Management* – The emphasis of Lean supply chain management is the identification and elimination of waste (see challenges above). And the concept for creating a Lean supply chain is pulling, not pushing, items through the supply chain (i.e., synchronizing supply with demand). Supply-chain models of "push type" and "pull type" are opposite in terms of a demand and supply relationship. "Push type" is represented by "make-to-inventory" (i.e., just-in-case inventory) in which the production is not based on actual demand; and "pull type" which is represented by "make-to-demand or -order," in which the production is based on actual customer demand.

  – Lean also recognizes the waste created by excess inventory, i.e., waste from increased transportation, motion, waiting, and defects (damaged or obsolete materials) as well as the need for superior supplier performance (quality and delivery).

    Compressed Process Lead Time (PLT) – The Order Fulfillment PLT, the time from the receipt of the order until the manufactured product, is in the hand of the orderer (buyer), should be continuously compressed through Lean waste elimination and other Lean concepts, e.g., Little's Law (WIP reduction), setup reductions, Overall Equipment Effectiveness (OEE) optimization, cellular manufacturing, visual management, etc. (see Figure 3.7).

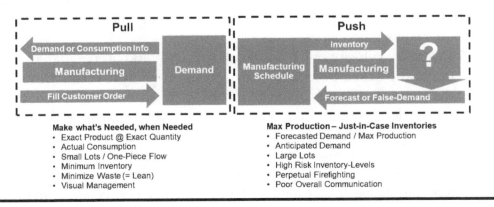

Figure 3.7   Lean: Push versus Pull.

■ *Supply Relations Management* – Maintain healthy supplier relationships. An important indicator of success in this industry is the health
of your supplier relationships. These connections should be maintained and cultivated on an ongoing basis, beyond the finalization of
your deal. The best supplier relationships are the ones with two-way
communication between the buyer and seller. Your objectives should
include mechanism(s) to maintain the health of your relationship, goals
for continuing improvement and value, performance measurement,
and a platform for conflict resolution. (*See Chapter 4 – Supply Relations
Management.*)

   – Improving supplier performance is in many ways a catalyst to a
   supply chain's success; and probably more precisely, poor supplier
   performance can doom a supply chain. Suppliers must deliver quality items within the required timeline, and proactive collaboration
   can be a prime enabler for this. The need for strong supplier performance must not be understated.

   – Contract Management – Savings are often negotiated during the
   procurement process, but they are rarely fully realized. This is
   most commonly because of a lapse in communication or lack of
   follow through on contract compliance. To combat this and realize those cost savings, as a best practice, companies are moving contract management under the supply-chain management
   and more specifically under supplier relations management.
   This allows the supply-chain management team to leverage its
   spend where there's a greater opportunity for reducing costs and
   mitigating risk.

   – Segment the Supply Chain, i.e., differentiate! Too many companies
   have one supply-chain approach for everything. This ineffective
   monolithic approach handicaps performance, wastes resources, and
   distracts the supply-chain organization (i.e., need to focus on the
   critical-few rather than be distracted by the trivial many). The best
   practice is to segment their supply after differentiating their commodities based on customer impact and supply risks. Instead of
   practicing one-size-fits-all supply-chain management, they manage
   based on business impact and supply risk.

■ *Utilize Meaningful Metrics* (a balanced scorecard) – There are numerous
measures for companies and their supply chains, but many (possibly
most) are measures for the sake of metrics with little "executable" purpose and without value in really measuring supply-chain performance

and driving continuous supply-chain improvement. To create a balanced scorecard, you should follow these guidelines:

- Metrics must drive improvement in safety, quality, delivery, cost and employee morale.
- All KPIs (Key Performance Indicators) are aligned with the overall business objectives of your company.
- Each KPI must have an "owner," whether that is an individual or a group of people.
- Design each KPI as a leading metric (rather than a trailing metric) so it would enable predicting of performance issues.
- KPIs should be actionable, providing timely, accurate data that process owners can interpret and appropriately react to.
- Each KPI should reinforce and/or balance others.
- Don't have KPIs that could potentially drive the wrong behavior.
- Each KPI should have a target or threshold indicating a minimum acceptable level of performance.

■ *Employ Supply-Chain Technology* – To be honest, I'm not a huge IT fan; as I think a lot can be accomplished through a robust pull-replenishment system and effective visual management. But providing visibility of inventory, order-status, etc., throughout the entire supply chain may assist in enabling a company in managing the customer, purchases/supply status, and/or manufacturing status through to delivery. Identify areas where technology can help improve and streamline processes.

■ *The Supply-Chain Organization* – Establish an appropriate and thoughtfully staffed supply-chain structure. Ideally, your supply chain will be staffed and structured in a way that maximizes effectiveness as well as efficiency to bring the most benefit to your organization. Most organizations these days find that a centralized strategy, implemented by specialized managers in their various business units, is the most optimal approach (this is a debatable item, as I have seen many centralized supply-chain organizations that are counterproductive and useless), but in theory, a certain amount of centralization would be desired. Reportedly, this combination leads to more harmony between strategy and implementation while also resulting in the best service. In staffing your supply chain, you should be more focused on strategy than simply transactional ability with your top leadership. These leaders should extend this strategic thinking toward creating value using strong interpersonal skills (such as communication and relationship management) internally as well as externally (see *Case-in-Point 4.2.*)

■ *Total Cost of Ownership* (TCO) – Best practice in procurement is to look at total cost of ownership rather than purchase price. Best-in-class companies have moved away from the procurement practice of selecting a supplier based completely on price. Instead, strategic sourcing involves understanding the total cost of ownership/consumption of a product. As a rule of thumb, the cost of acquisition for most products is only approximately 25 to 40% of the TCO, while the remaining percentage is comprised of operating, warehousing, and transportation costs, etc.

Supply-Chain Management Metrics

Metrics must drive improvement in safety, quality, delivery, cost and employee morale. And metrics should be structured in tiers to create an actionable balanced scorecard.

A sample of best-practice metrics are listed below:

1. On-Time-in-Full (OTIF) – On-Time-in-Full measures the percent of shipments received or shipped to customers that are 100% full of all required items and received 100% within the requested/confirmed delivery time windows
   - OTIF is calculated by dividing the number of on-time items by total items, and then multiplying the result by 100 for a percentage.
   - Fill Rate – The percentage of a customer's order that is filled on the first shipment. This can be represented as the percentage of items, SKUs, or order value that is included with the first shipment. It's calculated as: (1 – ((total items – shipped items)/total items)) * 100.
     • This metric is important for two reasons: It relates to customer satisfaction (do a large percentage of items take more than one shipment to fill?) and to transportation efficiency, which can be affected if multiple shipments are often needed to fill orders.
   - Perfect Order Measurement (POM) measures the percentage of orders that are error-free. Order errors can happen anywhere along the supply chain, but perfect order measurement is structured (tiered) to identify which links in the chain are most problematic. POM can be applied to each stage of the process: procurement, production, transportation, etc.

- The Perfect Order Measure calculates the error-free rate of each stage of a purchase order (e.g., error in order forecasting for procurement, error in warehouse pickup process, error in invoicing, and error in shipping orders, etc.).

2. Inventory – After measuring a manufacturer's service, i.e., OTIF, the next important metric is the inventory levels (usually measured as value or days of demand). But there are many ways to express the same metric.

 - Inventory Turns (a.k.a. Inventory Turnover) is probably one of the most common inventory measurements. It's simply the number of times that a company's inventory cycles (turnovers) per year. It is determined by cost of goods sold ($)/average inventory ($). The metric is stated as a number that reflects the number of inventory turns, or it could be stated as the Inventory Turnover Ratio (ITR).

 - This metric is also indicative of how much inventory is sitting around, a higher inventory turnover indicates an efficient supply chain.

 - This metric tells you whether you have issues with overstocking – or, conversely, with inadequate inventory levels to meet demand. A low turns number indicates too much is spent on holding costs and obsolete inventory taking up shelf space. A high turns number indicates that you may not have sufficient inventory on hand in case there are changes to the market or to customer demand (or it may mean that you have effectively sized and managed your inventory –.I like this scenario better).

 - Inventory Days of Supply (DOS) or Days-on-Hand (DOH)

 - DOS or DOH is the number of days that it would take to run out of supply if it was not replenished. It is calculated as inventory on hand/average daily usage.

 - SCM seeks to minimize inventory days of supply in order to reduce the risks of excess and obsolete inventory. There are other financial benefits to minimizing this metric – excess inventory tends to tie up operational cash flow.

 - By dividing the inventory on hand by the average daily usage, you will know what inventory is excess or obsolete and where your capital can be better spent.

 - Inventory Velocity (IV) is an inventory measurement that's not as commonly used as an inventory-metrics.

 - IV is the percentage of inventory we are projecting to be consumed within the next period. It helps the managers to understand how well the inventory on hand matched the demand. It is calculated by dividing the opening stock by the sales forecast of the following period. Tracking IV monthly will provide significant clues in terms of aligning inventory level to the optimal level for matching supply-demand and preventing excessive stock in the warehouse.

– Carrying Cost of Inventory is the amount it costs to store inventory over a given period. All the costs associated with inventory storage, e.g., labor, freight, insurance, space-rental, etc., are divided by the average inventory value times 100, which gives you this metric (a percentage). This is a seldom used metric, but it is a calculation that may be completed to quantify savings when reducing or eliminating inventory but seldom used as a metric.

– Inventory Accuracy is a comparison of the items in stock and the items recorded in the database. If the two counts don't match, there are issues with bookkeeping and data management, which can be fixed by implementing automated inventory control solutions such as barcode or RFID systems.

  • The inventory accuracy is usually determined by a cycle count, which is an inventory auditing procedure that falls under inventory-management. It's completed by a small subset of inventory, in a specific location, being counted on a specified day and being compared to the quantity in the "system."

3. Cash to Cash Cycle Time – The cash to cash cycle time has been mentioned throughout this book as a key element of supply-chain management. It's a key metric that has many drivers. I would not necessarily use this metric as a key performance indicator, but I would utilize it as a metric to drive improvement.

   – The cash to cash cycle time would be calculated as the number of days between paying for materials and getting paid for the product; i.e., materials payment date – customer order payment date. And since many materials and suppliers would be involved (1) you could take the worst case, (2) you could utilize a straight average, (3) take the highest value item, or (4) a weighted average materials payment date can be calculated.

   – Cash to cash measures the amount of time operating capital is tied up. During this time, cash is not available for other purposes. A fast cash to cash indicates a lean and profitable supply chain. It may also be reflective of an effective supply-chain management team.

- When Value Stream Mapping (VSM), the cash to cash cycle time would not normally be indicated, but it can easily be construed from the data; although payment terms may or may not be stated, *but* if I wanted to understand the cash to cash cycle time, then I would include it in my VSM.
- Some lowered tier measurements of the Cash to Cash Cycle Time are:
  • Day's Sales Outstanding: Measuring how quickly a customer's payment can be collected – and thus, put to use equals the day's sales outstanding metric. The formula here is receivables divided by sales, and then multiplied by days in the period. A low ratio here indicates accounts receivable efficiency in collecting needed revenue.
  • Average Payment Period for Production Materials: This metric is the average time that elapses between the receiving of raw materials and the payment for those materials. The longer the average pay period, the more favorable for the buying entity. It's best to pay suppliers within a reasonable amount of time but slow enough to have capital available when necessary.
4. Process Lead Time (PLT) – I would define this as the Order Fulfillment Lead Time. And this would be the metric that I would strive to accurately determine by Value Stream Mapping (VSM). It may be used as a performance metric, but I'd most likely use it as a metric for identifying improvement opportunities or as a baseline benchmark for my VSM activities.
   - Customer Order Cycle Time
     • Measures how long it takes to deliver a customer order after the purchase order (PO) is received. It would be calculated by: actual delivery date – purchase order creation date.
   - Supply-Chain Cycle Time: If inventory levels were zero, how long would it take to fill a customer order? By adding the longest times for each stage of the cycle, you can calculate this metric that evaluates the overall state of the supply chain. Stages with the longest lead times can be identified as opportunities for improvement.
5. Safety – Safety would measure whether the safety measures or metrics were achieved each day and marked on the board. Safety metrics might include:
   - No near misses
   - No safety violations

- No missed work due to injuries
- No unsafe work practices observed
- No safety glasses violations

6. There are many lower-tier metrics that may be cascaded-down to structure an effective Supply Chain Balanced Scorecard. Here are examples of lower-tiered metrics:
   - Logistics costs as % of sales
   - Warehouse costs as % of sales
   - Transportation costs as % of sales
   - Finished-goods inventory turns
   - Raw materials inventory turns
   - Inventory obsolescence
   - Work in progress days
   - Finished-goods days
   - Raw materials days
   - Inbound delivery in full
   - Inbound delivery on time
   - Outbound delivery in full
   - Outbound delivery on time
   - Manufacturing cycle time

Case-in-Point 3.1: Globalization

For this example, I'll share my personal experiences and lessons learned from my work experience in 23 countries.

I made my first trip to Asia in 1983; before Asia, I had traveled extensively throughout the US, Canada, Mexico, and Haiti, but none of that prepared me for what awaited this young, naïve redneck from North Carolina in Asia. Initially, I would allow my arrogance to supplant my inexperience.

I'll never forget arriving solo in Penang, Malaysia, for the first trip to Asia and having my first meal (lunch) outside in the stifling heat in the shadows of a snake temple (and it literally was an incense-laden temple that housed free-roaming snakes) as mange-riddled dogs roamed around my feet. An unbelievable ambience! My hosts (ethnic Chinese) asked me if I like KFC chicken, which of course I said yes; so I was served a chicken that supposedly had been fried but then chopped into various pieces so that nothing was even faintly recognizable. And I then I realized that Dorothy and Toto were right; I was not in Kansas anymore. I was basically ready to catch the next flight back to North Carolina. But I persevered for another couple of weeks before returning to the sanctuary of the US.

And I could continue to share hundreds of similar unpleasant and unbelievably wonderful encounters with you but that's not the intent of this case-in-point. My intent is to share with you the importance of understanding the cultures (business and social) of the countries that you engage in business with.

That first trip to Asia was to initiate a knowledge transfer of products and processes to our sister organization in Malaysia. And this was the first of many successful outsourcing initiatives to Malaysia and Thailand that I matrixed-managed over an eight-year period. A key to my success was that I made the effort to understand and appreciate their culture. And Penang (a former British colony) was a real melting pot of ethnic cultures consisting of Chinese Buddhists, Christians, Malay Muslims, and Indian Hindu. I quickly learned to be successful in this landscape; I needed to accept their ancient, rich cultures and to be humble in my business requests. I would successfully blend and align my US business requirements with their Asian business culture, and for approximately eight years (and hundreds of shipments) we had a business relationship that never yielded a late shipment or a significant quality issue. We had a truly win–win relationship in which we both learned from each other and had shared objectives.

After a couple of manufacturing joint-venture projects in Belfast and Poland, my next large expatriate assignment was a greenfield manufacturing start-up in southern *rural* China. My initial thought would be that I would 100% clone the manufacturing processes that we had in Canada and North Carolina. But as I started visiting many Chinese manufacturing sites and assessing the domestic supply-chain capabilities, I quickly realized that I needed to make our North American processes aligned with the available resources and equipment that were readily available in rural China (a remote area of Guangdong province). And I spent two years finding and assessing equipment suppliers, raw material suppliers, and service providers that would meet our needs. I modified our processes to meet the resources available in China; the results were that within the first year of production, we were meeting and exceeding the quality performance of my North American counterparts. I received a global corporate award for the quality/ cost results that I achieved in China. I didn't try to change more than a billion Chinese people, but rather adapted our processes to align with the local capabilities; the result was another highly successful project.

The point that I'm trying to stress is that I learned to adapt to the local culture, comply with stringent local regulatory and government policies, and still meet or exceed the expectations and needs of my North American customers.

I was once in a situation in which I joined an organization that had made some outsourcing decisions that immediately raised a red flag for me; instinctively, I predicted a catastrophic failure. And shortly thereafter, they incurred a catastrophic quality bust resulting in a huge negative financial and service impact on the company. The reason that I was able to predict this failure was my extensive experience within that specific industry in that specific country. And I think additional failures are inevitable, as their chosen supplier depends largely on undeveloped countries' migrant work-force which virtually creates a perpetual learning cycle. When a company is choosing an outsource partner, they must fully understand the cultural/business landscape of a country and the specific industry within that country and the probability of potential worst-case ramifications on their own business. Not planning for a potential worst-case scenario when utilizing overseas suppliers leaves your supply chain very vulnerable (and Murphy's law will eventually find you).

If you're using overseas suppliers, you better take business continuity planning very seriously. I have personally been involved where:

- A single-sourced packaging supplier was in a region devastated by a "100-year flood" that isolated it from all other regions of the same Asian country. Our cardboard packaging supply was interrupted for weeks! And these "100-year floods" seemed to be a regular occurrence in that country.
- Seaports and airports were closed by political protesters for weeks (in Asia).
- Suppliers who had their tier suppliers shut down (or eradicated) by tsunamis, earthquakes, floods, typhoons, etc.
- Borders were closed by cross-country political actions.
- Travel to a key outsource manufacturer was interrupted for months during wartime.
- Political tariff-wars were ongoing.
- The 1997 Asian financial crisis occurred.

Bottom line: I initially built my career by being able to effectively transfer knowledge, equipment, and materials for multiple outsourcing projects in Asia, a greenfield manufacturing start-up in China, and joint ventures in Europe, and I never had a major quality or delivery issue – because of the thorough planning and preparation and robust executable contingency plans I put in place (i.e., business continuity plans). And I have had to execute the contingency plans often – but preparation was key. And this preparation would not have been possible without thoroughly understanding the cultural, geographical, and business climate (and limitations) of every country involved.

Case-in-Point 3.2: Frozen Period

Company: An American multinational high-tech manufacturer
Background: This was a consultancy client, but the urgency for change was driven by their customer, a computer hard-drive assembler in Asia. The client manufactured a multipart subassembly that commenced as a semiconductor wafer in the US and then traveled between two Asian facilities to be completed as a subassembly to be supplied to the hard-drive assembler in Asia (a third Asian country). The total Process Lead

time (PLT) was 25-days, which was totally unacceptable to the hard-drive assembler, so they forced the upstream manufacturer to engage our consultancy services to reduce the PLT by 85–95% (i.e., a dramatic reduction in PLT).

The upstream subassembler required and worked off a weekly rolling schedule with a 13-week horizon.

> *Scope:* The scope covered from the wafer-fab "supermarket" in the US across the two Asian subassembly facilities to delivery to the hard-disk assembler in Asia.
>
> *Project Approach:* The approach was: comprehensive assessment, gap analysis of current-way versus customer (i.e., hard-drive assembler) expectations, define vision (i.e., new ways of working), validation and acceptance, and finally implementation across all sites (see Figure 3.8).
>
> *Solution:* The objective of our solution was straightforward; i.e., reduce PLT by 85–95%.

To reduce the PLT, we developed schemes for:

■ Improving productivity and/or line utilization.
■ Improving throughput by improving first-pass yields and reducing WIP.

Improvement initiatives that we implemented were:

■ Going from a forecast-driven weekly production schedule to a daily-pull schedule based on actual customer consumption. The customer would send a daily consumption fax (a.k.a. kanban-replenishment signal) to the subassemblers, and the subassemblers would manufacture today what was consumed yesterday. This was the major change, but all the other changes (listed below) were the enablers to

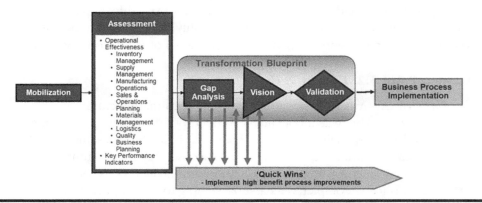

Figure 3.8 The Approach.

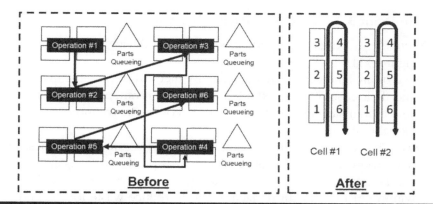

Figure 3.9   Conceptual: Functional versus U-Cell-Layout.

making this change successful; i.e., making the manufacturing cells lean, productive, and responsive to demand.

Improving labor productivity and line utilization by implementing manufacturing cells (went from workstations arranged by function to u-shaped cell design; see Figure 3.9).

■ Improving yields by eliminating excessive ineffective visual inspections, thus eliminating excessive handling and ineffective tweaking of components.

■ Minimizing WIP by going to single small lots of in-process subassemblies, thus reducing the cycle times which inevitably resulted in fewer damaged components.

The results (see Figure 3.10) of the above changes were:

■ 90% reduction in PLT (25 days to 2–3 days)
■ 20–100% improvement in labor productivity
■ 10–14% improvement First-Pass Yields
■ Approximately 60% reduction in in-process inventory (see Figure 3.10)

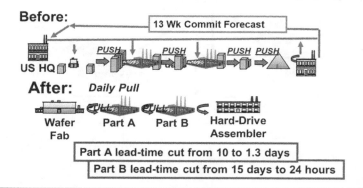

Figure 3.10   Overall Result Before/After.

Case-in-Point 3.3: The Green Packaging Story

Company: An American multinational medical-device manufacturer (see Figure 3.11)

Background: There's a growing trend by medical-device manufacturers and their customers to exhibit a strong environmental consciousness, so we brainstormed on how we could contribute to improving our global environment.

Scope: The scope was the corporation's highest-volume and highest-revenue product, a portfolio of surgical gloves produced in Asia.

Objective: The objective was to reduce the resources that we utilized within our manufacturing facility and to reduce waste for the end users. Our brainstorming activities identified our packaging materials as our largest opportunity to reduce environmental waste.

Project Approach: The approach was to create a value stream for the product portfolio denoting the opportunities for environmental waste reduction rather than our normal focus of reducing Lean waste.

Our Green Value Stream: As stated above, our focus would be our packaging material. All of our packing cartons were already made of recycled material, and we were utilizing the highest percentage of recycled material content possible while still meeting the packaging strength required for international shipping.

This portfolio of the gloves' inner packaging material is a high-grade plastic that tightly encompasses each pair of gloves, with the gloves positioned flat

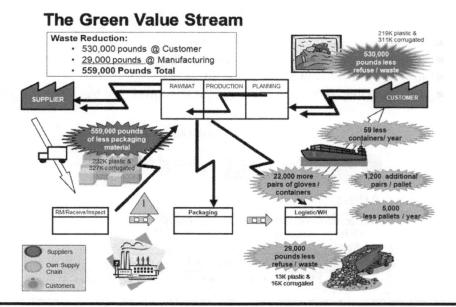

Figure 3.11   The Green Value Stream.

and unfolded. These gloves are tightly sealed and later will be sterilized. We conducted an analysis of our competitors' products and found that their gloves were packaged folded, thus basically using half the amount of plastic packaging material we used.

But before blindly proceeding and commencing with the "half-fold" configuration; we needed to:

■ Conduct life-cycle environmental testing to ensure that there would be no ill effects on the
■ functionality and physical attributes of the gloves over their lifetime. The gloves had to be tested in the simulated environment of a sea shipment container for all climates and seasons as well as under prolonged warehouse storage conditions (both climate-controlled and uncontrolled).
■ The second phase would be clinical tests with selective hospitals and clinics.
■ The final phase would be conducting customer data via voice-of-customer interviews/surveys with our customers and our competitors' customers.

Then, after determining that the "half-fold" packaging of our gloves had no negatives effects on the physical properties or functionality of the gloves, and that the end users were fully satisfied with the half-fold versus the unfolded gloves, we were ready to proceed with finalizing the packaging design.

Besides reducing the amount of plastic required for the individual interior glove packaging, the "half-fold" design allowed a larger quantity of gloves in each dispensing box and thus a larger quantity of gloves in each exterior corrugated cardboard carton.

The total saving in waste reduction was 559,000 pounds annually (almost 280 tons per year). And this environmental win–win was translated into a marketing differentiator.

In addition to the reduction in waste tonnage shown in Figure 3.12, the ability to ship more pairs of gloves per shipping carton also meant:

■ 5,000+ fewer wood pallets per year
■ 59 fewer sea containers per year

Annualized Savings (pounds)			
Areas of Reduction	Self-Manufacturing	Customers' Sites	Total
Total Waste Reduction	29,000	530,000	559,000
Plastic	13,000	219,000	232,000
Corrugated Cardboard	16,000	311,000	327,000

Figure 3.12   The Green Value Stream: Waste Reduction.

Case-in-Point 3.4: Justified by Sea but Premium Air Freight in Actuality

This case-in-point example is reflective of a situation that I often discovered as a consultant. This is an example of the metaphor that you "can't see the forest for the trees," but the meaning here is more of just looking at it from a different perspective; in particular, I was looking at the individual elements of the value stream instead of taking a 10,000-foot view of it.

> *Company:* An American Fortune 500 company with a very diversified high-tech product portfolio and an extensive global manufacturing footprint.
>
> *Background:* This was a consulting client, and we were engaged to conduct a comprehensive assessment of the global supply chain of their semiconductor division. During my initial assessment, the value stream for a high-volume subassembly that was being reported as the division "cash-cow" (i.e., extremely high profit margins) drew my attention because it just didn't pass the "smell test," so to speak. Therefore, I needed to dig much deeper into the specifics.
>
> *Scope:* The scope, within this case-in-point example, was a single high-volume, high-margin semiconductor-assembly product. The assembly consisted of three "semiconductor subassemblies" being assembled together on a substrate.
>
> *The Deep-Dive Assessment:* The manufacturing process for this assembly was roughly as follows.

The assembly consisted of three subassemblies and a final back end: 1) Optical subassembly, (2) Chip on board, (3) Surface mount on substrate, and (4) Final back-end assembly. Each of these four components required a different semiconductor/assembly technology, so it was a complicated assembly because its design fused four dissimilar manufacturing technologies into one assembly (see Figure 3.13).

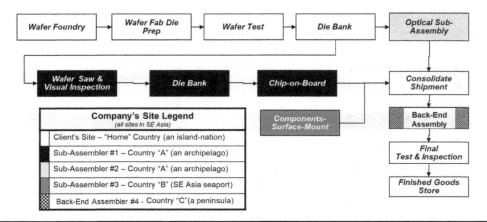

Figure 3.13   Overview of "Current" Assembly Process/Flow.

Our client was the electronic designer and buyer of this assembly, and to produce this assembly at the very lowest assembly cost, they sought experts in each of the four required technologies. After a competitive quoting process, they chose the four lowest-cost assembly options. The only issue was that these four assemblers were in three different countries which were all different than the buyer's country, so this assembly's components would traverse four countries. The transportation costs were a concern, but they calculated the optimal theoretical economic-quantity for ship-sea-shipments and the combination of assembly-costs and transportation cost and the established selling price resulted in a very attractive profit margin. The product had the highest profit margin within their division, and since this was one of the highest-volume product lines, this product line generated the most revenue and at the highest profit margins; i.e., it was the true "cash-cow" of the division.

The accounting scheme used by the client (globally) was heavily based on allocations instead of actual costs for everything but materials and labor, which in this example would be the purchased prices in lieu of labor/materials. Coincidently, at the onset of the overall project, the client asked that we do a quick perusal of their accounting scheme in comparison to an activity-based cost-accounting scheme. Activity-Based-Costing (ABC) is a costing method that identifies activities in a company and assigns the cost of each activity to all products and services according to the *actual consumption* by each.

So what our deep-dive analysis revealed was that over the past 12-months, zero of the subassembly shipments that had been budgeted for sea shipment were actually transported by sea. Actually, all shipments from/to the three subassembly facilities were by air, and what's worse, they were all shipped in small quantities which translates to hundreds of shipments at a premium air freight rate. The costs of the premium air freight and the frequency and quantity of shipments had fully eroded the profit margins, and these assemblies were being sold at a loss. Because of their absorption costing scheme, these high premium freight expenses were hidden, as they were spread over all product lines. Activity-Based-Costing would have captured this immediately, as the freight charges would have been immediately linked to the correct product.

The solution was simple in concept: just have all four "assemblers" quote for the full assembly; they awarded the contract to the bidder with the lowest overall price and established strict policies on shipments (frequencies, quantities, and mode), including a required escalation policy for any potential air shipment.

There are a few things to learn from this example:

■ Premium Air Freight – Logistics costs should not be allocated. Many companies have adopted a best practice of monitoring premium freight cost. Premium freight is defined as additional charges paid to a transportation provider to expedite shipments in order to meet a required date, or as any abnormal shipping expenses.

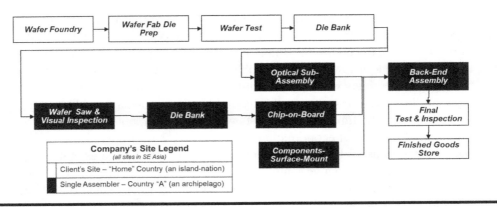

Figure 3.14 Overview of "Future" Assembly Process/Flow.

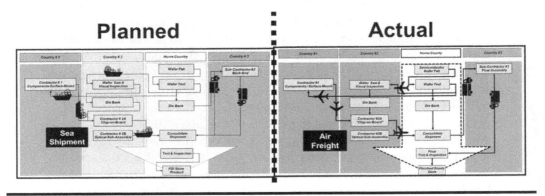

Figure 3.15 Planned versus Actual Transportation Modes.

- This is a good example where it wasn't enough to focus on the realistic total cost of ownership, as the focus was really on the aggregated purchase.
- They really didn't assess the business-continuity risk of having four assemblers working in series in three countries. And if there's a quality issue after it's assembled, who's going to be accountable for the resolution?
- The value stream is beset with waste (non-value-added activities); transportation (four assemblers and three countries plus the receiving country), inventory (buffer inventory required at all locations), motion (packing and unpacking at multiple locations), and waiting (logistics queues/delays, documentation processing, etc.) (see Figures 3.14 and 3.15).

Case-in-Point 3.5: Inventory Velocity

This case-in-point example is about companies' point of view regarding inventory carrying-cost (cost of holding the inventory). I have been employed by a couple of American companies (both Fortune 500 companies) that I would consider industry leaders in operational excellence, but although both put an emphasis on reducing inventories, neither utilized "carrying costs" in calculating cost savings, etc. And I think this inherently "leaves money on the table." I think if you really want to relentlessly focus on reducing all inventory, then you must track the reduction in carrying costs as well, as everybody likes to have that quantitative bottom-line benefit of their effort. I assume that some companies choose not to consider this cost, because when inventory is reduced, it doesn't have an immediate impact on the P&L sheet and is possibly considered a cost avoidance. But I think the cost-avoidance debate is futile; who cares if you ultimately are going to have fewer expenses because you're procuring and holding less inventory? Back in my much younger days, we used an 8–11% carrying cost, which I always thought was too low, but it still quantified my inventory reduction efforts.

I have been involved in many instances where companies have rented/ bought extra warehouse space or full warehouses to house their increasing inventory levels, so how 100% of that cost is not directly attributed to inventory carrying-cost is beyond me – and beyond common sense.

I have had a passion for inventory reduction throughout my whole professional career, as I always viewed inventory as "money sitting around gathering dust."

The last example in inventory velocity that I'd like to share is that I had a third-party consulting engagement with another Fortune 500 company with an objective to substantially increase their profit margin, but they took all inventory reduction off the table, as their global operations leader thought that just-in-case inventory should be the objective. Their inventory turns were very, very low, and they had just recently added another distribution warehouse. So the company wanted us to aggressively pursue increasing their margins, but they insisted on taking one of the largest opportunities off the table. But I strongly feel that we could have added double-digit improvement to their margin if we were able to attack the "elephant in the room." But it was not even a discussable point with them. And this company wasn't ready for any type of significant change; they're like many companies that dream of dramatic changes to their margins but drag their feet on accepting dramatic changes. To them, the status quo is their "winner-winner: chicken-dinner."

Case-in-Point 3.6: Burning Platform Thailand

A fast-moving consumer goods manufacturer in Thailand had a burning platform.

Its business issues were:

■ Current supply chain consists of four central warehouses and 18 sales offices.

The results were:	Improvement
Improve Service Level (On-Time-In-Full)	>85%
Increased Inventory Turns	250%
Reduce Overall Inventory	40%
Reduce Inventory Carry Costs (annual savings)	$560k
Reduce Warehouse Operating Expense	$15.5k
Reduce Obsolete Inventory (cost avoidance)	$400k

Figure 3.16   Results.

- It takes an average of 75 days for products to flow through the supply chain.
- The biggest component of supply-chain costs is fixed selling expenses, followed by the cost of delivering products from sales offices to customers.
- Service level (on-time-in-full) of 60%.
- Losing sales of almost half a billion Thai-baht (US $15.9 million) a year because products are not available in the right quantities at the right place and the right time.

Our approach was:

- Complete as-is assessment, develop to-be processes and business case.
- Develop new warehouse deployment plans.
- SKUs reconciliation and impact on warehouses after SKUs rationalization.
- Production and Sales A-B-C comparison.
- Review options for improving product flow in warehouse.
- Improve current warehouse operations.
  - Reallocate time of logistic functions
  - Warehouses layout
  - Flexible manufacturing

See Figure 3.16 for summary of quantitative improvements achieved through this approach.

Chapter 4

Supply Management

Supply-Management Overview

Supply Management is the process of identifying, acquiring, and managing the products or services needed to operate a company/business. Traditionally, this would have been called procurement or possibly strategic sourcing, but the role and responsibilities have evolved over the years.

And the purpose of supply-management practices and procedures is to keep supply costs stable and use resources effectively to increase the profits and efficiency of the business.

Figure 4.1 highlights the key elements that make up supply management, which are as follows:

1. Materials/Inventory-Management – This is the nucleus of the supply management function.
2. Procurement – This is the traditional purchasing function, primarily a transactional activity in today's supply management.
3. Logistics – This is the inbound and outbound transportation function.
4. Supplier Relations Management – This is where a lot of the focus lies in today's supply management. This is the area that can be leveraged to drive your organization to world-class status.
5. Total Cost of Ownership – This should be a major area of emphasis for the supply-management organization; this takes you beyond focusing on the purchase price.

Supply Management

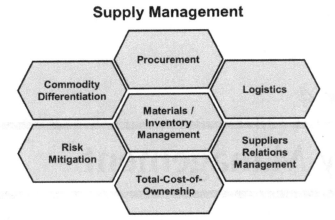

Figure 4.1   The Key Elements of Supply Management.

6. Risk Mitigation – This is, given globalization, an element that cannot be overlooked; it can make/break your company.
7. Commodity Differentiation – This is an area most companies have not effectively utilized, but it should be one of the key drivers for all the strategy for all the other elements of supply management.

Supply-Management Elements: An In-Depth Look

Let's take a more in-depth look at these elements:

1. *Materials Management and Inventory-Management* – This is the nucleus of the supply-management function.
   – Materials Management
     • Materials management is the primary function of the supply-management organization within the enterprise. Materials management involves the planning, acquisition, flow, and distribution of production materials from the raw material state to a saleable product state.
     • Materials-management activities include procurement, inventory-management, receiving, stores and warehousing, in-plant materials handling, production planning and control, traffic, and surplus and salvage. The organizational functions and direct responsibilities may vary slightly across different business entities.

- Since materials management, as described above, is the heart and soul of supply management, the terms supply management and materials management are often treated as interchangeable. The same is true of the functions of each of them.
- Disposition/Investment Recovery
  - Disposition is the act of moving goods out of one's internal organization to another organization due to loss of value, obsolescence, excess inventory, or product change. Investment recovery refers to a systematic, centralized organizational effort to manage the surplus/obsolete equipment/material and scrap recovery/marketing/disposition activities in a manner that recovers as much of the original capital investment as possible. Where applicable, these activities should be linked to a robust, effective corrective action/preventive action (CAPA) system that drives root-cause analysis and permanent effective countermeasures. Additionally, disposition/investment recovery activities should be part of a structured, systematic Material Review Board (MRB) or Material Disposition Review (MDR), or any form of nonconforming and/or excessive material management.
  - Inventory-Management
    - In my view, inventory-management is the second-highest important activity (after purchasing) of a supply-management organization. Inventory is where a company can harbor a lot of dollars, intentionally or unintentionally, and in either case, that's a negative for me. But I'll provide more detail on the impact of inventory-management later in this book.
    - Inventory-management consists of:
      - Making decisions about which items to stock at which location.
      - Determining how much stock to keep on hand at various levels of the operation.
      - Deciding when and how much to buy.
      - Managing (expediting) shortages and back orders.
      - Controlling pilferage and damage.

2. *Procurement*
   - Procurement and purchasing are organizational functions, and in most cases they're sub-functional groups of materials management. I often use the terms procurement and purchasing interchangeably,

but in our modern times, there has been a differentiation of the two terms.

- Procurement, typically, is the "purchasing" function that controls quantity, quality, sourcing, and timing to ensure the best possible total cost of ownership. Purchasing refers to the major function of an organization that is responsible for the *acquisition* of required materials, services, and equipment.
- Purchasing is more transactional, whereas procurement is more tactical or even strategic.

3. *Logistics*
 - Logistics is the process of planning, implementing, and controlling the efficient, cost-effective flow and storage of raw materials, in-process inventory, finished goods, and related information from point-of-origin to point-of-consumption in alignment with customer requirements. Depending on how a company chooses to organize (or classify) their supply-management/logistics activities, there may be many sub-functions under Logistics, such as:
   • Transportation/Traffic/Shipping (a.k.a. Inbound/Outbound Logistics)
     ■ Transportation, traffic, and shipping are terms describing the movement of materials, products, etc., over distances. Traffic is a materials-management activity that controls buying, scheduling, auditing, and billing of common and contract carriers.
   • Warehousing/Stores/Receiving
     ■ Warehousing or physical distribution refers to a range of materials management activities that involve shipping, receiving, internal movement, and storage of raw materials and finished goods.
     ■ Receiving is the business function that is responsible for verifying that the goods received are the goods that the organization ordered. This involves inspecting and accepting incoming shipments.
   • Distribution
     ■ Distribution refers to the process by which commodities move to final customers, including the return of goods. Activities include storing, transacting, packaging, and shipping.

4. *Supplier Relations Management* (a.k.a. Supplier Relationship Management)
 - Supplier Relations Management (SRM) is the function of supply management for managing all interactions with third-party organizations

that supply goods and/or services to an organization to maximize the value of those interactions. SRM entails creating collaborative relationships with key suppliers to uncover and realize new value, and reduce the risk of failure. These relationships can deliver greater levels of innovation and a competitive advantage that most probably couldn't be achieved by operating through a traditional transactional type of a purchasing arrangement. With SRM, the focus is on the relationship. In today's world, managing the supply base is about strengthening relationships that can make or break your business. Earning your suppliers' trust with honest communication, listening to their concerns, and involving them in your processes ultimately makes them a vested partner in your business.

– SRM is becoming more and more important for best-in-class supply-chain organizations, causing a shift in the procurement function. SRM is undergoing a major transition. Gone are the days where simply managing spend and finding the best deal possible within your supply base is enough – or easy. In today's global economy, there are so many factors to consider when choosing and managing a supplier.

SRM has six primary tasks:

1) Basic Supplier/Contract Management – SRM is about managing the ongoing contracts with all suppliers more intensely. Contract management activities can be categorized into three areas: service delivery management, relationship management, and contract administration. The SRM team must work toward achieving (or exceeding) the suppliers' service /performance requirements of all internal stakeholders. Contract administration refers to developing appropriate procedures and filing all relevant documentation. Suppliers' performance is much more than compliance. Establishing strong contract relationships and ensuring buyer and supplier compliance to those agreements is one part of the SRM team's responsibility in delivering value.

   • Expectations are changing. The supply-management function is expected to know where they are vulnerable and bolster their teams for success. Teams that put a greater emphasis on qualitative and quantitative supplier data analysis will be able to quickly and succinctly identify weak spots, risks, and opportunities in the global supply chain – improving the strategies and plans needed to manage the suppliers, and ultimately both businesses, for continued success.

- It's mutually beneficial. If a company is aligned with its suppliers and treats them as partners, both businesses will experience higher success rates, decreased risks, and enhanced collaboration and innovation.

2) Strategic Sourcing – The selection and initial management of suppliers with a focus on achieving the long-term goals of the business.
   - The sourcing process covers the supplier selection process and related contract development. The overall goal of this activity is frequently to reduce the number of suppliers and to enable managing the suppliers. You want to create partnerships rather than a large landscape of transactional suppliers.
   - Supplier segmentation is an important part of strategic sourcing. Supplier segmentation is defined as the process of dividing suppliers into distinct groups with different needs and characteristics or behavior based on or aligned with the commodity differentiation strategies (*see Supply-Management element #7, Commodity Differentiation*).

3) Supplier Development - Is about improving the suppliers' capabilities and performance so that both customer and supplier work in harmony to perform better, faster, and cheaper, i.e., a "buying" company's team (quality, operational excellence, supply manage-ment, etc., staff) works with selected suppliers to:
   - Improve quality – Within a focused and collaborative supplier relationship management strategy, there is significant opportunity to bring about improvements in supplier quality as an outgrowth of investment in regular meetings with the supplier that focus on all aspects of business performance. Further, it includes the sharing of data related to product failures, etc. and addresses potential warranty, service, reparability, and maintenance issues.
   - Deploy operational excellence techniques to identify and mini-mize waste and non-value-added activities, to increase suppliers' productivity, to reduce process lead times, etc. Possibly reducing costs and sharing the benefits, i.e., win–win opportunities. Effective SRM can deliver not only big savings but big opportunities. How are you developing lasting relationships with your suppliers?
   - Continuously improve or develop new products/services to gain a competitive advantage.

     Studies have found the top SRM teams that have successfully aligned with their key suppliers have improved supplier capabilities of innovation, quality, reliability, and cost/price reductions and agility to reduce risk factors. Greater value can be achieved for both businesses, something that would be difficult to achieve if operating independently. It delivers big opportunities. Successful SRM yields a faster time to market, transactional efficiency, competitiveness, risk management, and large financial gains – all of which not only contribute to your bottom line but also allow you to deliver a quality and cutting-edge product, putting you ahead of the market.

4) Tier-supplier management of critical suppliers requires understanding and monitoring their supply chains (i.e., the supplier's tier 1 and lower suppliers). Tiered-supplier management integrates an organization with its key first-, second-, and third-tier, etc. suppliers. The goals are typically to reduce costs, cycle times, and in-process inventory and to improve customer response time, forecasting, quality, product development, collaboration, and flexibility. It's an integral part of a successful supply-chain management program. It may also be a source of competitive advantage for companies that can successfully establish it as a standard practice. It's important to understand lower-tier suppliers':

- Geographical landscape, to assess the potential impact of natural disasters, political unrest/ stability, currency fluctuations, infrastructure reliability, human rights issues, etc.
- Potential commercial liabilities, e.g., financial stability, delivery / quality reliability, etc.
- Inventory levels

It is possible to be proactive in monitoring the lower-tier suppliers by requiring the primary supplier to provide the following information on their tier 1 and 2 suppliers:

- Ongoing delivery and quality performance
- Regular site-audit reports
- Corrective and preventative action activities
- A current process failure mode and effect analysis

Regulatory compliance certifications such as ISO, Quality Management System, etc. (see Figure 4.2).

5) Quality
- Supplier quality is often handled by a company's quality department in collaboration with the supply-management team. One important aspect of managing supplier quality is some type of CAPA. An effective closed-loop CAPA system is key to achieving

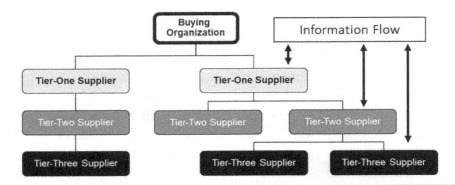

Figure 4.2   Tier-Supplier Management.

the quality levels of the supplied items that meet the expectations of all stakeholders. Never take shortcuts in the deployment of a robust, effective CAPA system. I'd also, strongly recommend utilizing a continuous Process Failure Mode and Effect Analysis (PFMEA) approach for driving continuous improvement by the supplier.

6) Supply-Base Rationalization
   • The idea of supplier-base rationalization is that an appropriate (often lower) number of suppliers means that the supply-management organization will reap lower prices through leveraged volume, standardized service, and lower costs to manage transactions and the supply base.
   • Furthermore, it will be easier to monitor supplier performance, and because these suppliers have been identified as "key" or "the best fit" for the required goods and services, the relationships can grow, fostering integration, trust, value-added services, and innovation. Supply managers will be able to optimize suppliers' capabilities, ultimately bringing the buying firm and its suppliers greater success.
   • The initial drivers for doing supply-base rationalization are often cost related. Supply managers recognize the enormous excess cost associated with an undefined or inadequately managed supply base.
     – *Maverick spending.* When users have the authorization to spend arbitrarily or outside supply management, the firm is not able to apply prudent negotiating or contracting expertise.
     – *Obsolescence.* Problems due to obsolete parts or maintenance services are more likely if original purchases are made outside of a managed supply base.

- *Price.* The more spend is dispersed across a wide scope of suppliers, the less the firm can leverage volume for lower-priced goods and services.
- *Transaction costs.* The higher the number of suppliers, the most costs incurred for processing and back-end functions
- While controlling the above factors is appealing, there are more strategic drivers for supply-base rationalization; it can be a means to an end for optimizing supply-base excellence.
  - *Innovation.* Deeper relationships with suppliers allows a firm to capitalize on innovation produced by the supplier.
  - *Customer of choice.* In times of need or of new projects, the purchasing firm may be considered the customer of choice.
  - *Deeper relationships.* Stronger relationships with the retained suppliers can produce more trust, rewards sharing, and opportunities.
- Accepted best practices for rationalizing the supply base include:
  - Identifying current spend volume, per category and per supplier.
  - Determining a supply-base strategy for each category of goods and services (typically segmented based on high/low-volume and high/low criticality).
  - Selecting the appropriate number and specific suppliers for each category, based on that segment's strategy, considering:
    - ■ Supplier capabilities
    - ■ Firm's ability to manage the suppliers
    - ■ Customers' need for a range of choices
    - ■ Firm's tolerance for risk
    - ■ The commodity market's competitive environment
  - Defining the desired relationship with the retained suppliers, emphasizing continuous improvement and value-added performance.
  - Managing the supplier relationships as defined above; in most cases, this translates to a more integrated relationship, deeper communication and information sharing, and increased levels of trust.
  - Ongoing monitoring of customer satisfaction and supplier performance.

5. *Total Cost of Ownership* – The scope of sourcing extends beyond supplier-price negotiation and considers the total cost of ownership. Total

Cost of Ownership (TCO) is the purchase price of an item plus the life-cycle management of that item. When evaluating alternative items *and suppliers* in a purchasing decision, companies must look not only at an item's short-term purchase price but also at its long-term cost impact, which is its TCO. The item with the lower TCO is the better value for the long term.

1) When determining an item's (or service's) TCO, the following are the basic elements that must be considered:

- Purchased Price – This is the base that you start with, but in terms of overall TCO, this may be a small percentage of the TCO.
- Shipping Costs – A supplier's geographical location has a major impact on shipping cost, as costs and complexity obviously increase as the distance between the supplier and the receiving point increases. And if the supplier in on a different continent, there's the multimodal transportation factor that creates a far greater degree of costs and complexity. Additionally, you must plan for agent and brokerage fees as required. And if you're planning on ocean shipments, then you might as well budget a few expedited air shipments a year. Potential tariff increases make import costs an unstable financial variable.
- Shipping Time – Shipping times can be a substantial time variable for imported items, as you must account for documentation creation, customs clearance, etc. Ocean transport times can easily range from two to eight weeks or more, depending on the country's location and infrastructure. Inventory buffers must be appropriately sized to accommodate for shipping-time variability.
- Inventory – In addition to tradition cycle-stock inventory levels; buffer inventory must be held to accommodate for shipping-time variability and to hedge against a potential supply interruption due to political unrest, natural disasters, etc. These costs should include the buffered inventory value plus preservation/storage costs, financing costs, and risk of obsolesce.
- Quality Costs – Supplier quality issues may, characteristically, lead to:
  - Production stoppage due to material shortages/ delays.
  - Lower production yields and/or lower product quality, which often leads to dissatisfied customers.
  - Increased inspection (or rework).
  - Costs.

- – Higher warranty or product returns costs.
- – Loss of sales from dissatisfied customers.
- Supplier management costs (including travel costs for supplier governance) – These costs are often overlooked, but provisions should be made for costs incurred for traveling to build/strengthen relationships, to provide technical /production support, and to resolve any unforeseen supply-chain disruptions or quality issues.
- Foreign currency fluctuation – Potential foreign currency fluctuations if paying in foreign currency.
- Intellectual property protection costs
  Financial/commercial obligations – Payment terms, administrative/banking fees, etc. (see Figure 4.3).

6. *Risk Mitigation* – Given globalization, this is an element that cannot be overlooked; it can make or break your company. Risk mitigation under supply management should be focused on supply continuation, i.e., the continuous uninterrupted flow of required materials, supplies, services, etc.
   - – Distant sourcing and extended global supply chains are not only raising levels of supplier risk but are creating more diverse forms of risk. If supply-management organizations are to mitigate these very

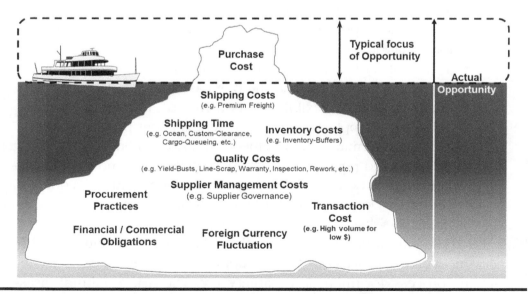

Figure 4.3   TCO: Purchased Price is Only the Tip of Any Cost-Reduction Opportunities.

real supply-chain risks, they must gather and manage information on suppliers on a global basis.

- Supply-chain risk means managing the entire supply chain, not just tier-1 suppliers. All tiers, distributors, carriers, ports, transportation hubs, warehouses can be the site of a lengthy delay or disruption of your supply. Keys to supplier risk mitigation are:
  - Sourcing new suppliers impacts your whole supply chain – It's easy to get lost in the mechanics of sourcing new suppliers and not foresee the impact on the whole supply chain. Dual-sourcing suppliers within the same country or geographical region may not hedge you against natural disasters, political unrest, trade/ tariffs disputes, etc.; it may handicap you the same as sole sourcing. Where are the lower-tier suppliers located? What are the costs/risks of potential new sources? Transportation costs, tooling costs, and geography-specific risks have cost considerations that must factor into the sourcing process. Think: Total Cost of Ownership.
  - In considering your supplier risks, it must go beyond the specific supplier, and you must consider the whole supply landscape, e.g., the countries that your supply originates in and those it must traverse, the modes of transport and handling, the logistical hubs/ ports, the sensitivity and protection of the intellectual property, and the customer-specific contractual requirements (e.g., safety compliance, country of origin, human rights, political unrest, forced labor, etc.).
  - You must start with a "balanced scorecard" of sourcing requirements that extend beyond the purchase price, such as delivery/ quality reliability, flexibility/responsiveness, innovation, sustainability, etc. Supplier risk management is about protecting your supply performance requirements and how to ensure that you get the expected performance. These requirements and your expectations must be included in your negotiations and subsequent contracts. Do you need third-party insurance, etc., to protect your financial risks?

The bottom line is that potential risks need to be embedded in the sourcing process. Potential suppliers must be vetted, early in the process, for financially stability, etc. The risk of natural disaster, political embargo, civil unrest, etc., should be identified across the supply landscape. Regular site inspections, and mandatory progress and performance metrics reporting, etc., must be included in the contract.

7. *Commodity Differentiation* – A key part of supply management is developing a supply strategy, and, to me, the first step is to establish a baseline analogy of your current supply (procurement) landscape. And do to that I would collect data on the following criteria:

   – Classifications by commodity, i.e., an affinity-type grouping of purchased items by commodities, e.g., electronics, plastics, packaging materials, metals, mechanical assemblies, consumable supplies, chemicals, outside services, etc. The actual commodity groupings will vary across industries, so that's why I suggest starting by doing an affinity-type grouping of purchased items.

   – After the commodity groups have been identified, we need to start aligning the purchased items with their appropriate commodity group, and identifying:

   • Number of items per each commodity group.
   • Number of purchase orders issued per each commodity group.
   • Total dollar spend per each commodity group.
   • Total number of suppliers per each commodity group; distinguish domestic from import.
   • Average lead time (days) per each commodity group.
   • Average annual inventory per each commodity group.
   • Obsolete, excess, slow-moving inventory ($-value) per each commodity group.
   • Annual scrap ($) per each commodity group (see Figures 4.4 through 4.6).

After baseline data has been obtained, the next step is to start to formulate a supply strategy. And to complete a strategy, I'd start with a Kraljic-type of matrix. The key to the Kraljic approach is differentiation, i.e., you can't apply the same acquisition strategy to every commodity grouping (one size doesn't fit all).

The matrix is divided into four quadrants along two axes; the y-axis represents business impact and the x-axis represents supply risk, and the quadrants are then positioned based on each quadrant's relationship to business impact (low-to-high) and supply risks (low-to-high).

The four quadrants are defined as:

1) Common
2) Competitive

Process Based Procurement Commodities

#	Commodity	Items	#	Commodity	Items
1	Aluminum	Bare fin / Pre-coated fin (normal / blue / gold)	11	Packaging	C.C. Case,sleeves, baseboard, top board
2	Copper	Groove tubes & Bare tubes	12	Hardware	Bolts / screws / washer /nuts / adhesives
3	Copper assembly	Multi-bent tubes, tube assemblies, valves, manifold tubes, capillary tubes , others	13	Sub-contract	Terminal assembly, electronic parts assembly, accessories box
4	Steel	Steel sheets/coil	14	Chemical	Paints / Cleansing agents
5	Metal stamping	Pressed parts	15	Others	All others, badges, tapes / Adhesives / etc
6	Resin	Plastic resins ABS, PS, etc	16	Refrigerant	R22
7	Plastic Injection	Injection molded / extrusion parts / flexible pipes bands	17	Foam polystyrene	Shock absorbers
8	Insulation Material	Sound proof material, Filters, Butyl tape, Foam,Poly E, Foam Poly-U, EPT Seal	18	Electrical	Power supply cord complete, remote controller / switches, S. H. Capacitors, transformer / valves / thermostat / etc.
9	Compressors	Compressors	19	Electronics	Printed circuit board, integrated circuit, resistors / capacitors / etc
10	Fan motors	Fan motors, toroidal motors	20	Rubber	Bushings / anti vibration bushings / etc

Figure 4.4   Example: Commodity Grouping *(Commercial Equipment OEM).*

3) Strategic
4) Constrained

Business impact would be defined as a composite of:

- Profitability to the business
- Functionality/performance impact on end item
- Value to the customers

Commodity	Annual Value	Number of SKUs	Average Inventory			Number of Suppliers	Average Lead Time (days)	Purchase Orders
	2007 Planned Purchases (Php in millions)		Value (Php in millions)	Coverage (days)	Obsolescence (Php in millions)			No. of PO's
Raw Materials								
Active	-	179				181	98	747
Excipient	-	285				284	88	1002
Total Raw Material	2351.8	464	1,504.0	233.4	43.5	465	93	1749
Imported Finished Goods	610.0	106	-	-	-	35	116	543
Imported Bulk	143.3	-	-	-	-	-		-
							Average	
Total	3105.1	-	-	-	-	500	105	2,292

Figure 4.5   Example: Macro Commodity Procurement Baseline Analysis *(Pharmaceutical Manufacturer).*

Commodity	Annual Value Value (Php in millions)	Number of SKUs	Average Inventory Value (Php in millions)	Coverage (days)	Obsolescence (Php in millions)	Number of Suppliers	Average Lead Time (days)	Purchase Orders No. of PO's	Average PO Value (Php in millioms)
Packaging Materials									
Bottles	634.7	65	15.2	10.1	1.5	1	61.4	216	2.94
Boxes	384.7	775	193.5	211.2	42.9	4	46.0	2450	0.16
Corrugated Box	302.9	104	5.6	7.8	0.5	1	35.4	240	1.26
Caps	260.4	54	16.5	26.6	0.1	6	75.9	182	1.43
Flexible Foil	175.3	224	52.7	126.3	6.9	1	67.2	532	0.33
Plastic Container	104.2	33	27.7	111.6	0.9	6	62.9	107	0.97
Dropper Assembly	79.4	6	10.6	56.1	0.7	3	62.5	50	1.59
PVC Film	36.4	32	53.6	618.8	7.2	2	63.6	99	0.37
Tin Can	29.5	13		0.0		1	46.0	24	1.23
Sticker Label	24.9	130	7.9	133.1	1.1	1	48.3	384	0.06
Labels	24.3	338	17.9	309.1	3.9	4	42.5	904	0.03
Inserts	16.9	310	10.8	268.7	2.8	3	41.0	1113	0.02
Aluminum Blister Foil	16.2	46	23.2	600.3	8.1	2	85.0	115	0.14
Collapsible / Aluminun Tubes	9.5	29	8.9	394.2	0.3	2	45.0	69	0.14
Others	12.0	15	24.3	850.5	8.1	6	varies	35	0.34
Total Packaging Materials	**2111.3**	**2,174**	**468.4**	**93.2**	**85.0**	**43**		**6,520**	**0.73**

Figure 4.6 Example: Commodity Procurement Baseline Analysis – Packaging Materials *(Pharmaceutical Manufacturer).*

Supply risk would be defined as a composite of:

■ Availability and location of viable suppliers
■ Opportunity for an alternate material or parts substitution (low opportunity = high risk)
■ Degree of customization/uniqueness (high degree = high risk)
■ Availability of technology (to manufacture)

So:

■ Low-Medium Business Impact and Low-Medium Supply Risk = Common
■ Medium-High Business Impact and Low-Medium Supply Risk = Competitive
■ Medium-High Business Impact and Medium-High Supply Risk = Strategic
■ Low-Medium Business Impact and Medium-High Supply Risk = Constrained (see Figure 4.7)

The characteristics of purchased items that would follow under the Common (a.k.a. Trivial) category are characterized by:

■ Commoditized items:
  – Reasonably interchangeable goods or materials that are bought and sold freely as an article of commerce.
  – Items that are mass-produced and unspecialized (common use).

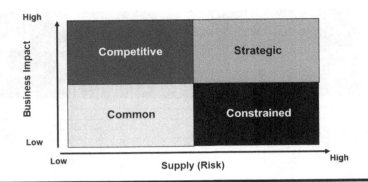

Figure 4.7 Commodity Categorization Matrix *(based on the Kraljic model concept).*

- Many sourcing options; cataloged items, sold by third-parties/distributers, etc.
- A buyer's market, i.e., many sourcing options with competitive pricing.

And revert to Dr. J. Juran's Pareto Principle; i.e., the critical-few versus the trivial-many. So these are common/trivial items (i.e., the trivial-many); therefore, don't spend too much time and cost managing and acquiring these items; i.e., make the end-to-end acquisition process simple and cheap.

The supply-management strategy for Common items should be based on the objective of *minimizing the cost of acquisition*.

The key elements of the Common supply-management strategy are:

- Simplify the procurement process as much as possible, e.g., blanket purchase agreements, purchasing cards, non-complex supplier relationships, etc.
- Pull/replenishment deployment, minimum or no planning, self-scheduling.
- Minimize administrative and logistics costs.
  - Articles removed from materials requirements planning system.
  - Focused storage at point of use.
  - Vendor-managed replenishment based on "pull" signals where applicable.
  - Simplified, reusable packaging.
  - Pay upon receipt.
- Inventory Turn Target: 2–4 turns/year (imported items) and 12–24 turns/year (local-manufactured items).

The characteristics of purchased items that would follow under the Competitive (a.k.a. Leveraged) category are characterized by:

- Items in this classification have the potential for more specialization than the Common items but still have many sourcing options.
- Buyer's market with substantial opportunity for leveraging suppliers obtaining competitive pricing with strategic partnerships.
- More impactful to a product's functionality than the Common items.

The supply-management strategy for Competitive items should be based on the objective of *minimizing the TCO*. The key elements of the Competitive supply-management strategy are:

- Maximization of buying leverage (consolidate requirements) with suppliers to obtain the lowest TCO.
  - Single source (alternatives are readily available by definition).
  - Repetitive supply contracts.
- Search for the lowest-cost supplier by soliciting competitive bids and establishing benchmarks.
  - Source globally, favoring weak-currency countries (LCC – Lost Cost Countries).
- Inventory Turn Target: 6–12 turns/year with VMI (Vendor-Managed Inventory)/VMR/consignment whenever possible.
- Planning driven by Material Requirements Planning (MRP)/Sales and Operations Planning (S&OP).
  - Call-off by "pull" signal where applicable.
- Repetitive supply contracts with long-term visibility driven by MRP and actual demand through local material call-offs (e.g., pull signal).

The characteristics of purchased items that would follow under the strategic category are characterized by:

- This is probably the most important quadrant of the matrix, as it represents items that have the highest impact on the business and have the highest supply risks. This is where you'll need the highest portion of your supply-management efforts focused; i.e., this is your Pareto Principle's "critical-few."
- Items in this category would have a large degree of specialization, thus limiting the potential sourcing options, which creates high supply risk.

The supply-management strategy for Strategic items should be based on the objective of *strategic alliances with suppliers to ensure supply reliability (i.e., delivery reliability > 98%) and minimizing TCO via a win–win, buyer–seller environment*. The key elements of the Strategic supply-management strategy are:

- Develop strategic alliances with key suppliers to gain and/or preserve competitive advantages; the supplier relationship must be carefully constructed and managed, i.e., establish long-term partnerships (supply contracts) with industry leaders.
  - Single source: requirements >10% of supplier capacity.
- Plan requirements linked to 5-yr business plans and/or customer contracts.
  - Repetitive supply contracts driven by MRP, and actual demand through regional and local material call-offs (e.g., pull signal).
- Establish cross-functional sourcing team with clearly defined improvement objectives.
- Inventory Turn Target: 6–12 turns/year with VMI/VMR/consignment whenever possible.
- Engage in the free exchange of information:
  - Shared technology roadmaps and marketing plans.
  - Total cost transparency along the full value chain.

The characteristics of purchased items that would follow under the Constrained (a.k.a. Critical or Bottleneck) category are characterized by:

- Typically, Constrained items have specialized applications and are often limited by products' functionality and/or customers' requirements.
- More of a seller's market than buyer's market, with typically few sourcing options.
- This category is mainly characterized by the high supply risk; limited suppliers usually required for very customized applications/functionality.
- Constrained items may individually have a potentially high business impact but differ from Strategic items, as the impact is limited to a smaller overall volume of customer demand.

Constrained commodities, though of low value, consume disproportionate supply-management resources because of their limited availability or immature technology.

The supply-management strategy for Constrained items should be based on the objective of *minimizing supply risk*. The key elements of the Constrained supply-management strategy are:

■ Shift to a product from Constrained to Common or Strategic.
  – Locate suppliers with the latest technology who can ensure availability, even at some extra cost.
  – Reposition product on strategic grid:
    • Change specification/design to standard.
    • Adopt a lower-risk alternative technology.
■ Secure supply:
  – Conduct global search for alternative sources.
  – Establish long-term contracts with supplier guarantees.
  – Strengthen supplier relationship.
■ Defect rate and delivery reliability are critical (see Figures 4.8 and 4.9).

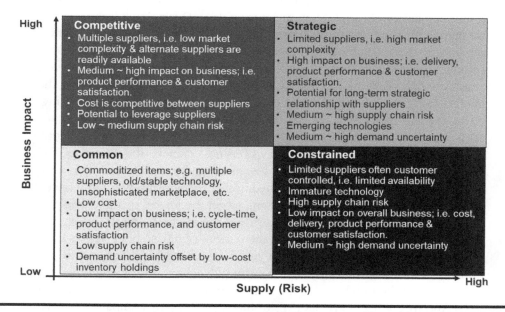

Figure 4.8   Representative Commodity Categorization: Attribute Characterization by Quadrant.

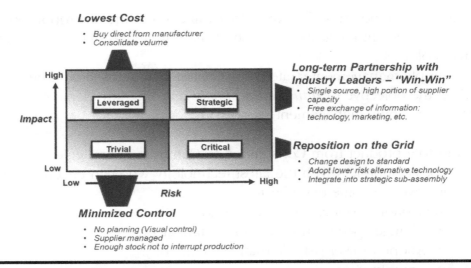

Figure 4.9   Summarized Supply-Management Optimization Strategy.

Case-in-Point 4.1: Supply-Management Findings from a Voice-of-Customer (VoC)

A few years ago, when I was conducting a Voice-of-Customer (VoC) for a high-tech manufacturing client, my interviewee was one of my old bosses from my telecommunication manufacturing days. During our discussion, we started chatting about the subject of purchasing, and he stated that the purchasing dynamics have changed a lot since the old days (circa 20 years ago), when he might have encountered a scenario where a loyal production employee had been injured (for whatever reason), and he'd have to find the injured employee a less physically challenging desk job such as purchasing (a buyer, etc.), as the boss really just needed a warm body to buy material via an MRP-system or something similar. It was a task that basically anybody could perform. But that won't work in today's business climate; the person performing a supply-management function must manage the *supplier* as much as the commodity. Twenty years ago the buyer–seller relationship was fairly adversarial, with the buyer relentlessly driving to get the lowest possible price from the seller and with the buyer's key performance metric being PPV (Purchase Price Variance); i.e., the reduction in the current purchase price versus the purchase price from last quarter, last year, or whatever time period you want to use. Additionally, the buyer was consistently acting as an insistent expeditor to ensure that the purchased items were received on time. Wow, the good old days! And that "buyer/expeditor" role still exists in many companies today.

Supply management, in contrast to the buyer/expeditor approach, is built around a collaborative approach, i.e., full exposure (transparency). Supply management is about building a win–win environment with a few key strategic supply partners.

Also, when I was conducting the VoC with my former boss, I made another interesting finding. As I stated earlier, my client for this VoC was a high-tech manufacturer, a semiconductor manufacturer to be exact, so when I asked my former boss to rank his top five semiconductor manufacturers/suppliers, my client ranked in the top five, which was great since my former boss had more than 100 semiconductor suppliers. And when we examined his semiconductor suppliers' scorecards, my client had the highest overall score (based on quality, delivery, price, etc.), but the interesting finding was that the supplier he rated number one (a couple of spots above my client) was not one of the top ten scorecard achievers. Most surprising of all was that the supplier he rated number one had only an average delivery performance. So how could this supplier be ranked number one? And to my former boss, the answer was very simple: It was the relationship, and mainly the transparency of the relationship, that mattered most. This highest-rated supplier's delivery performance was average, but the differentiator was that this supplier was proactive and always informed his customers in advance of any order delays, etc. (I should note that during that commercial era, semiconductor demand far exceeded the supply, so customers were on allocations, etc. It was a seller's market.) Additionally, this supplier would be as responsive as possible to any demand fluctuations that inevitably occurred. So it was the collaborative nature of this supplier–customer relationship that placed this supplier far ahead of its competition.

Case-in-Point 4.2: Supplier Development

During my employment with a medical-device manufacturer in Asia, I spent a considerable amount of time working with our suppliers, i.e., suppliers of material and services to our Asian manufacturing facility, and suppliers of finished products that would be exported to our end customers in the US and Europe. I was a regional director of operational excellence, with my primary responsibility being the development of our internal staff in Asia. But as a global corporation, my employer had a strong commitment to the development of its suppliers (and even its customers) in the effective deployment of Lean Six Sigma concepts, tools, and methodologies. Our goal was to improve the order fulfillment of our suppliers, i.e., shorten lead times, improve productivity, improve quality (especially their problem-solving skills, reduce inventory, reduce inspections, etc.).

The last one, "reduce inspections" may seem strange, because why wouldn't we want our suppliers 100% inspecting everything, and maybe double- and triple-inspecting everything? First, inspection typically creates extra waste, e.g., slower-moving inventory, higher queueing and wait times, excessive handling (which may lead to handling damage), etc. But our primary resistance to excessive inspection was a symptom of a lack of confidence in their processes' capability to meet our specifications. We preferred to see their and our time spent improving the capabilities of their processes.

In general, we knew that if we could improve their processes, then we would almost assuredly see an improvement in their reliability in terms of quality and delivery, so It was worth our investment in our key suppliers (a good application of the Pareto Principle, i.e., develop 20% of our suppliers to supply 80% of our demand).

We did hope to reduce the operating expenses of our suppliers, and we'd have liked to see (okay, we expected) them share the savings, but the key is *share*. The purchased products were low-margin items for us both, so any mutual improving in cost/price is a huge win–win for all.

In another instance, a service supplier that I collaborated with was our "sterilizer" supplier. They provided a service of sterilizing our in-house manufactured product after it was packaged and ready for shipment overseas. Our in-house process was relatively short, but the transporting and queueing of our product for sterilization and then the subsequent transport/queue at a seaport could potentially be an extremely long process with excessive handling and transporting. For us to be proactive in improving this process in every way possible would reap great rewards, especially in the reduction of our lead times.

With many of these product suppliers, we would Value Stream Map (VSM) their processes (with them), and we would assist and challenge them in identifying breakthrough projects that could give us both a potential competitive advantage. We wanted to utilize the "open kimono" approach for both of us. And if the process changes didn't expose any of our proprietary attributes, the suppliers were free to incorporate the improvement with their other customers. Typically, we were the largest single customer for the suppliers that we engaged in these development initiatives, but we equally wanted a similar developmental relationship with other strategic suppliers, as it was always healthy for the overall commodity landscape to have multiple sustainable, viable, and reliable suppliers.

After my contract expired, I decided three years in Thailand were enough, so after a few offers, I joined one of the suppliers that I had previously assisted on their development journey. The interesting item, more than a year later, was that my former employer in Thailand wanted to visit my new employer/client and engage in a VSM workshop. My old employer knew that I had joined this company and definitely knew/trusted my capabilities, but the whole objective of this VSM initiative was not to just create a new VSM (the last one that I had done with the supplier was probably three years old). It was also to collaborate in the development of the VSM and for the customer to clarify their needs and expectations of their supplier, and thus through collaboration and brainstorming, there would be a mutual agreement of the future state that the customer wanted from the supplier. The fact is that my former employer, as a corporation, was committed to globally developing strategic suppliers and strengthening long-lasting partnerships. And I think this corporation's growing market share, growing stock value, continual climb in the group of elite Fortune companies, etc., is somewhat reflective of their commitment to operational excellence throughout their global supply chain.

And an added note, a VSM between customer and supplier should probably be revised jointly every 12–18 months.

Case-in-Point 4.3: Differentiated Procurement Strategy – The Kraljic Model Approach

Company: A Japanese multinational electronics OEM corporation.

Background: This was a consultancy client, and the stated objective of this Supply Chain Operational Optimization project "was to reduce cost and process lead times within the Manufacturing, Procurement, Planning and Quality areas through the introduction of industry best practices, the simplification and standardization of processes, efficiency improvements, and the reduction in inventory levels."

Scope: Limited to the procurement processes and strategies.

Project Approach: To assess the current purchasing landscape and then utilize the Kraljic model concept to develop a future-state procurement strategy.

"Case-in-Point 9.1" (Chapter 9) reflects a comprehensive assessment of the company's total supply. But for this case-in-point I'll limit my summary to the key findings of the current *procurement* ways of working.

We started by segmenting the annual spend by commodity, and the commodity groupings are based on common materials, technology, and manufacturing processes. Figure 4.10 reflects the segmenting of all purchased items into 20 commodity groupings.

One of the key findings from the supply-chain assessment was the lack of a differentiated purchasing strategy, as the purchase-sourcing strategy was the same for all purchased items, with no regard to annualized value-of-spend or commodity type. So we utilized the Kraljic model concept to devise a strategy for each quadrant of our purchasing matrix, i.e.,

#	Commodity	Items	#	Commodity	Items
1	Aluminum	Bare fin / Pre-coated fin (normal / blue / gold)	11	Packaging	C.C. Case, sleeves, baseboard, top board
2	Copper	Groove tubes & Bare tubes	12	Hardware	Bolts / screws / washer /nuts / adhesives
3	Copper assembly	Multi-bent tubes, tube assemblies, valves, manifold tubes, capillary tubes , others	13	Sub-contract	Terminal assembly, electronic parts assembly, accessories box
4	Steel	Steel sheets/coil	14	Chemical	Paints / Cleansing agents
5	Metal stamping	Pressed parts	15	Others	All others, badges, tapes / Adhesives / etc
6	Resin	Plastic resins ABS, PS, etc	16	Refrigerant	R22
7	Plastic Injection	Injection molded / extrusion parts / flexible pipes bands	17	Foam polystyrene	Shock absorbers
8	Insulation Material	Sound proof material, Filters, Butyl tape, Foam,Poly E, Foam Poly-U, EPT Seal	18	Electrical	Power supply cord complete, remote controller / switches, S. H. Capacitors, transformer / valves / thermostat / etc.
9	Compressors	Compressors	19	Electronics	Printed circuit board, integrated circuit, resistors / capacitors / etc
10	Fan motors	Fan motors, toroidal motors	20	Rubber	Bushings / anti vibration bushings / etc

Figure 4.10 Commodity Groupings.

Leveraged (a.k.a. Competitive), Strategic, Trivial (a.k.a. Common), and Critical (a.k.a. Constrained or Bottleneck).

The commodities were further categorized based on the commodity groupings' attributes:

- *Trivial* commodity groupings' attributes:
  - *Mass-produced common-use items*
  - Items having minimal impact on the functionality of the end product
  - Low-to-medium supply risk
- *Leveraged* commodity groupings' attributes:
  - *Mass-produced common-use items but with some specialized functionality incorporated*
  - Items having medium-to-high impact on the functionality of the end product
  - Low-to-medium supply risk
- *Strategic* commodity groupings' attributes:
  - Medium-to-high technology items
  - *Items having medium-to-high impact on the functionality of the end product*
  - Medium-to-high supply risk
- *Critical* commodity groupings' attributes:
  - *Limited sourcing opportunities*
  - Items having low-to-medium impact on the functionality of the end product
  - Medium-to high supply risk

Figure 4.11 reflects the categorization of commodity groupings based on their commodity characterization, and the bubbles (ovals) are sized relative to the commodity's annual spend.

Figure 4.12 represents some of the procurement data collected during our initial assessment.

During the initial assessment, we had these key findings:

- Too many total purchase orders overall: 460,000 purchase orders over 12 months
  - And almost 50% of the total purchase orders were issued for *Trivial* commodities. This is a bad practice as, in many cases, the administrative cost will exceed the value of the purchased items.
  - 28,000 purchase orders (6%) had to be modified or canceled.
- They have 187 active suppliers
  - Approximately 40% of the total suppliers are for *Strategic* commodities
- 54% of annual spend ($) is for *Strategic* items

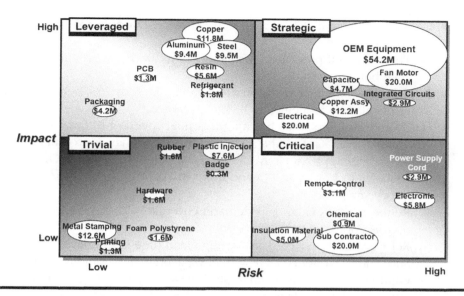

Figure 4.11   Commodities Categorized by Supply Strategy.

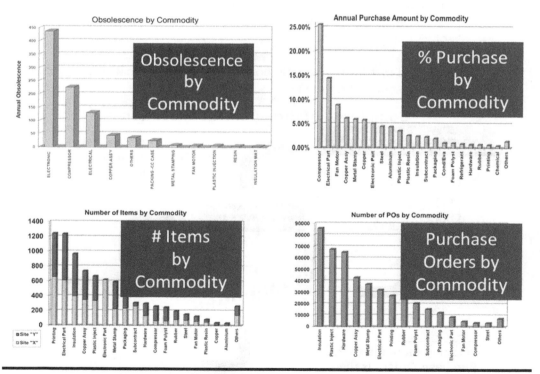

Figure 4.12   Representative Graphs of Procurement Baseline Data.

- Insulation material: 18% of all purchase orders but only <3% of total spend ($)
  - There are 400 purchased insulation items, with the only major variance being length.
- Total purchased items are approximately 8,360, with 26% being Trivial, 23% Critical, 18% Strategic, and 33% Leveraged.
- Hardware (fasteners, etc.) has a total annual spend of $1.6 million which is only 0.7% of total spend, and this group has approximately 300 items and approximately 65,000 (14%) purchase orders (PO), so that equates to $24 value/PO and more than 200 POs per item/year.
- Inventory snapshot:
  - Rubber: DOH (a.k.a. days demand coverage) = 72 days; average lead time is approximately 15 days.
  - Refrigerant: DOH = 65 days; average lead time is >30 days.
  - Subcontracted Items: DOH = 58 days; average lead time is >15 days.
  - OEM items (internal purchases): DOH = 5 days; average lead time is approximately 45 days.
  - Copper: DOH = 5 days; average lead time is approximately 30 days.
  - 7.5% of purchased items ($) is classified as excess.
  - 60% of obsolete material (total value approximately $300 k) is electronics/electrical averages 30 days' lead time and an average DOH of 21 days.

The findings and metrics reveal a plethora of bad supply-management practices, which are summed up in Figure 4.13.

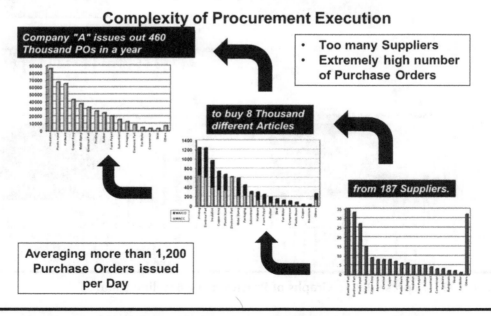

Figure 4.13   Compounded Complexity of Poor Supply-Management Strategy.

Based on the procurement assessment, the following "To-Be" strategy was devised for each quadrant of the purchasing matrix:

"To-Be" strategy for Leveraged commodities will be:

■ Source for lowest total cost supplier
  - Buy direct from manufacturer.
  - Source globally, favoring weak-currency countries.
■ Maximize leverage by consolidating Company "A" volume:
  - Form a buying cooperative.
  - Single source (alternatives are readily available by definition)
  - Reduce variability, e.g., standardize packaging and use labels or online printing
■ Issue PO for long lead time/imported commodities:
  - Minimize processing cost through elimination of non-value-added activities.
■ Reduced supplier lead time:
  - Less than 14 days.
■ Delivery reliability >98%:
  - Supplier certification and zero defect.

"To-Be" strategy for "Strategic" commodities will be:

■ Strategic supplier partnership agreements:
  - Reduce lead time to two days.
  - Machine reservations.
  - Orders are either based on daily replenishment plan for bulky, expensive items or Kanban signal for common A items.
  - At completion of a production lot, approved automatically by back flush (VMI).
■ Price Reduction
  - Cost Transparency: Total Cost Analysis
■ Eliminate Purchase Orders
  - Orders based on daily replenishment plan or Kanban signal.
  - Orders/Kanban signal transferred automatically.
■ Minimize suppliers
  - Localization of suppliers.
  - Reduction of the number of suppliers.
■ Eliminate incoming quality inspection:
  - 0% defect rate from the supplier.
■ Reduce inventory stocks into 0.5 to 2 days:
  - 48 hours delivery.

"To-Be" strategy for "Trivial" commodities will be:

■ Vendor-Managed Two-bin system for "C" items, which are small, cheap parts

- That are readily available:
  - Hardware (nuts and bolts)
  - Metal parts
  - Rubber
- Minimize administrative and logistics costs
  - Articles removed from MRP.
  - Vendor-managed replenishment based on "visual" signal.
  - Eliminate PO and process cost (Purchase Cards, Material Call-Offs, Blanket POs, etc.).
  - Delivered directly to production line.
  - Simplified, reusable packaging.
  - Eliminate incoming inspection.
  - Payment approval upon reception.
- Minimize suppliers
  - Reduction on the number of plastic/metal suppliers.
- Two weeks' inventory – maximum
- Eliminate material shortage.
  - Delivery lead time, reliability, and defect rate less critical because of inventory coverage.

"To-Be" strategy for Critical commodities will be:

- Reposition commodity on strategic grid:
  - Change design to standard or simplify process, e.g., procure insulation material in roll form and cut to order at point of use.
  - Adopt a lower-risk alternative technology.
  - Integrate into completed part or subassembly, passing supply responsibility to supplier, e.g., subcontractor.
- Secure supply:
  - Consolidate demand for all articles in a commodity with a single local distributor, e.g., electronic.
  - Conduct global search for alternative sources.
  - Build inventory to cover shorter of redesign time or product life cycle.
  - Establish long-term contracts with supplier guarantees.

Critical commodities, though of low value, consume disproportionate supply-management resources because of their limited availability or immature technology (see Figures 4.14 and 4.15).

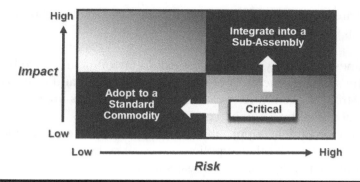

Figure 4.14   Primary Strategy for "Critical" Items is Repositioning.

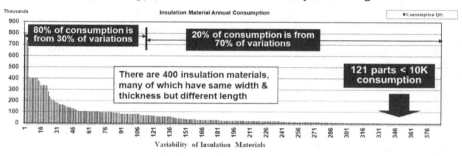

Figure 4.15   Proliferation of Insulation SKUs.

Case-in-Point 4.4: Supplier Rationalization
Single-Sourcing – My Personal View

Many companies are trending toward single-sourcing, but I'm not sure that's a great strategy.

There are obvious benefits to single-sourcing, such as:

1. Single-sourcing means less effort to qualify a single versus multiple sources; less administrative effort (e.g., less paperwork) in dealing with only one supplier.
2. Potentially better quality.
3. Potential for better supplier innovations.
4. Giving all your volume to one source maximizes your leverage based on the economies of scale rationale, and provides the opportunity to emphasize this during negotiations, etc.
5. Potential to leverage long-term contracts (although suppliers may have concerns about committing too many resources to a single major customer, thus shrinking their customer base, which could be risky for them).
6. The supplier should feel a special obligation to help the buyer in terms of availability, etc. Again, in the process of awarding this business to the supplier, the fact that the buyer's company is relying on the supplier for material availability should be made clear.

But there are significant risks that I think outweigh the benefits of single-sourcing, such as:

1. Business continuity is the largest risk in my opinion; you're basically at the supplier's mercy," but there's also the risk that the supplier has a catastrophic event (fire, weather, political, etc.), has financial problems, gets acquired by a competitor, etc.
2. In periods of tight supply, the company may be at a disadvantage in being able to ask other suppliers to accept orders. The company has become dependent on that single source.
3. Other suppliers may lose interest in trying to compete for the business if they see that a sole source situation is likely to persist, i.e., shrinking supplier base and losing some economic competition.

Personally, I'm not a fan of single-sourcing, as I have witnessed single-source supplies being disrupted by fire, labor strikes, political unrest, flooding, port closures, tsunami, etc., and even suppliers making their own business decisions to discontinue a product or service. I think you must treat suppliers like life, i.e., be prepared for Murphy's Law.[1]

What I am a fan of is dual suppliers with some SKU overlap, i.e., cross-sourcing.

Dual-sourcing is the supply-chain management practice of using two suppliers for a given component, raw material, product, or service; cross-sourcing includes overlapping the purchases from two suppliers. Cross-sourcing is a method of expanding the supplier base without increasing the number of suppliers.

For an example of cross-sourcing, let's consider a scenario of two suppliers, X and Y; X is the single source for five items, and Y is the single source for five other items. X has the manufacturing capability to produce some (i.e., not all) of the items that Y can produce. Y has the capability to produce some of the items currently being manufactured by X. Thus, a buyer may move items among the suppliers fully or partially. Therefore, the opportunity exists to keep the supplier base intact while moving items to ensure the continuity and/or adequacy of supply.

The challenge for the buying company is the supplier qualification and selection process. In addition to product quality, two important factors are the supplier's ability to produce several different products (or families of products) and the flexibility of its manufacturing system. The overall objective is the selection of suppliers that can be flexible partners in meeting the company's requirements.

When dealing with the suppliers, it must be a win–win situation. Given the fact that two sources have the capability to produce the same items, the company's risks have been reduced by cross-sourcing. Cross-sourcing can also be done at the corporation, with dual suppliers supplying multiple sites with a larger array of items. The capability of having dual sources within the existing supplier network can be activated by altering the mix of products at either supplier. Risks are reduced, and a win–win environment is the result. I worked for one company that leveraged this concept extremely effectively. They spread their outsourced products across three suppliers, and even had a couple more with their process "pre-certified," so if demand rose sharply or something happened to the other three, there was a contingency plan in place. And the three prime active suppliers were fully aware of the multiple supplier/cross-sourcing scheme being deployed by the company, as everything was as transparent as possible. The suppliers had facilities across two countries. During my few years associated with this company, the outsourced products were *effectively* moved by at least six suppliers. And it should be noted that originally these low-margin outsourced products were self-manufactured, but since there were so many viable outsourcing options the self-manufacturing facility was sold, which resulted in a major reduction in overhead. And with these being low-margin commoditized products, the elimination of overhead and reduction in operating expenses was potentially a major competitive advantage.

Another single-source type of scenario involved a self-manufacturing pharmaceutical company that had a major dilemma, as they needed to create some manufacturing redundancy but didn't want to expand their business because there were labor unions, community issues, etc., that made expansion highly undesirable. And there were no realistic suppliers or regional manufacturers to outsource the items, but to have any potential risk-mitigation opportunities they urgently needed multiple sources. The solution was that the company had to develop new sources, which they did by creating a couple of new business entities which had their own facilities, management teams, etc. These new sources (i.e., suppliers) were basically an extension of the manufacturer's operations but operated in different regions of the country with non-unionized facilities as independent business entities. Often under special situations, manufacturers are required to develop their own sources such as in this scenario, and often it's just components or items with limited sourcing options, so to ensure business continuity they must be developed with the creation of redundant viable sources (i.e., risk-mitigation options) being a higher priority than price/cost.

End Note

1. Murphy's law is an adage that is stated as: "Anything that can go wrong will go wrong."

Chapter 5

Inventory-Management

Inventory-Management Overview/Purpose

Inventory is listed as an asset on a company's balance sheet, and inventory is typically defined as the finished goods available for sale or the raw materials used to produce finished goods. But it also includes the items needed to maintain production support activities (e.g., consumables, maintenance and repair, etc.) and to provide customer service. Inventory is often categorized based on its flow through the production cycle, i.e., raw materials, work-in-process, and finished goods. And inventory represents one of the most important assets of a business because the turnover of inventory represents one of the primary sources of revenue generation and subsequent earnings for the company's shareholders (see Figure 5.1).

Inventory's primary purpose is to meet customers' demand. Inventory is an expensive asset and must be carefully managed and controlled. Inventory-management is the supervision of these non-capitalized assets (inventory) and stock items.

There are several important technical terms that pertain to an inventory's purpose and status:

- *Cycle stock*. Cycle stock is the most active inventory component and the most critical to prevent production being interrupted. Its amount is based on daily demand, replenishment times, lot-sizing rules, etc., as items are received and consumed (see Figure 5.2).
- *Safety stock*. Safety stock is inventory that's carried in excess of demand expectations to provide potential coverage for uncertainty in demand

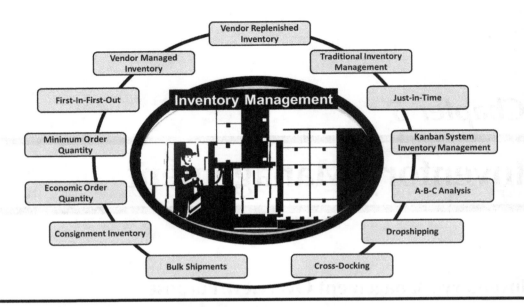

Figure 5.1   Inventory-Management Techniques/Concepts.

(a.k.a. demand volatility), variations in replenishment lead time, supply-quality uncertainties, and forecast errors (see Figure 5.2).

■ *In-Transit.* In-transit inventory in the transportation network, including inventory shipped from a supplier but not yet received by the customer. And this is an area of growing major importance in the days of globalization, i.e., items shipped by sea can be in-transit for several weeks. The overall supply-chain network design impacts the amount of in-transit inventory.

■ *Obsolescence.* Obsolescence is a concern within inventory-management, as out-of-date inventory, most often, becomes a write-off against profits on the P&L statement. There are many potential causes of obsolete

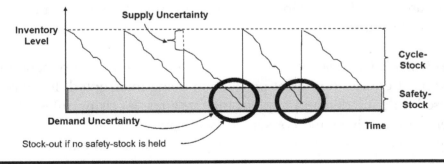

Figure 5.2   Cycle Stock & Safety Stock.

inventory, with the worst cause being overproduction or over-buying. Obsolescence can also occur from the effects of poor preservation or the loss of usefulness (i.e., no longer needed).

■ *Hedging.* Hedging is purchasing inventory in advance to mitigate the impact of anticipated price increases or shortages, and in today's political environment to offset anticipated embargoes, tariffs, etc.

■ *Anticipation.* Anticipation (a.k.a. just-in-case) is the stocking of additional inventory to cover projected trends of increased demand from seasonality, plant shutdowns/vacations, supplier price increases, possibilities of labor disruptions, and forecasted special events such as sales promotions.

■ *Decoupling.* Decoupling is creating independence between supply and the use of material; in production, this is often done by deploying "supermarkets." Decoupled products are inventory that is purposely collected between operations so that fluctuations in the production rate (cycle times) of the supplying operations do not limit the output of the next operation. A customer-order decoupling point is a point where inventory is carried to buffer at least part of the manufacturing system from individual customer orders. The selection of customer-order decoupling points is a strategic decision that determines customer lead times and inventory investment.

Inventory Holding Costs

The cost to hold (or carry) inventory has been a debatable point since the inception of inventory-management, as accounting departments' approaches to inventory costs vary greatly across companies; and some companies just ignore holding costs, see *Case-in-Point 3.5* as a case-in-point reference to a company's view of inventory carrying costs.

See Figure 5.3 for a breakdown of the costs associated with holding inventory.

Types of Inventory in the Supply Chain

Inventory is a broad term, so we'll tend to further classify it by its current state within the supply chain:

■ *Raw materials.* Raw materials require added value to be transformed into saleable or usable parts. The generally accepted accounting view of raw materials is purchased items that will be converted into components and products through manufacturing.

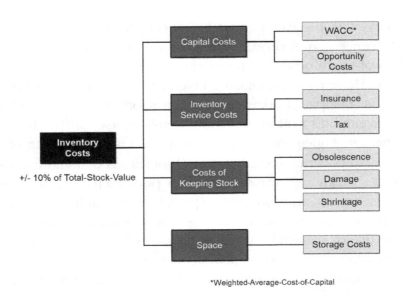

Figure 5.3   Inventory Costs.

- *Work-in-Process (WIP)*. WIP refers to items in various stages of completeness within the manufacturing process, including all material that has been released for initial processing and processed material awaiting inspection. A value-added process (condition) applied to a raw material transforms it to WIP.
- *Finished Goods*. Finished goods are those items on which all manufacturing or service operations have been completed. They are products available for delivery to the customer.
- *Semi Finished Goods*. Semi finished goods (SFG) is a term that I don't hear as much today as I did in my earlier years in manufacturing. Semi finished goods are items that are partially complete and usually temporarily stored in that unfinished-state, which could be done for means of decoupling or late-differentiation. And there are scenarios where semi finished goods can be sold as-is, particularly, as service parts.
- *Distribution*. Distribution refers to inventory located in the distribution system that is separate from manufacturing inventory. It includes finished-goods items in transit and items in storage awaiting delivery to a customer.
- *Maintenance, Repair, and Operating Supplies (MRO)*. MRO refers to items used to support general operations and maintenance (such as spare parts) and consumables used in the manufacturing process and supporting operations.

■ *Service Parts.* Service parts, i.e., spares, repair parts, or replacement parts, are interchangeable parts that are kept in inventory and used for the repair or replacement of failed units. Service parts are usually a segment of distribution inventory.

Inventory Turns

Inventory turns has always been a major measuring stick for determining how effective a company is at managing its inventory. There are other metrics such as Days-on-Hand, Days of Coverage, Average Days-on-Hand, etc., but inventory turns has always remained a critical metric and often a metric seen as a reflection of the total health of a supply chain.

Inventory turns is a measure of how quickly (velocity) materials are moving through a facility or through an end-to-end supply chain and is calculated by dividing some measure of the cost of goods by the amount of inventory on hand.

The most common method of calculating inventory turns is to use the annual cost of goods sold (before adding overhead for selling and administrative costs) divided by the average inventories on hand during the year (see Figure 5.4).

Using the cost of goods rather than sales revenues removes a variation unrelated to the performance of the supply-chain operations, i.e., fluctuations in selling prices. And using an annual average of inventories rather than an end-of-the-year figure removes another source of common variation; i.e., an artificial drop in inventories at the end of the year to "make the numbers."

Inventory-Management Techniques (Concepts)

Inventory-management is like the dilemma that Goldilocks faced, i.e., the bed was too hard (inventory too high), or the bed was too soft (inventory too low) or the bed is just right (inventory=demand). The bad thing is that Goldilocks had a far higher probability of finding the right mix than most companies have in optimizing their inventory level. But the goal for inventory-management is

$$\text{Inventory-Turns} = \frac{\text{Annual Cost of Goods Sold}}{\text{Average Value of Inventories During the Year}}$$

Figure 5.4   Inventory-Turns Calculation.

simple in theory: have enough inventory to meet customers' demand. So the inventory-management dilemma is to maintain the minimum amount of inventory to meet the customers' demand, i.e., to have no stockouts.

Inventory-management's prime objective will always be to provide *uninterrupted* production, sales, and/or customer-service levels at the *minimum cost*. But the fact is that you'll have to make a strategic business decision: do I keep "too" much inventory, or do I let customer service (On-Time-in-Full) potentially suffer? I will discuss later how to statistically optimize that, but most often a company is not willing to hold the *seemingly* excess inventory to ensure an OTIF of 99.95%; thus, inventory-management will, always be a game of give and take.

Inventory-management is performed through an assortment of business processes (operational and transactional) ensuring that the right inventory is available per customers' demand at the lowest operational costs. Inventory-management ensures that the core manufacturing processes of a company keep running efficiently by optimizing the availability of inventory.

Possessing a high amount of inventory for a long time is usually not advantageous for a business because of storage costs, spoilage costs, and the threat of obsolescence. However, possessing too little inventory also has its disadvantages, e.g., the business runs the risk of market share erosion and losing profit from potential sales. Inventory-management forecasts and strategies, such as a Just-in-Time (JIT) inventory system, can help minimize inventory costs because goods are created or received only when needed.

So to accomplish the objectives of maintaining an *uninterrupted supply* of materials to meet customers' demand at the *minimal operational cost*, there are several inventory-management techniques for you to consider.

Inventory-Management Techniques

1. Traditional Inventory-Management
   - Traditional inventory-management systems attempt to solve the inventory-management dilemma (supply = demand) through better forecasting, improvements in the order point/order quantity process, or by adjusting safety-stock levels.
   - The basic questions for traditional inventory-management are:
     • Should more be ordered?
       ■ How long does it take to get more?
       ■ How much will be used at this time?
     • How much should be ordered?

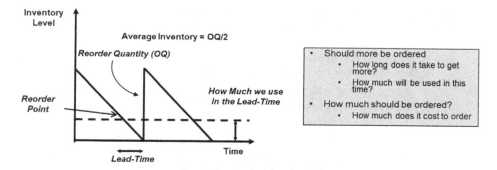

Figure 5.5   Basic Questions/Structure for Traditional Inventory-Management.

■ How much does it cost to order?

See Figure 5.5 for the basic elements of traditional inventory-management.

– Figure 5.5 reflects the basic questions that need answering and reflects the cycle stock (or cycle inventory). And a cycle is the lead time required to replenish the stock (reorder and receive). The other factor would be the amount of safety stock to be maintained.

   • Safety stock is required to cover:

      ■ Forecast error over lead time period.

      ■ Variances in lead time (delivery) performance.

      ■ Potential supply-quality losses.

   • And typically you would use a service factor (Z) to determine the multiplier for sizing the amount of inventory to be stored, so given a normal distribution of ability to fulfill orders, we can choose a level of customer service which will then determine how much safety stock to carry. See Figure 2.2 for a diagram of the service factor (Z) determination (see Figure 5.6).

   • The formulas for calculating the amount of safety stock is shown in Figure 5.7.

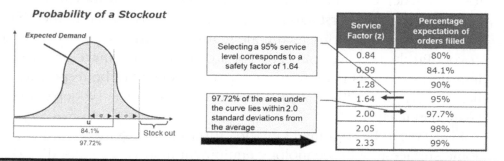

Figure 5.6   Service Factor Based On Normal Distribution and Service Target.

The Safety Stock component is the additional inventory held to protect against unexpected changes in demand and supply

- Uncertainty in demand results from:
  - Forecast error in the customer commit
- Safety stock to cover demand uncertainty is calculated by

$$SS_{Demand} = Z \times S_f \times D_{avg} \times (LT)^{1/2}$$

- Uncertainty in supply results from:
  - Supplier on-time delivery
  - Incoming supplier quality

- Safety stock to cover supply uncertainty is calculated by

$$SS_{Supply} = Z \times S_r \times D_{avg} \times (LT)^{1/2}$$

- Where
  - SS = safety-stock
  - Z = service-factor
  - S_f = forecast error = standard deviation of commit forecast at full replenishment lead-time
  - S_r = reliability error = (1-(Supplier on-time delivery %)(Supplier incoming quality %))
  - D_{avg} = average daily demand based on the previous month's actual demand (units/day)
  - LT = full replenishment lead-time (days)

Figure 5.7   Formula for Determining Safety Stock.

- However, order quantities, safety stock, and lead time represent only a minority of the sources of inventory problems. Many inventory problems are the result of poor execution, poor communication, and/or poor decision making.

2. Just-in-Time (JIT): A JIT system of production makes and delivers just what is needed, just when it is needed, and just in the amount needed. A JIT system operates very much the same as a traditional inventory-management system, but the *mentality* would be different, and there would be less tendency to have "just-in-case" inventory; thus, there would be a strong need for an accurate forecast. In JIT, you would want to create a large, frozen window where limited forecast changes would not be allowed; JIT, for the most part, would be evolving to a make-to-order scheme with a longer quoted lead time for customers' orders.

   JIT is a term that first surfaced (circa early 1980s for me in the US) as an overall manufacturing technique that was an American clone of the Toyota Production System (TPS). For a company to manage its inventory in a JIT fashion, its manufacturing operations need to be responsive, flexible, etc., or in 1997-onward terminology, you must be deploying Lean Manufacturing.

   In the early 1980s, I made my first trip to Japan to inspect/validate some surface-mount-technology equipment that we purchased, and I had the opportunity and pleasure to visit and study many non-Toyota

Japanese companies that were deploying JIT. And they were fully immersed in a JIT inventory-management system where they wanted their suppliers to deliver the raw material to their dock just-in-time so that their manufacturing could complete the finished product just-in-time to be delivered to the customer just-in-time to meet the promised delivery schedule – there were no just-in-case inventories in the processes.

– The benefits/advantages of a JIT system:
  • Lower inventory holding costs – With inventory purchased or produced at short notice, there's no need to have any inventory not clearly designated for a firm order.
  • Improved cash flow – Without the need to hold large volumes of inventory always; advanced expenditures are reduced.
  • Less dead stock – Because inventory levels are aligned with actual customer demand, there's less risk of excess and obsolete inventory.
– The barriers/disadvantages of a JIT system:
  • Limited responsiveness to order fulfillment – If a customer orders a product and you don't yet have it in stock, you run the risk of not being able to fulfill the order in a timely fashion.
  • Little room for error – Doing JIT right means having accurate demand forecasts and insights into customers' buying habits at all times. Any miscalculation could have a significant negative impact on business operations.

To optimize a JIT inventory-management system, a company could replace its forecasting technique with a pull/replenishment system; or many companies will adopt a hybrid system of forecast, most often for "C" items and sometimes "B" items, and a kanban system for "A" items.

3. A Pull/Kanban System reflects one of the driving principles of an Enterprise Lean system, i.e., creating "pull" and "kanbans" is a key enabler of the pull system. Lean-manufacturing systems use the kanban as a technique to keep inventory levels as low as possible; the process pulls materials through the production or distribution process. The kanban system provides a signal for reordering or replenishing inventory. A kanban system is an inventory-scheduling system that allows companies to stock only needed components and parts in the production or distribution process.

A "pull" system is characterized by items being produced only as demanded for use or to replace items taken for use. In inventory control, pull systems withdraw inventory as demanded by operations. This contrasts with a "push" system, in which items are produced on a schedule in advance of customer need.

In a pull system, kanban signals enable actual demand or usage to initiate the flow of materials. The term "kanban" is a Japanese word that, roughly, translates to a "sign" or "signal." A kanban gives a signal that provides authorization and instructions for the production or withdrawal (conveyance) of items.

The mechanics of a kanban system are simple, as it generates two types of two signals, Production or Withdrawal. Production and withdrawal kanbans work together to create a pull system (see Figure 5.8).

– *Production kanban* signals an upstream process of the type and quantity of products to make for a downstream process. In the simplest situation, a card corresponds to a "kanban" of parts, which the upstream process will make for the next downstream process or supply to a decoupling-storage (e.g., supermarket). A production kanban allows the production system to start with the production and, also, describes the item that should be produced. Like all kanban systems, it is based on the principle of WIP limitation.

– A *withdrawal kanban* signals the kind and quantity of product which a manufacturing process should withdraw from a preceding process (or supermarket). This is also known as move cards or conveyance kanbans. Whenever a component is to be shifted from one production part to another this type of kanban are used for signaling. The card is connected to a set number of parts that are taken to the working place where they are needed. When these parts are

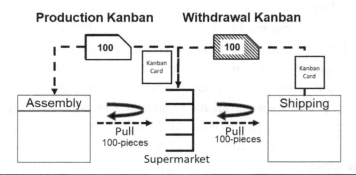

Figure 5.8   Example Traditional Kanban Card Production & Withdrawal Kanban Cycle.

used, the cards are returned as a signal for sending the same part with the same number back (i.e., to replenish the kanban).

The benefits/advantages of a Kanban system:

- Kanbans synchronize the supply with true demand/consumption; it's a pull-replenishment system, i.e., demand/consumption pulls replenishment from the supply.
- A properly designed kanban system requires minimum or no intervention by procurement staff, production schedulers, material planners, etc. It's self-managing when properly deployed.
- A kanban system allows a company to optimize inventory levels and fulfill customer-service expectations.

The barriers/disadvantages of a Kanban system:

- Staff discipline – A lot of kanban systems required kanban cards to be managed by material handlers, water spiders, expeditors, etc., and when the processes are not diligently adhered to, issues will arise.
- Kanban-sizing – This shouldn't be a barrier or a disadvantage, but many companies attempt to implement kanbans without proper training, preparation, etc., and many companies fail, and they may not know why.
- Kanban-sizing must be periodically monitored to adjust for potential demand fluctuations, seasonality, new product introductions, etc.

Another integral part of most pull systems is a *supermarket*. A supermarket in a manufacturing environment is a location where a predetermined amount of inventory is maintained to supply downstream processes. Each item in a supermarket has a specific location from which a material handler withdraws materials and/or products in the precise amounts needed by a downstream process. And it does operate like your typical grocery supermarket: a "customer" (a downstream activity) takes what they need and then a "supplier" (an upstream activity) replenishes the supermarket. Actually, in the 1950s, Toyota developed their just-in-time system around the American retail supermarket concept.

- In a supermarket-enabled pull-production system, each process has a "storage area" (supermarket) that holds a controlled amount of each product that is produced by that process. An upstream process simply produces to replenish what is consumed (or withdrawn) from its supermarket. Typically, as the material is withdrawn from the supermarket by the downstream process, a kanban will be sent upstream to authorize the upstream process to replenish what was withdrawn.

The potential disadvantage of a supermarket system is that it must carry an inventory of all part numbers that the processes produce, which may not always seem feasible if the quantity of part numbers is large. So to be effective, the strategy for a supermarket must link to a company's manufacturing run strategies *(see Chapter 6)*, which would define manufacturing replenishment intervals, manufacturing replenishment lead times, etc.

Another form of pull production is sequential pull production, which is a pull system that utilizes a mechanism such as a heijunka box *(see Chapter 6)* to assist in scheduling the replenishment of kanbans.

Most of my experience with pull production has centered around a hybrid of the sequential pull system and a pure supermarket. There's a decoupling of downstream customer demand from some upstream operations; once an external customer demand triggers the process by pulling its needs, that will trigger upstream activities, but the activities will not be fully synchronized, as the upstream replenishment processes may be sequentially scheduled in accordance with the upstream manufacturing run strategies.

But we often need to decouple the system and utilize supermarkets. This is an asynchronous system, as many of the upstream parts will be manufactured at a different rate than the customers' actual consumption. Upstream parts replenish production kanbans; but most often a customer order signals a withdrawal kanban, which is synchronous with the customer demand, But the pull signals to replenish the supermarkets are asynchronous and are being pulled by the customers' demand (consumption) (see Figure 5.9).

Regardless of the form, kanban signals instruct processes to make products, and they instruct material handlers to move products. And as previously stated; the former use is called production kanban (or make kanban); the latter use is termed withdrawal kanban (or conveyance or move kanban). Kanban signals can be in many forms, including:

– *Kanban Cards.* Kanban cards are the best-known and most common example of a kanban signal. The kanban card contains all the information required to allow manufacturing and other departments to communicate what needs to be produced and what materials in what quantity are needed for the production process – all via the kanban cards.

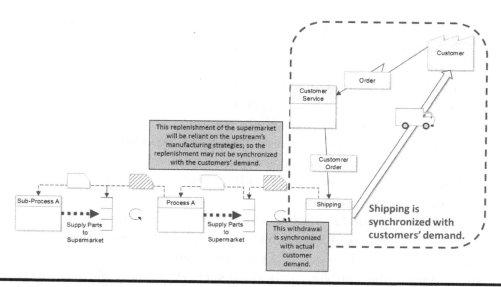

Figure 5.9   Example of Pull System Utilizing Supermarkets.

- Kanban cards are often placed in parts buckets. When the production team runs out of parts in the bucket, the kanban card is sent back to the receiving department or inventory department with the next order of parts. The receiving or inventory department delivers the amount of parts listed on the kanban card in a bucket with a new card included/attached.

- In environments with various products to manufacture, the kanban cards are used to schedule production. They differentiate batches, specifications, and order of production. Then there are "traveler kanbans," which are attached to the batch of products as it goes through the various stages.

- One disadvantage of the kanban cards is that along the way, they could be lost. When this happens, there is decreased production and shortages may occur. Significant staff discipline is required when relying on physical kanban cards as your replenishment-signals.

  - *Colored-balls* or any other device that can convey the needed information while preventing the introduction of erroneous instructions.

  - The *absence of materials*, etc., in a marked floor area can be a signal for replenishment (color-coded markings and/or labels can designate what type of material and quantity to be replenished).

    - An empty bin, container, or cart can trigger replenishment.

- *Electronic* kanban signals can be automatically generated by an Enterprise Resource Planning (ERP) system or other types of IT systems.
- *Andon Lights* can be a signal to replenishment.
- *Fax Kanban* (see *Case-in-Point 3.2*).

 Triangle Kanban. The triangle kanban activates a max–min situation that has a designated reorder point. And when this reorder level is reached, a triangle kanban is released to trigger production to produce more. Figure 5.10 shows an example of a triangle kanban.

Lot-Making Board is another form of a kanban-pull scheme. A lot-making board involves creating a physical kanban for every container of items in the system. As the material is consumed from the supermarket, the kanban cards are detached and brought back to the producing process and displayed on a board that highlights all part numbers and displays each of the kanban cards in the system.

- A returned kanban card placed on the board in the shadow space indicates inventory has been consumed in the market; unreturned cards represent inventory still in the market. As predefined trigger points are reached, the production operator knows to begin making products to replenish the material in the market.
- A lot-making board allows information to come back to the production process more often, signals what has been taken away, and

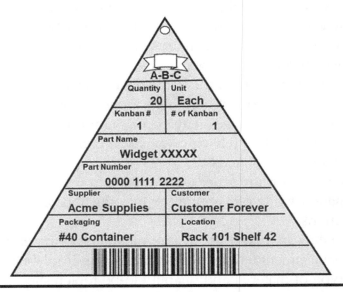

Figure 5.10 Example of a Triangle Kanban.

uses smaller increments than the signal kanban. It also provides a visual representation of inventory consumption and highlights emerging problems in the central market. However, it may require many kanban cards, and the cards must be brought back in a timely and reliable manner for the batch board to be accurate. Discipline is required on the part of schedulers and supervisors not to build inventory in advance of when needed.

2-Bin System – For many experts of this initiative, they agree that the two-bin system is the quickest and the easiest to practice. This is mainly because it's easy to understand, and once put in place, supply areas only come up with the specified quantity based on the frequency of product used.

– This system requires two bins that come with components that indicate the needed units to produce. The first bin's contents indicate usage quantity, and when used up, the bin is sent to production for refilling. At the same time, the second bin will be used until it is emptied. The first bin will only be returned in place as the second bin is back to the production area.

– The number of bins could be increased as required by the organization. What is essential is that these containers are dedicated for the components and not used for anything else. Everyone must understand the sole purpose of the bins and the very important signal they send out in the whole production process.

CONWIP is a kanban system that's based on the premise of "constant work in progress." The system is geared toward a high-mix, low-to-medium volume manufacturing environment, where you have a finite capacity and you manufacture to true customer demand but because of limited capacity, sequencing of the customers' orders is required based on a priority scheme.

The basic mechanics of the CONWIP scheme are:

– A CONWIP card by default does not include a part number. The part to be produced is defined when the CONWIP card returns to the beginning of the loop. There the card meets the backlog queue, i.e., a list of different part numbers that are waiting for production. This backlog queue is sorted according to overall priority. The most urgent products are produced first, as soon as a CONWIP card becomes available, if there is raw material available.

Someone must determine the backlog sequence (i.e., decide which part is more urgent than another one). The CONWIP scheme

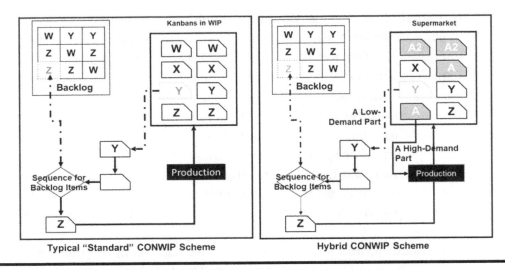

Figure 5.11   Standard & Hybrid CONWIP Scheme.

requires a lot of human intervention and manual planning/scheduling skills (see Figure 5.11).

– On the other hand, if you produce to order, a traditional kanban system would have difficulties. If every product you make is potentially unique, then you would need a unique kanban for this product. But since kanban are always assigned a part number, this will be difficult. CONWIP, on the other hand, has no part number assigned by default to the CONWIP card. Hence, any part number can be assigned (temporarily) to the CONWIP part, even if the part is produced only once. Therefore, CONWIP is well suited for made-to-order high-mix, lower-volume parts. However, for higher-volume made-to-stock production, you'd need a well-defined production sequence or you may end up with great difficulty fulfilling your customers' orders.

– The CONWIP may be a good option for your "C"s and, possibly, "B"s, but probably not your "A"s. So a hybrid system that has kanbans assigned to the high-runner part types and utilizing the CONWIP scheme for the low-volume parts might work; thus, whenever a kanban card comes along, the part number of this kanban is produced, and whenever a CONWIP card comes along, the most urgent part from the backlog of low-volume parts is produced. See Figure 5.11 for an example of CONWIP/Kanban hybrid-scheme.

The K_{max} K_{min} System is probably my "favorite" kanban system. It has the benefits of being a kanban system and the simplicity of a max–min

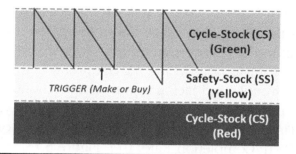

Figure 5.12   Inventory Levels of a K_{-max} K_{-min} System.

system. The sizing is amazingly simple and is based on the historical demand for the past 12-months (which is good practice for all inventory-management schemes).

As a best practice, the safety stock should be driven by the standard deviation of both the historical demand and the historical delivery performance for the past 12-months as well. And if the supplier has a poor quality history, then an adjustment for quality variability should also be considered (see Figure 5.12).

For more details on a K_{-max} K_{-min}, see *Case-in-Point 5.2*.

A Kanban Board is a workflow visualization and management tool. It makes the tasks that a team or organization need to handle stand out in a visual way that is accessible to everybody. This makes this approach much more flexible and allows it to be useful in a much wider variety of applications and environments. The Kanban Board is separated in columns which represent the discrete steps in a process that an item needs to go through to transform its status from impending to complete. Sticky notes are added to represent each task, and the team reviews the status of each action to determine how to move it to the next phase. That may require the task to be reassigned to someone else or for leadership to get involved to help it move forward. The function of the Kanban implementation is to allow a team to prioritize, organize, and optimize their own workflow while facilitating communication by providing clear visual information for all tasks.

4. WIP Cap

The primary function of a WIP Cap is to limit the amount of WIP within a process, but a secondary function is to set up the WIP Cap so that it's also a virtual kanban, i.e., a signal to replenish the WIP Cap. And since the WIP Cap is setting the maximum level of WIP, it's also establishing the minimum level before signaling for replenishment. To create this visual-kanban, you'll mark off areas as green-yellow-red, which means that if you have material in the green area, then you're good; material in the yellow area (empty in green), then you need to replenish; and if material is in the red-area (empty in green and yellow), then you're in trouble and facing a potential stockout.

Use Little's Law to determine your WIP Cap quantity, i.e., WIP Cap = (Lead Time x Completion Rate), which is based on Little's Law of: Lead Time = (WIP/Completion Rate) (see Figure 5.13).

5. A-B-C Analysis
  – Based on the Pareto Principle, also known as the 80-20 rule, stating that 80% of the overall consumption value is driven by only 20% of the total items, A-B-C analysis is a popular technique for segregating inventory into three categories: "A," "B," and "C," based on annual consumption (units/pieces), inventory value $), or cost significance.
    • A": Items of high value (70%) but small in number of SKUs (10%)
    • "B": Items of moderate value (20%) and moderate in SKUs (20%)

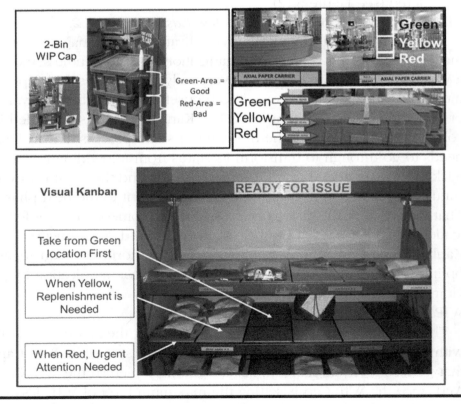

Figure 5.13   Examples: WIP Cap/Visual-Kanban.

- • "C": Items of small value (10%) and large in number of SKUs (70%)
 – Best practice is to manage each category separately and as required, as not every category needs the same amount of attention and effort. A-B-C analysis allows for the prioritization in terms of managing different goods and inventory, where selective control and allocation of funds and human resources are deployed.

 For instance, "A" items should be eyeballed constantly and put under special and tight inventory control because the need for reordering will be more frequent and continuous. On the other hand, items in Category C require minimum attention and can be kept under simple observation, employing a rather hands-off approach (see Figure 5.14).

6. Drop-Shipping

 This inventory-management technique eliminates the cost of holding inventory altogether. When you have a drop-shipping agreement, you can directly transfer customer orders and shipment details to your manufacturer or wholesaler, who then ships the goods directly to your customers. Thus, you do not have to keep goods in stock, and you get to save on upfront inventory costs and benefit from a positive cash flow cycle. Drop-shipping is, also, a form of retail fulfillment that can be applied to a company's contract manufacturers, outsourced items, etc.

7. Cross-Docking

 Cross-docking is a technique, like drop-shipping, where a company can minimize the need for transitional warehouses and their associated costs, while removing the risks involved with the additional handling and storage of transitional inventory. Cross-docking is a practice where

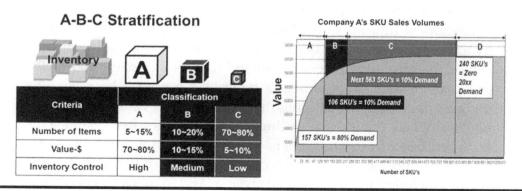

Figure 5.14 A-B-C Analysis of Inventory.

incoming semi-trailer trucks or railroad cars unload materials directly onto outbound trucks, trailers, or rail cars with little or no storage and handling in between.

– Essentially, cross-docking means you move goods from one transport vehicle directly onto another with minimal or no warehousing. You might need staging areas where inbound items are sorted and stored until the outbound shipment is complete and ready to ship, though. You will also require an extensive fleet and network of transport vehicles for cross-docking to work.

• Provide a central site for products to be sorted and similar products combined to be delivered to multiple destinations in the most productive and fastest method. This process can be described as "hub and spoke."

• Combine numerous smaller product loads into one method of transport to save on transportation costs. This process can be described as "consolidation arrangements."

• Break down large product loads into smaller loads for transportation to create an easier delivery process to the customer. This process can be described as "deconsolidation arrangements."

8. Bulk Shipments

This method banks on the notion that it is almost always cheaper to purchase and ship goods in bulk, so you plan to reorder products and replenish your inventory less frequently than you usually would. Bulk shipping is one of the predominant inventory-management techniques in the industry, which can be applied for goods with high customer demand.

– The downside to bulk shipping is that you will need to lay out extra money on warehousing the inventory, which will most likely be offset by the amount of money saved from purchasing products in huge volumes and selling them off fast.

9. Consignment Inventory – Consignment inventory is the inventory owned by the supplier/producer but held by a customer. The customer purchases the inventory once it consumed (i.e., incorporated into their own products) or sold. Consignment is typically a way to delay paying for the material and delay entering the inventory into your system, but it's highly unlikely that they're getting this "service" for free. Manufacturers are often eager to have suppliers' materials in consignment, as consigned inventory is not on the accounting books of the manufacturer (it's not included in their balance sheets). And manufacturers often feel that they're getting something for free, but that's probably not true, as

most suppliers will incorporate a "holding cost" into their selling price. Remember the adage "[T]here's no such thing as a free lunch," which means that you'll pay for it in some way or another.

- When demand is reasonably known and stable, consignment inventory is not recommended. If a customer is pressuring consignment to reduce his costs, a supplier is probably better off offering longer payment terms rather than consignment inventory. This should achieve the same objective without creating the added burden of managing consignment inventory by both parties.
- There are potential scenarios where consignment is beneficial to a supplier, mainly in a reseller or retail situation where the supplier wants their product promoted by the customer and readily accessible to end users. The benefit to the customer in this scenario is that they do not expend capital until it proves profitable to them, meaning they only purchase it when the end user purchases it from them or until they consume the inventory for their operations.

10. Economic Order Quantity – EOQ

Economic order quantity (EOQ) is the ideal order quantity a company should purchase for its inventory given an average demand, item's value, stockholding rate (% of value), and other variables. This is done to minimize variable inventory costs, and the equation for EOQ considers stockholding costs and ordering costs. See Figure 5.15 for sample equation.

In addition to the EOQ for purchased items, there's an EOQ to determine optimum manufacturing quantity based on setup cost and holding cost. The graph in Figure 5.16 shows the relationship between setup and holding costs.

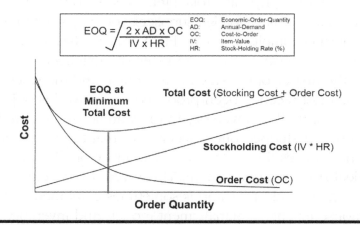

Figure 5.15   EOQ Equation for Purchased Items.

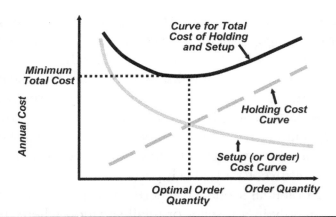

Figure 5.16   EOQ Equation for Manufactured Items.

11. Minimum Order Quantity

A minimum order quantity (MOQ) is the lowest set amount of stock that a supplier is willing to sell. If you can't purchase the MOQ of a specific product, then the supplier won't sell it to you.
 – All MOQs vary, depending on the product.
 – High-ticket items that cost more to produce will usually have a lower MOQ than low-ticket items that are easy and cheap to produce.

First In First Out (FIFO) Inventory Control – First In First Out is a commonsense best practice to manage the "aging" of your materials and/ or inventory. But I have also been surprised over the years (especially outside the US) by the number of companies that don't strictly enforce this, and it's often caused by laziness, as their storage racks have limited front-back access, so they'll just place the newer items in front of the old items rather than physically rotating the items. So if you're outsourcing internationally or have foreign suppliers; you may want to reinforce the need for strict compliance to the FIFO principle (see Figure 5.17).
 – A FIFO warehouse system is an inventory-management system in which the first or oldest stock is used first, and the stock or inventory that has most recently been produced or received is only used or shipped out until all inventory in the warehouse or store before it has been used or shipped out. This ensures that the oldest stock is used first and reduces the costs of obsolete inventory. It is also considered the ideal stock rotation system. This inventory system is commonly used in many industries and is sometimes combined with other warehouse inventory-management models and inventory systems such as the EOQ modeler or other multiple-order inventory models.

Figure 5.17   FIFO: Simple but Important Inventory Control Principle.

- The FIFO method of inventory valuation is a cost flow assumption that the first goods purchased are also the first goods sold. In most companies, this assumption closely matches the actual flow of goods, and so is also considered the most theoretically correct inventory valuation method.

12. Vendor-Managed Inventory

The goal of Vendor-Managed Inventory (VMI) is to provide a mutually beneficial relationship where both sides will be able to more smoothly and accurately control the availability and flow of goods.

- In VMI, a manufacturer or distributor assumes the role of inventory planning for the customer. Extensive information sharing is required so that the manufacturer/distributor can maintain a high degree of visibility of its goods at the customer's location. Instead of the customer reordering when its supply has been exhausted, the supplier is responsible for replenishing and stocking the customer at appropriate levels. Wal-Mart has mastered VMI and is the company against which many other organizations benchmark themselves.

- Customer Benefits – When the supplier can see that its customer is about to exhaust its inventory, the supplier can better prepare to replenish the customer because the supplier can then better schedule its own production/distribution. Customers will reduce/eliminate stockouts because they will not have to reorder goods at the last minute without knowing whether the supplier has the capability to restock without interrupting the customer's operations. Therefore, part of VMI's goal is to reduce the uncertainty that arises when the supplier is blind to the customer's inventory status.

- Supplier Benefits – As long as the supplier carries out its task of maintaining predetermined inventory and avoiding stockouts, it will be able to lock in a VMI-supported customer for the long term with or without a contract. This will produce a steady and predictable flow of income for the supplier and reduce the risk that the customer will switch suppliers (Switching would be too costly for the customer). A VMI arrangement will allow the supplier to schedule its operations more productively because it is now monitoring its customer's inventory on a regular basis. Furthermore, reductions in inventory will be achieved once the supplier develops a better understanding of how the customer uses its goods over the course of a year.

13. Vendor-Managed Replenishment (VMR)

When a manufacturing company uses many components for their finished goods, they find that they can spend a lot of time in forecasting, ordering, and receiving thousands of items. In many cases, these items are supplied by only a few vendors.

- As companies try to improve customer service and reduce costs, they are looking to their suppliers to provide them with a service that benefits them and provides the vendor with a level of security. One way in which this can be achieved is for companies to adopt a vendor-managed replenishment (VMR) program.
- This is like the vendor-managed inventory (VMI) programs that companies use but has several differences.
- VMR versus VMI
  • In the VMI model, the vendor will own the inventory and will replenish inventory based on pre-agreed min–max quantities. The customer owns the inventory once it is removed from the warehouse and can sometimes have liability for inventory that has not been removed.
- With VMR programs, the customer owns the inventory and the vendor is responsible for replenishment to pre-agreed, demand-driven min–max quantities. Therefore, with VMR, the customer has liability for the goods once they arrive from the vendor, whether they have been used or not.
- With the VMR model, the customer must be vigilant that the min–max levels that they agree to do not allow for too much inventory to be delivered, as they will own whatever inventory is supplied by the vendor.

Inventory-Management Best Practices

There are numerous best practices included in the previous inventory-management techniques; actually, each technique is a potential best practice if applied effectively. But there are also other best practice activities relevant to inventory-management; below are a few that I believe to be of significant importance:

Inventory Accuracy – One activity to assist in maintaining accurate inventory data is "cycle counting." Cycle counting is an inventory auditing procedure, where a small subset of inventory, in a specific location, is counted on a specified day. Cycle counts contrast with traditional physical inventory in that a full physical inventory may stop operation at a facility while all items are counted at one time. Cycle count compares the balance-on-hand based on this actual physical count versus the quantity, item, etc., that are supposed to be there per current inventory-records (database, IT systems, or any record-keeping system). Cycle counting is about continuously counting samples of inventory and utilizing that data to drive root-cause resolution of any discrepancies uncovered. When a root cause is identified and resolved, then the proper countermeasures must be implemented and deployed throughout all relevant operations.

Best practice in deploying cycle counting is to utilize an A-B-C scheme; such as the "A" items are counted often, probably once per month, "B" items are counted less often, maybe per calendar quarter, and "C" items are counted even less often, perhaps once per year.

The key to cycle counting is to drive permanent resolution of uncovered issues; without root-cause problem-solving initiatives to address discrepancies found by cycle counting, I would argue that your cycle counting effort is wasted and useless.

Pooling Inventory – In a multiple-warehouse distribution landscape, strategic decisions as to where items, and their quantities, are warehoused is important to optimizing the various inventory levels in relation to customer-service objectives. Stocking every item in every warehouse is probably not necessary. Pooling inventory strategies are deployed when items have highly variable demand across stocking locations. Inventory centralization is a potential strategic solution, although you must be cognizant of potential longer delivery lead times and increased expediting efforts and shipping costs. Always think total cost. There are advantages and disadvantages to centralizing inventory (see Figure 5.18).

Postponement – Postponement (a.k.a. late-differentiation) strategies purposely delay the completion of items at designated points in the supply chain until the customer order is received. Thus, postponement is a business strategy which maximizes possible benefit and minimizes risk by delaying further investment into a product or service until the

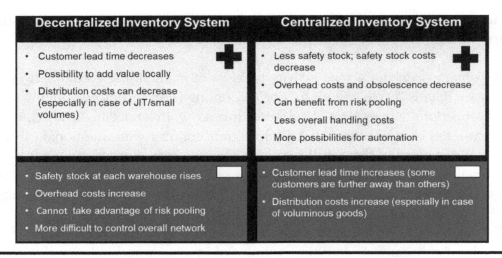

Figure 5.18   Pluses/Minuses of Decentralized & Centralized Inventories.

last possible moment. Postponed activities could include labeling, packaging, manufacturing and/or assembly. Dell's computer build-to-order online store is, probably, one of the most effective applications of this (see "Dell's Push-Pull System").

Lean Inventory-Management – The deployment of Lean techniques within inventory-management (and throughout the supply chain) is a trending best practice. See the section "Lean Concepts in Inventory-Management" (see Figure 5.19).

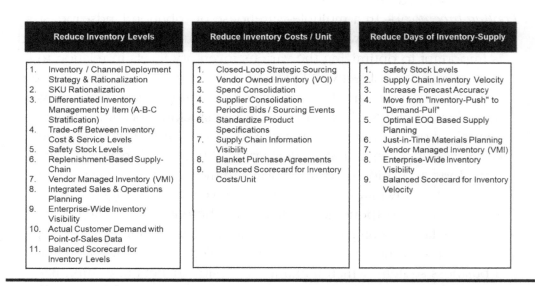

Figure 5.19   Best-Practice Inventory Optimization Techniques.

Dell's Push-Pull System

Dell's computer build-to-order online store is probably one of the most effective applications of late (or delayed) differentiation. And Dell's system is often referred to as a "push-pull" system, as it's a combination of both.

Basically, Dell manufacturers (pushes) a few "standard" products to its warehouses, and then customers go online and configure (pulls options) the "standard" unit to fit their needs. And although it's being called a push-pull system by many, to me it's just a superb example of late-differentiation.

The Dell push-pull system has three essential supply-chain principles:

1. Minimal inventory counts of consumables and configurable components, thus avoiding obsolescence and minimizing inventory holding costs.
2. Custom-made finished goods are sold directly to the end users, allowing Dell to easily sell on other products and services through this direct interface with the end users (its customers).
3. Strong direct end-user customer service. Dell's customers get direct service with no middlemen.

And a few best-practice characteristics of the Dell system are:

■ The "standard" base equipment is primarily stocked per a max–min scheme.
■ The "options" that the end users are able to pull from its stock are based on forecasts but are retained at minimal, very manageable levels (there are short lead times for replenishing the stocked "options").
■ The short lead times involved give Dell a competitive advantage in supplying its customers and delivering new products to market.

Lean Concepts in Inventory-Management

Many companies are initiating Lean inventory-management techniques to assist in increasing flexibility and/or responsiveness to customers' fluctuating demand, to lower operating expenses, and to improve overall supply-chain performance. Lean supply-chain and inventory-management techniques enable companies to improve efficiency and increase profits.

Lean terminology and concepts will be mentioned and featured predominantly throughout this book, with an initial heavy dose in Chapter 3. But I don't think there's any one area in the supply chain that can benefit more from Lean concepts than inventory-management.

Lean can be defined as the "relentless pursuit to eliminate waste," and that definition can be extended by stating that Lean strives to provide maximum value to customers while consuming the minimum amount of resources as possible, i.e., maximum value at minimum cost.

Lean's inception (although it surely wasn't known as Lean at that time) can be attributed to work by Henry Ford in the 1920s, as Ford wanted to manufacture automobiles that would be affordable to all Americans. In 1913, Ford established the first-ever moving assembly line and, essentially, the first one-piece flow. In the 1970s and 1980s, the Toyota Production System (JIT, etc.) started gaining traction. And in the 1990s, the term Lean was coined, and in today's Lean environment, we're focusing our attention on the five key principles of Lean, which were, probably, introduced to many of us by the book: *Lean Thinking: Banish Waste and Create Wealth in Your Corporation* by Womack and Jones.

And these five principles (*Value, Value Stream, Flow, Pull, and Perfection*) have great applicability to lean management:

1. *Value*. "Value" is defined as the creation of value from the customer's perspective, i.e., something that's directly beneficial to the customer. And one way that Lean assists us in creating value is by the identification and elimination of waste (i.e., non-value-added activities). The seven wastes, denoted by the acronym TIMWOOD, are:
   – Transportation waste
   – Inventory waste
   – Motion waste
   – Waiting waste
   – Overproduction waste
   – Over-processing waste
   – Defects
   See Figure 5.20.
2. *Value Stream*. In inventory-management, the value stream starts with the acquisition of materials and supplies, continues through the

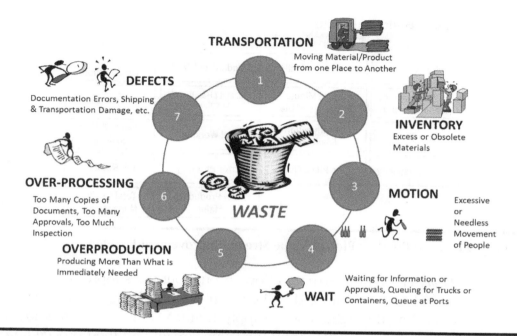

Figure 5.20 Obtain Value by Eliminating Waste (a.k.a. Non-Value-Added Activities).

manufacturing transformation stage, and then continues to the distribution to the customer. Value Stream Mapping (VSM) is a tool/methodology that we utilize to identify opportunities to improve the overall performance of the value stream. And through Lean initiatives, we'll strive to improve many of the performance attributes of inventory-management:

– Identify and minimize non-value-added activities (including all forms of waste).
– Reduce process lead times.
– Improve flow, including the reduction of WIP, etc.
– Synchronize production execution with customer demand.
– Create production/capacity flexibility (increase capability to be responsive to customers' demand volatility).

We'll utilize key Lean concepts/techniques to realize the performance improvements mentioned above. We have a Lean toolkit of concepts/ techniques that I'll refer to as the Lean Building Blocks, (see Figure 5.21). Some of the Lean concepts/techniques that are very relevant to a Lean value stream transformation are pull/kanbans, manufacturing cells, setup time reductions, one-piece flow/small batch sizes, production smoothing, create flexible capacity, etc.

Lean Building Blocks

Flow		Standards	Culture
Pull & Kanbans	Leveled Production	Standardized Work	Workplace Organization
Cellular Manufacturing	Single Minute Exchange of Die	Std. Mat'l Handling & Locations	Teams
Takt Time	Communication & Feedback	Visual Workplace	Training & Multi-Skilling
Flexible Capacity	One Piece Flow	Error Proofing	Job Rotation
		Total Productive Maint.	Total Quality Management

Figure 5.21 Lean Building Blocks: Value Stream Improvement Enablers.

Flow. Fluid, uninterrupted flow throughout the supply chain is essential for an optimized and efficient supply chain. To implement proper flow throughout your supply chain, VSM is a great methodology for removing waste from the value stream and then proceeding to ensure that all process steps flow smoothly with no interruptions, delays, or bottlenecks. Think of "flow" as a river (or another form of water); when it's free of obstacles, it flows freely, but when obstacles exist, the flow is turbulent (see Figure 5.22).

Pull. Pull is synchronizing what you make with what was consumed. It means that downstream's demand, consumption, or replenish signal identifies what needs to happen upstream. The basis of a pull inventory system is that inventory is only moved when a

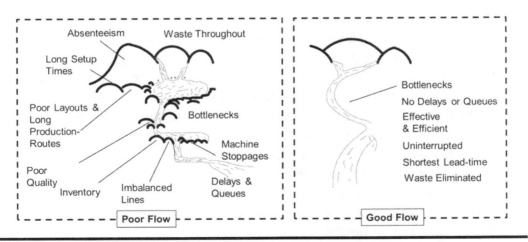

Figure 5.22 Develop Unobstructed Flow.

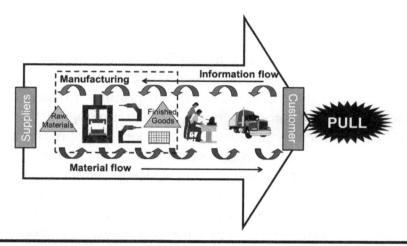

Figure 5.23   Pull Throughout the Supply Chain.

customer order is placed. Within the supply-chain landscape, pull identifies the quantity required, therefore signifying how many and what needs to be produced, which then signifies what needs to be acquired on the supply side. And one of the prime components of a pull system is the kanban. See Figure 5.23 for an example of a supply-chain pull system.

Pull is an element of Just-in-Time (JIT), and the primary goal of JIT, in terms of inventory-management, is to reduce safety stock to a minimum and to order/produce just enough stock to meet customer demands. The JIT approach has its potential risks (in terms of customer service), but it greatly reduces the cost of holding and maintaining inventory; there are trade-offs.

3. *Perfection.* Perfection is the perceptual "continuous improvement" of your organization, top-to-bottom. It's a culture of always striving to improve. Perfection in the supply chain could be defined as "constantly delivering the perfect order" (i.e., no documentation errors and the exact quantity ordered delivered within the required time frame with zero defects).

There are several Lean tools and/or methodologies that will allow you to identify opportunities for improvements in inventory-management, such as:

■ *Value Stream Mapping*: The value stream consists of all the activities or processes necessary to deliver a product or service to the customer. Value Stream Mapping (VSM) is a technique using flow charts to identify the key elements and activities in the processes and flow of material, product, and information. In VSM, each activity is identified as either a value- or non-value-adding activity. Lean management seeks to minimize and eliminate non-value-adding activities from all processes.

During the VSM process, the objective is to identify non-value-added items; e.g., inventory, waiting/queues, transporting of materials and product, motion, overproduction, etc. And after mapping, the team should strive to identify improvement solutions; e.g., pull/replenishment scheme, cellular manufacturing, leveled production, one-piece-flow, streamlined layouts, task elimination (especially inspections), etc.

The VSM effort should hopefully create a plethora of improvement opportunities which should then be prioritized by benefit (e.g., monetary, customer value, etc.) against effort (e.g., implementation costs/time, external or internal barriers, etc.). I personally prefer to plot the benefits versus effort on a Benefit & Effort (B&E) diagram (see Figure 5.24).

■ *Kaizens*: A kaizen (a.k.a. kaizen workshop or event) is a group activity commonly lasting five days in which a team identifies and implements a significant improvement in a process (see Figure 5.25).

■ *Workplace Organization (a.k.a. 5S)*: The basics of workplace organization are to remove clutter, optimize ergonomics, employ visual management, improve product and material flow through workstations, and minimize operator motions, etc. 5S is a technique to eliminate waste

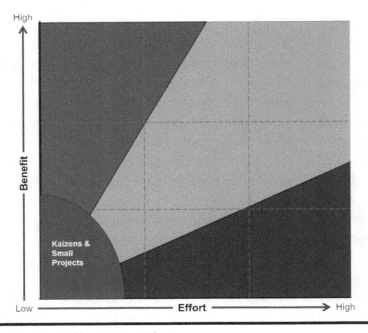

Figure 5.24 Benefit & Effort (B&E) Diagram.

Monday	Tuesday	Wednesday	Thursday	Friday
Finalize Problem or Opportunity (Consensus)	Value Stream or Process Mapping (current state)	Mid-Week Review	Implementation & Validation	Complete Control Plan, Action-List & Final Report
Data Collection Plan	Identify potential Countermeasures	Complete initial Process FMEA		
Data Collection		Finalize Countermeasures		Management Report-Out
Value Stream or Process Mapping (current state)	Value Stream or Process Mapping (future state)	Implementation & Validation	Complete Standard Work, FMEA, Control Plan	X

Define	Measure	Analyze	Improve	Control

Figure 5.25 Example Kaizen Workshop Agenda.

by thoroughly cleaning and simplifying the work environment to make activities instantly and visibly obvious. Visual management enables ease of understanding the status and current performance levels of the workplace. This is accomplished by making any issues visually stand out, such as missing tools, low or excess inventory, and out-of-place products (see Figure 5.26).

■ *Setup Reduction (a.k.a. Single-Minute-Exchange-Die [SMED])*; The goal of SMED is to reduce the time to set up or changeover equipment, product lines, etc. The goal is not to increase capacity volume but to increase capacity flexibility, accommodate smaller lots, reduce queues, etc. The key principle of SMED is to accomplish as much as possible to prepare for a new setup or changeover *prior* to the machine or line being stopped (this is referred to as external activities) so that the effect of the production stoppage will be minimized. And setup changeover activity performed while the equipment or line is stopped is classified

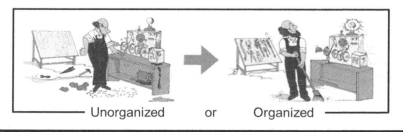

Unorganized   or   Organized

Figure 5.26 Workplace Organization: Everything Has a Place, and Everything in Its Place.

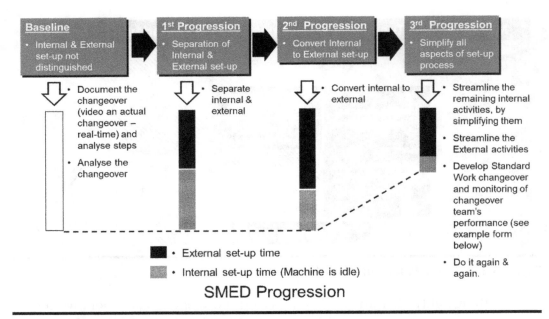

Figure 5.27   Single-Minute-Exchange-Die (SMED) Stages.

as "internal." "Single-Minute-Exchange-Die" is terminology from Toyota that represents reducing all setups, etc., to less than ten minutes (i.e., a single minute digit). See Figure 5.27.

Case-in-Point 5.1: Kanban Board/Lot-Making Board

Company: A German conglomerate's Power-Distribution OEM Division.

Scope: The scope covered a manufacturing facility in China.

Background: This was a consultancy client. The scenario that we faced was that their process involved a large fusion-type oven, and it was imperative that this oven be fully loaded with a complete set of assemblies for each fusion cycle. The assemblies were a combination of precision-machined mechanical parts and electromechanical subassemblies that were fabricated in-house in a job-shop mode with widely varying cycle times. In the current situation, they relied on an ineffective, complex scheduling system which rarely produced the right quantity and/or mix of the right components at the right time. The company already had several sets of gravity-flow storage racks to store the machined parts and subassemblies, and they meticulously but ineffectively tried to manage the inventory in the racks to provide the needed combinations of components for the fusion oven, but they never could get the right combination at the right time.

Project Approach: The obvious solution was to implement a kanban replenishment system and to convert the gravity-flow racks into a "supermarket." So the steps to implementing the solution were:

- Gather the process-routing and cycle-time data on the various machines and parts, fabricated subassemblies, and the subsequent assemblies by executing an RBWA (Routing-by-Walking-Around).
- Calculate the kanban-sizing based on daily demand, machining, fabrication, and assembly cycle times, and include a small amount of safety and buffer stock.
- Some of the subassemblies were heavy, so there were limits on the quantity per container and thus how many containers in a kanban that must be taken into consideration.
- Determine the required part mix to fulfill the fusion loading requirements, and complete an A-B-C alignment accordingly.
- Convert the flow racks into a supermarket (pre-fusion oven). In the true sense of a supermarket, we dedicated rows of the racking to specific component part numbers and maximum/minimum quantities of kanban. The number of rows and the number of kanbans varied greatly, dependent on the downstream demand, So we developed a simple system to maintain a proper FIFO (First-In-First-Out) flow.
- Create a kanban board to assist in managing the min–max scheme, as kanban cards of consumed kanbans were located on the board until the proper number of kanban card accumulated, signaling the correct quantity to launch a new production-make lot of those components (see Figure 5.28).

In the above example, the production launched when all the green slots were filled with kanban cards; if you placed a kanban in the yellow slot, that was a warning; and if you made it to a red slot, then there was a risk of having a component shortage which would shut down the fusion oven, thus stopping all downstream production.

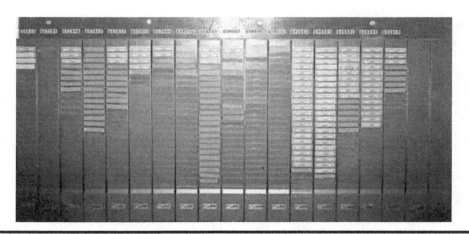

Figure 5.28   Example of Kanban Board/Lot-Making Board.

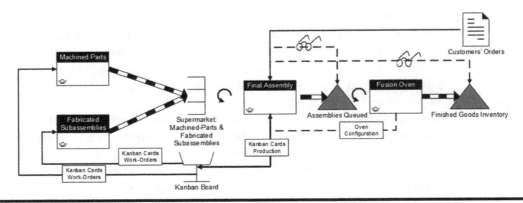

Figure 5.29   New Kanban Inventory-Management Scheme.

The process flow of the new Kanban Inventory-Management scheme was (see Figure 5.29):

■ Receive Customer Order.
■ Final Assembly planner checks inventory status at Finished-Goods and Oven-Queue.
■ Final Assembly planner verifies oven-configuration requirements.
■ Final Assembly planner pulls required parts and subassemblies from the supermarket.
■ Final Assembly planner releases kanban cards to kanban board.
■ Final Assembly planner releases kanban cards/work orders to Machined Parts and Fabrication Subassemblies when trigger point reached.
■ Machined Parts and Fabrication Subassemblies work centers complete Work Orders.
■ Material handlers move completed kanbans to the supermarket with kanban cards.

Key features of the new scheme:

■ The kanban cards control the number of parts and subassemblies produced; previously, there was always an excess of certain items and stockouts of others (more stockouts than excess). The kanban cards ensured the proper mix.
■ The kanban cards allowed the machined parts and fabrication subassemblies work centers to be level loaded.
■ The new scheme required very minimal planning of the kanbans; the system was basically self-scheduling.
■ The fusion oven was run at an optimal level and unplanned downtime due to machined part and fabricated subassembly stockouts being fully eliminated.

This kanban supermarket scheme was a great success, eliminating unplanned idle time at the fusion oven, removing unevenness through the pre-oven activities, and eliminating the laborious scheduling activities. The divisional managing director praised my solution; in particular, he praised its simplicity and fit-for-purpose. I was later called back by the managing director to design a similar solution for a second China facility.

Case-in-Point 5.2: K_{-max} K_{-min} System

Company: An American Fortune Global 500 health care services company.
Scope: The case-in-point example occurred at a medical-device manufacturing site in Asia.
Background: The site managed their inventory via a K_{-max} K_{-min} system.

The components of a K_{-max} K_{-min} system are:

■ K_{-max}=Maximum Kanban Quantity=the maximum amount of inventory to be in stock.
■ K_{-min}=Minimum Kanban Quantity=the *trigger point for replenishment.* Kanban refill quantity should be K_{-max} quantity minus the current balance-on-hand in the kanban.
■ CS=cycle stock=DD×LT.
■ DD=daily demand.
■ LT=time required to replenish the consumed inventory.
■ SS=safety stock=2–4 weeks (see Figure 5.30).

This company did not have an elaborate information-technology system to manage the inventory but relied on a simple database to monitor the balance-on-hand and to manually react accordingly. This system was very effective for them.

My only issue with this process is the safety stock is not "statistically/ mathematically" calculated but is maintained at two weeks for "A"s/"B"s and four weeks for "C"s.

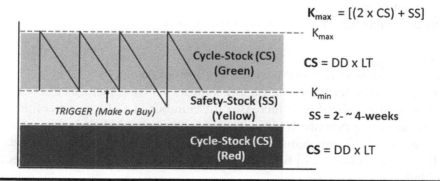

Figure 5.30 K_{-max} K_{-min} Inventory-Management.

But by utilizing this system for inventory-management, this site was able to have inventory turns at approximately 12+and still have an on-time customer-service level of greater than 98% for "A"s and greater than 95% for the remaining products.

Case-in-Point 5.3: Comprehensive Supply-Chain Assessment and Optimization

Company: An electronics manufacturing services company in Asia

Background: This was a consultancy client, and their biggest issue was too much raw material and work-in-process inventory. The CEO was under tremendous pressure from his board of directors to reduce inventory.

Project Approach: The project consisted of five phases:

1. Assessment
2. Gap Analysis
3. To-Be Design
4. Validation
5. Implementation

The project objectives were:

■ To reduce the raw material inventory levels (work-in-process was later included in the scope, but the focus would be raw material).

■ To develop and implement consistent raw material inventory-management processes/policies which optimize customer service and inventory levels based on current supply-chain capabilities (e.g., demand volatility, supply reliability). Review of current customer and supplier agreement/ways of working and their impact as drivers of raw material inventory.

■ To separate strategic and tactical activities associated with the procurement of materials.

■ To establish a strategic supply-management strategy.

Baseline:

Figure 5.31 shows the initial baseline-assessment data.

Figure 5.32 reflects the complexity that occurs from having customer-specific part numbers, as it increases the number of SKUs by threefold, i.e., so there are potentially three (or more) stocking locations and part numbers for the same items. The complexity was driven because of the lack of standardization in finished-goods SKU creation. It could had been avoided.

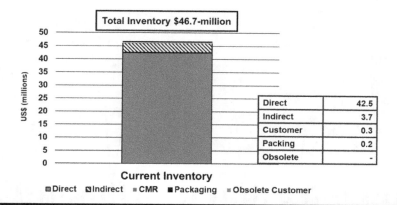

Figure 5.31   Baseline Inventory Data.

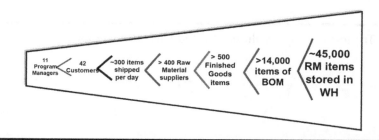

Figure 5.32   Complexity driven by lack of SKU nomenclature standardization.

Figure 5.33 shows a triple chart for a high-volume printed-circuit-board assembly (PCBA). The target inventory for the printed-circuit-board (PCB) is four weeks and for finished-goods inventory is one week.

Figure 5.34 shows the commodity-purchased distribution, and the annual-purchasing analysis revealed:

- Total annual purchase is US$80 million, with 15,400 POs (40+POs/day)
  - *30% of total is Integrated Circuits (ICs), with approximately 8 PO/day.*
  - *12% of total is PCB, with approximately 3 PO/day.*
  - *<1% of total is Label, Carton, and Tape with approximately 3 PO/day.*
- Total Suppliers > 450
  - *80% of amount is to 65 suppliers (14%).*
  - *20% of amount is to 385 suppliers (86%).*

Figure 5.35 shows the positioning of the high-PO commodities on the grid according to an evaluation of its risk and impact determines the supply strategy with which it can be procured most effectively.

There was a simple high-level RBWA done for the manufacturing process (see Figure 5.36 for a summary).

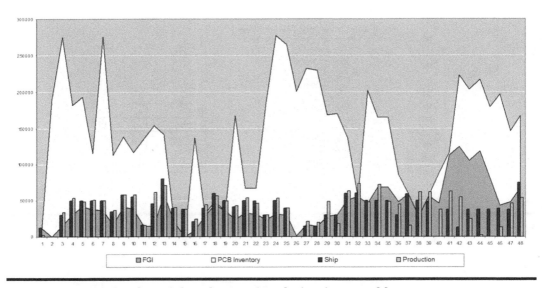

Figure 5.33   Triple-Play High-Volume Printed Circuit Assembly.

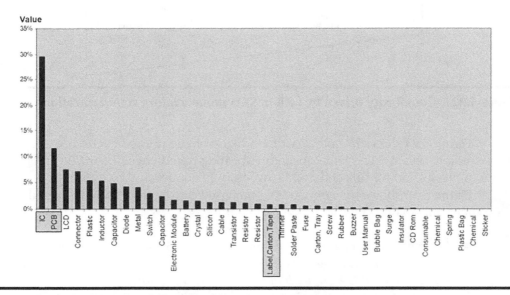

Figure 5.34   Supplier – Commodity Purchasing Analysis.

■ Only 28% of the operation is value-added to the processing of the product, so 72% of the operation is non-value-added (48% pure waste and 24% NVA-but needed). Other observations and findings were:
  – The Weekly Production Master Schedule (WPMS) is a plan based on the Master Delivery Schedule (MDS) per operation (e.g., SMT, B/E).
  – Each operation follows its own WPMS (i.e., fragmented scheduling).

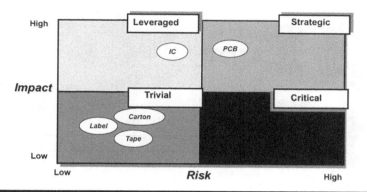

Figure 5.35 Commodity Impact – Risk Matrix.

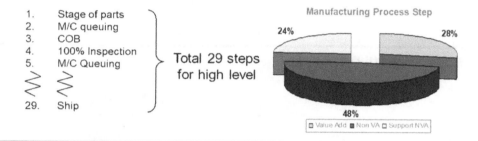

Figure 5.36 High-Level RBWA Summary.

- Prior operation can manufacture or pull in work orders that are not required at succeeding operations (i.e., pushing material downstream).
- Work orders might wait in other operations at times due to the availability of supplies (i.e., not synchronizing supply with demand).
- There are nine hand-offs within manufacturing (i.e., non-value-added activity resulting in more non-valued-added activities such as unnecessary waiting and queueing).

Figure 5.37 reflects a spaghetti diagram that was constructed from the RBWA data and observations. The spaghetti diagram, RBWA, and observations revealed:

- ■ The parts travel greater than three-quarters of a mile to manufacture the product (this is highly excessive for a PCBA).
- ■ The operations are arranged in functional-based order.
- ■ The processes are done in a straight-line concept.
- ■ Conveyors are built into the layout of production, where operators sit down and wait for the workload to be processed.
- ■ There are assigned locations to stage WIP inventory.

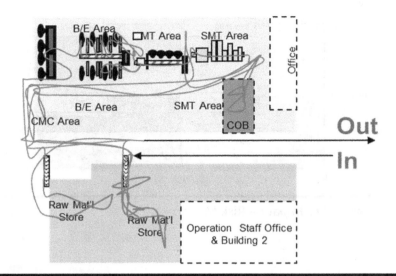

Figure 5.37   Spaghetti Diagram.

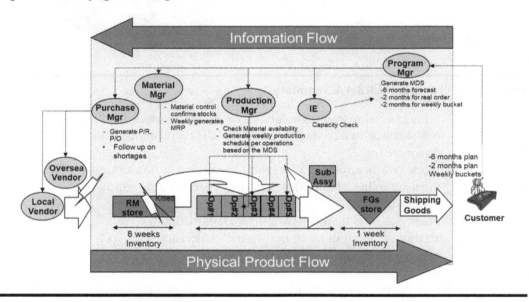

Figure 5.38   Current Supply-Chain Model.

- Production performs 100% inspection on all operations.
- There are assigned areas where the product can be reworked (touched-up)

The current supply-chain model is shown in Figure 5.38.

Based on initial findings, the opportunities shown in Figure 5.39 would be considered improvement countermeasures to the current way of working.

Planning and preparation consume 50% of the cycle time and there are more than 24 hand-offs to start production (Figure 5.40).

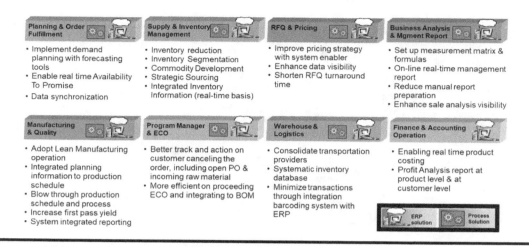

Figure 5.39   Early Findings & Opportunities.

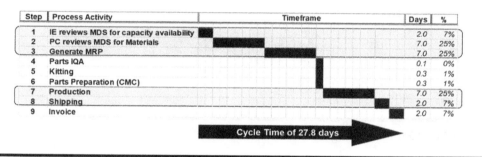

Figure 5.40   Current Order-Fulfillment Process.

Order processing and production planning:

- Multiple cycles of process due to the requirement to check material and capacity availability.
- RCCP is done manually outside MFG-Pro.
- Approximate one-week loss in material checking process after MDS/MRP generated.
- Critical processes like Weekly Production Scheduling still being done manually.
- Unable to generate synchronized production schedule directly from the system (see Figure 5.41)

Demand-planning model (Figures 5.42 and 5.43)

Based on a customer-service level of 80%, inventory can be reduced by 33% to $28.5M. This results in savings of $14.0M and greater customer satisfaction than at present (see Figure 5.44).

Target Inventory Level Model prediction shows order excess stock comprises 46% of total inventory, while cycle stock, 23%. Thus, the focus should

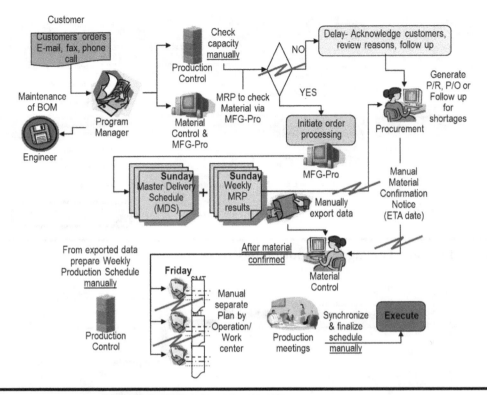

Figure 5.41   Oder-Planning Model.

be to reduce minimum order quantities and cycle times (i.e., more frequent orders) (see Figure 5.45).

Commodity group "A" makes up 30% of the total target inventory. Order excess continues to be the highest component, at 41% of the commodity's inventory, reinforcing the need to reexamine MOQs (see Figure 5.46).

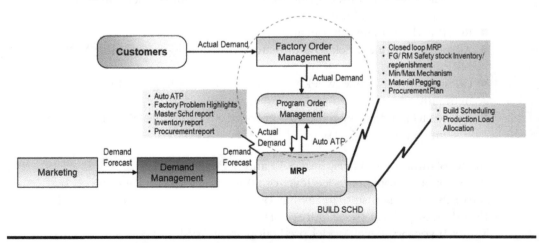

Figure 5.42   Demand-Planning Model.

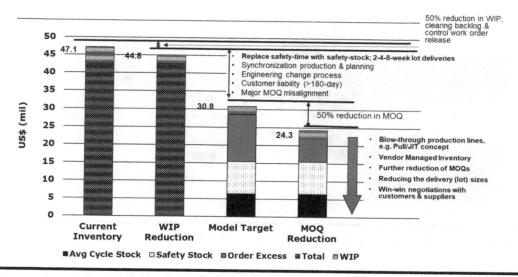

Figure 5.43   Inventory Improvement Opportunities.

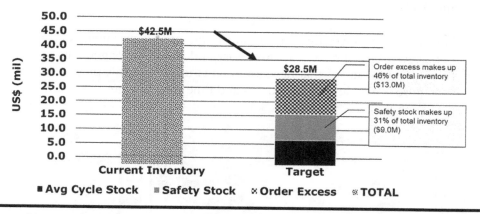

Figure 5.44   Inventory Improvement Target.

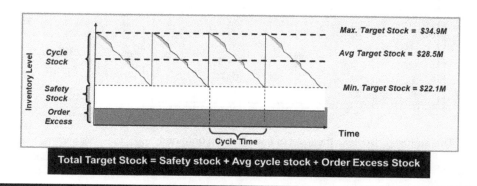

Figure 5.45   Inventory Improvement Target.

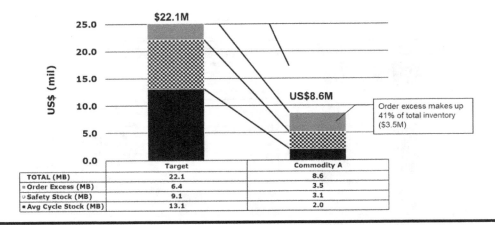

Figure 5.46   Inventory Improvement – Commodity "A" Target.

There were 19 initiatives identified to be implemented to reduce the inventory and improve inventory-management and supply management (see Figure 5.47).

Priority 1 – Initiatives that have a direct and immediate impact on the key focuses of this project, i.e., inventory and supply management.

Priority 2 – Initiatives that have an indirect impact on this project and/or require a high level of resources and time to complete.

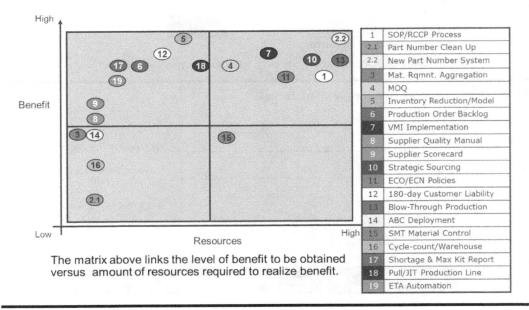

Figure 5.47   Inventory- & Supply-Management Improvement Opportunities.

#	Improvement Initiatives	Responsible	Priority	Project Charter Confirmed	Project Charter (weeks)
1	SOP process with RCCP planning		1	yes	11
2.1	Part number clean up		1	yes	7
3	New Material Requirement Aggregation using ABC classification		1	No charter, only follow up actions required	Done
4	MOQ review/ MOQ SAP configuration		1	yes	9/11
5	Inventory Model/ how to use inventory target to manage the inventory level		1	27-Jul	6
6	Clean up backlog & Production Order Controlling Process		1	yes	7
12	180-day customer liability policy		1	yes	17
15	Control storage & movement of SMT material in reels on shop floor		1	26-Jul	9
7	VMI Implementation (Phase1 &2)		2	yes	17
8	Develop Quality Assurance Manual		2	yes	11
9	Develop Supplier Scorecard		2	yes	11
10	Strategic Sourcing Implementation		2	yes	16

Figure 5.48   Inventory- & Supply-Management Improvement Opportunities Priority Summary.

#	Improvement Initiatives	Responsible	Priority	Project Charter Confirmed	Project Charter (weeks)
11	ECO/ECN policy change		2	yes	13
14	Enterprise wide deployment of ABC classification using Pareto Analysis		2	No charter Only follow up actions required	N/A
17	1. Shortage report development to have visibility of material requirements considering PO confirmed date 2. Max Kit additional report to roll up BOM requirements vs availability of the materials after sales order is pull-in to support production release decision		2	No charter, to follow up with MIS Plan	6
19	To automate the update of the ETA date from data source for each released purchase order		3	N/A	N/A
2.2	New Part Numbering System		3	N/A	14
13	Layout production line to accommodate blow-through operation		3	N/A	14
16	Cycle count/ physical count based on material value/turnover Redesign warehouse physical layout		3	N/A	16
18	PCBA semi finished goods BOM is created for multiple FG/ required Kanban execution for replenishment of SMT production line (link to VMI implementation #7)		3	N/A	N/A

Figure 5.49   Inventory- & Supply-Management Improvement Opportunities Priority Summary.

Priority 3 – Initiatives that are out of the scope of this project but are important to the overall performance of Company "A" (see Figures 5.48 and 5.49).

Benefits (Best Practices) – Inventory Management (see Figures 5.50 through 5.53).
  Benefits (Best Practices) – Supply Management (Figure 5.54).

Initiative #	Initiative (short name)	Benefits	
		Intangible	Tangible
1	Sales & Operation Planning	• Customer order commitment linked to production capability	• Reduce WIP as plan = production's capability, no excess • Improved customer service (OTD) • Reduce inventory (synchronization of production and planning)
2	Consolidate "common" parts numbers	• Reduce complexity and data in SAP. • Increase system efficiency.	• Reduce inventory by reducing redundant stocking locations of "same" part • 4,900 part numbers reduced to 1,200 with a current part-number base of ~17,000. This is a 10% reduction. With an optimized initial inventory target of $28.5-million, and a conservative approach (5%), the Balance-Sheet (BS) savings would be $1.4-million, the annualized P&L savings = $0.1-million (inventory carrying cost of 8%).
3	Material requirement aggregation	• Reduce overall administrative costs	• Savings are redundant to implementing the inventory model. See Initiative #5 below.
4	MOQ optimization	• Reduce overall administrative costs	• Excess inventory attributed to high MOQ is $13.0, so if we assume a conservative 30% improvement, then a BS savings of $4.6-million and P&L of $0.4-million • Reduced total cost of ownership

Figure 5.50 Inventory-Management Benefits & Best Practices.

Initiative #	Initiative (short name)	Benefits	
		Intangible	Tangible
5	Utilization of Inventory Model, i.e. statistically determined safety-stock	• Improve customer service (80% OTD target)	• Savings are redundant to implementing the inventory model. Savings based on reducing inventory from $42.5- to 28.5-million. A BS savings of $14.0-million and a P&L savings of $1.1-million. • Floor space savings – warehouse • Administrative costs savings
6	Clean-up production order backlog	• Reduce "congestion" within the production area • Improved customer service • Improved cash flow	• Reduce backlog from US$12-million to US$2-million • BS savings = US$10-m / P&L = $1.3-m • Reduce overall manufacturing cycle-time
11	ECO process	• Reduce overall administrative costs	• Reduce material obsolescence • Reduce excess inventory
12	180-day Customer inventory liability		• A May 2006 snap-shot had inventory over 180-days at a value of $5.6-miilion BS savings = $5.6-million P&L = $0.4-million

Figure 5.51 Inventory-Management Benefits & Best Practices.

Initiative #	Initiative (short name)	Benefits	
		Intangible	Tangible

13	**Enhance production layout**	• Improved customer service
		• Reduce administrative activities
		• Minimize non-value added activities
			• Reduce mfg. cycle-time from 17-days to 5-days (70% improvement)
			• WIP reduction (US$4-million) by 70% to $1.8-million
			  BS savings = $4.4-million
			  P&L = $0.4-million
			• Improve floor space utilization
			• Reduce material handling

14	**Enterprise-wide deployment of A-B-C strategy**	• MC and Procurement effectively spend time on the priority material, i.e. high value	• Reduced overall cost of ownership of top priority material • Improved management/control of 80% of the material value
15	**Control the storage/management of SMT material**	• Improve customer service • Improved visibility of SMT material availability • Minimize warehouse contamination from partially used reels	• Minimize administrative activities • Prevent material "losses" • Reduce changeover times & effort

Figure 5.52   Inventory-Management Benefits & Best Practices.

Initiative #	Initiative (short name)	Benefits	
		Intangible	Tangible
16	**Improve warehouse process and data integrity**	• Improve FIFO compliance • Shorten response time commitment to customers	• Minimize administrative activities • Prevent material "losses" • Reduce inventory levels, e.g. misinformation lead to duplicate orders being placed for material
17	**1. Shortage report development (considered PO confirmation date)** **2. Max Kit additional BOM roll up report**	• Ensure the availability of the materials for a product	
18	**Introduce a Pull/JIT production line**	• Satisfy customer's request • Improve customer service • Reduce manufacturing response time	• Reduce manufacturing cycle-time • Reduce overall inventory level

Figure 5.53   Inventory-Management Benefits & Best Practices.

Initiative #	Initiative (short name)	Benefits	
		Intangible	Tangible
7	**Reduce inventory levels through VMI, etc.**	• Improve customer service	• Reduce inventory levels • Improve floor space utilization • Improve cash flow • Reduce administrative costs
8	**Supplier Quality manual**	• Improved supplier reliability • Improved supplier communications	• Reduction in administrative costs
9	**Supplier Scorecard**	• Improved supplier reliability • Justification for eliminating poor performers • Improved supplier communications	• Reduction in administrative costs
10	**Strategic Supplier Partnerships**	• Improve customer service • Reduction in inventory levels	• Reduction in total cost of ownership (3~7%, annually) • Substantial reduction in administrative costs

Figure 5.54   Supply-Management Benefits & Best Practices.

Case-in-Point 5.4: Dynamic Inventory Model

The company in this case story was a Fast-Moving-Consumer-Goods (FMCG) (a.k.a. Consumer Packaged Goods [CPG]). The company was a global manufacturer of personal care products, household goods, etc., which meant that these products typically sold quickly and had to be replenished quickly. And if for some reason a product is sold out (no stock on the shelf), a consumer has many options of competitors' products to choose from, and/or a retailer may give the vacant shelf space to a competing brand. So stock-outs in a retail environment must be avoided, and that's one major reason why FMCG companies are known for having the best supply-chain process. And this particular company was no different, as they are globally recognized for their effective supply chain. But the manufacturing site of this case story was in Indonesia, an archipelago of more than 10,000 islands, which created major logistics challenges. And, as the fourth most populous country in the world, Indonesia was a large consumer market, but it was spread over a large land area with many very remote consumer areas.

The other major challenge was its product portfolio that consisted of over 22,000 SKUs. And this was a larger portfolio than most country's manufacturing sites had to manage, as it offered a larger range of packaging types and sizes (from individual one-use sachets to large economy family sizes).

The company had a complex distribution network that had included a finished-good warehouse at their three manufacturing sites, a couple of large central distribution warehouses, ten sales depots (smaller regional warehouses), and even smaller stocking locations at 11 sales offices.

The company had a global standardized homegrown legacy ERP (Enterprise Resource Planning) system that was effective for most processes, but it didn't have a robust inventory-management system and it wasn't set up to handle the many stocking locations that existed in Indonesia's consumer landscape. And all of the above-mentioned factors made Indonesia one of the most challenging supply chains within this Fortune Global 500 company.

The ERP system did allow real-time sharing on SKU inventories at all stocking locations, and the company survived by all the stocking locations working together and sharing the inventory as needed, which was an inefficient and costly way of doing business, but they made it work.

The consulting firm that I was employed by was asked to assess their distribution strategy and develop a Microsoft Excel-based robust inventory-management model for them.

Our assessment included:

■ Gathering historical demand data for all stocking locations and an A-B-C stratification of demand at all stocking locations (the demand profiles varied significantly by geographic location).

- Calculating current-state replenishment process lead times for each SKU based on manufacturing site and current distribution strategy.
- Calculating standard deviations for demand and process lead time variations by SKUs.
- Constructing a current-state matrix of the various sales offices and current replenishment routes and transportation mode (land, sea, and both).
- Understanding existing manufacturing run strategy (the frequency that SKUs are manufactured, i.e., daily, weekly, biweekly or monthly).

The results of our analysis also included the following:

- There were 184 SKUs that were 80% of the demand volume, and we established that these SKUs must be stocked at locations and manufactured and shipped on a daily basis to minimize inventory.
- There was a large group of SKUs (>15,000) that we basically found to be inactive; these items would only be manufactured and shipped from factories on demand, i.e., no held inventory at any stocking location.
- The other approximately 5,000 SKUs will be maintained at the central distribution centers and sales depots, and will be managed by max–min levels of inventories. We will statistically calculate the max–min setting of a customer-service level of 98% for "A"s (184 SKUs) and 95% for the other approximately 5,000 SKUs.

The company had requested (and we provided) a robust Excel inventory model, so that various scenarios could be modeled and the company could quickly know the impact on inventory levels. The model would recalculate new standard deviations, etc., on a weekly basis and adjust the SKUs max–min as needed.

The resulting metric was a 20% reduction in the total network inventory levels, and overall transportation costs were reduced by 30%.

Chapter 6

Manufacturing Execution Strategies

In this chapter, I will discuss aligning your manufacturing strategy to assist in optimizing your supply chain. And by strategy, I'll be looking at the manufacturing execution model. Manufacturing is the crucial element of the supply chain, as it's the element of the supply chain that produces the product to be distributed to the customer (see Figure 6.1).

The objectives of a manufacturing execution strategy are to develop the ability to:

- Deliver On-Time-In-Full (OTIF).
- Manufacture at the highest quality level.
- Respond to changing and potentially volatile customer demand
- Operate using minimal resources, i.e., lowest operating expense.
- Align with the enterprise's short- and long-term vision.

And the above objectives should be an enabler optimizing your supply chain.

The basis of an effective manufacturing execution strategy should be derived from Lean Six Sigma principles, thus leveraging the Lean Building Blocks (see Figure 5.21).

The building blocks which are most crucial to the manufacturing execution strategy are:

- Takt Time – The available production time divided by customer demand. The manufacturing execution strategy must be designed to accommodate varying takt time (i.e., customer demand).

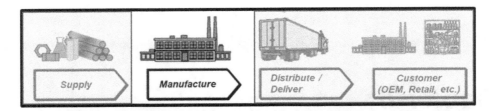

Figure 6.1   Manufacturing is the Crucial Element of the Supply Chain.

- Pull and Kanbans – Pull is about synchronizing production with customer demand; actual demand or consumption of an items triggers its replenishment. And a key component of a pull system is the kanban, a replenishment signal.
- Leveled Production – Production rate that remains constant irrespective of fluctuations in demand.
- Cellular Manufacturing – A manufacturing approach in which equipment and workstations are arranged to facilitate small lot, continuous-flow production.
- Single-Minute-Exchange-Dies (SMED) – A process for changing over production equipment, manufacturing line, etc., from one product or part number to another in as little time as possible. SMED refers to the target of reducing changeover times to a single digit, i.e., less than ten minutes.
- Flexible Capacity – Changing production (equipment, lines, staffing, etc.) to accommodate change in customer demand without losing significant effectiveness.
- One-Piece-Flow – Producing and moving one item at a time (or a small and consistent batch of items) through a series of processing steps.
- Training and Multi-Skilling – Creating manufacturing flexibility starts with creating staff flexibility.
- Total Productive Maintenance (TPM) – A set of techniques to ensure that every machine in a production process is capable of performing its required tasks every time it's required. Unlike traditional maintenance, which relies almost solely on maintenance personnel, TPM involves operators in routine maintenance, improvement projects, and simple repairs. Operators will perform daily activities such as lubricating, cleaning, tightening, and inspecting equipment and often minor equipment adjustments and/or setups (see Figure 6.2).

    The benefits of an effective TPM are:
    - Safer working environment
    - Improved equipment reliability – uptime

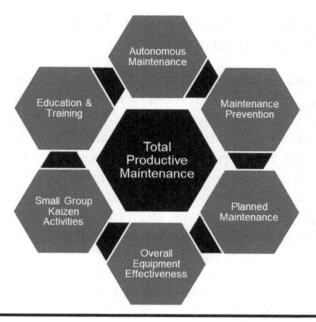

Figure 6.2   Six Core Elements of TPM.

- – Increased capacity
- – Increased productivity
- – Improved quality
- ▪ Total Quality Management (TQM) – A structured approach to overall organizational management. The focus is to improve the quality of an organization's supply-chain operating and all supporting activities/processes (see Figure 6.3).

Figure 6.3   Eight Core Elements of TQM.

Steps to Creating a Successful and Effective Lean-Manufacturing Strategy

- Start small and focus on trying to answer this question for all staff: "What's in it for me?" You only gain traction with Lean when people start to see the benefit for them. Get them engaged in small initiatives. Think about starting up SGAs (Small Group Activities). An SGA is a small collection of people related by common objectives who collaboratively work together to achieve common goals.
- Use metrics that drive Lean behavior and staff-engagement, such as:
  - SGA improvement initiatives, i.e., a rule of thumb that each SGA should target a minimum of four improvement initiatives per year.
  - Kaizens per year, i.e., a rule of thumb that a company should target one kaizen per year per every 10–20 employees.
  - Participation levels for participating in Lean-activities; e.g., Lean training, SGAs, kaizens. Individual participation would be based on hours of participation such as 40 hours per 12 months for all non-direct, including management, and 20 hours for direct.
- Use a site-wide program to identify and eliminate wastes: transportation, inventory, motion, waiting, overproduction, over-processing, and defects.
- Use Value Stream Mapping to drive improvement initiatives.
  - Optimize flow of materials, product, and information.
  - Reduce lead times.
  - Identify and eliminate non-value-added activities.
  - Minimize inventory levels.
  - Reduce operating expenses.
  - Simplify processes.
  - Define a short-term future state and a long-term ideal state.
- Utilize visual management, such as:
  - Hour-by-Hour production boards (track making takt)
  - Safety, Quality, Delivery, Cost, and Employee (morale) metrics (S,Q,D,C, & E) at the cell/line levels.
  - 5S audits and scoring: workplace organization and housekeeping.
  - Floor markings, labeling, and signage.
  - WIP control; e.g., WIP caps.

Every-Product-Every-Interval

Every-Product-Every-Interval (EPEI) is a manufacturing concept that would be described as a best practice as an element of most manufacturing strategies; actually, for many manufacturing strategies, EPEI is the prime premise of the strategy. The underlying principle of EPEI is production leveling, i.e., to distribute the demand evenly across a period of time (the "I" in EPEI). For example, you break your daily production quantity in lots as small as feasible and distribute these lots evenly throughout a period (a.k.a. Interval). The longer the interval the more leveled the overall demand is, but the harder it is to actually follow the planned-sequence. And that's where the A-B-C stratification becomes important, as shown in some of the manufacturing strategies listed later. See Figure 6.4.

Additionally, EPEI represents the frequency with which different products (SKUs) are produced in a production process or production system. It's good for an EPEI to be as small as possible in order to produce small lots of each part number and minimize inventories in the system.

However, a machine's EPEI will depend on changeover times and the number of part numbers assigned to the machine. A machine with long changeovers (and large minimum batch sizes) running many part numbers will inevitably have a large EPEI unless changeover times or the number of part numbers can be reduced. So SMED is important to reducing a machine's changeover so that more SKUs can be produced in smaller lots.

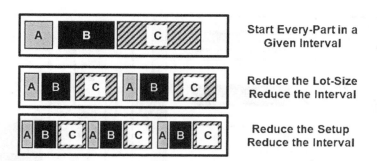

Figure 6.4   EPEI – The Mechanics of the Concept.

Manufacturing Execution Strategies

Most manufacturing strategies incorporate many of the Lean Building Blocks as they are best practices for efficient manufacturing operations. And all acceptable strategies will include some "pull" principles.

Differentiated Manufacturing Execution Strategy

Differentiated manufacturing (Figure 6.5) is based on the premise that you don't manufacture your "A"s the same as you do your "B"s and "C"s. And you would use the Pareto Principle (i.e., 80–20) to stratify your products, such as:

- "A"s are your high-volume products, your "High Runners"; potentially 5–20% of your SKUs and 70–80%.
- "B"s are your medium-volume products, your "Repeaters"; potentially 10–20% of your SKUs and 10–15%.
- "C"s are your low-volume products, your "Strangers" potentially 70–80% of your SKUs and 5–10%.
- "D"s are your lowest-volume products, your "Outsiders"; these products fall outside the Pareto Principle based on the total unpredictability of their demand. And these products are prime candidates for rationalization scrutiny and potential obsolescence.

So after stratifying your products, the next step is defining a manufacturing-execution strategy per the A-B-C-D groupings.

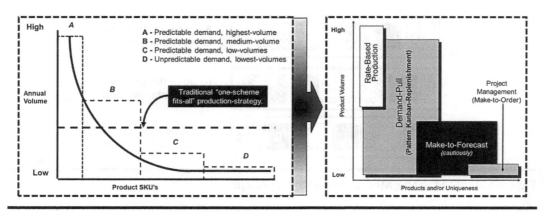

Figure 6.5   Differentiated Manufacturing Execution.

For the High Runners ("A"s), these products are consumed at a very high rate with minimal to no demand volatility, so they are great candidates for rate-based production, i.e., you produce an exact quantity of an exact SKU on a repeated schedule, preferably, daily. This is a type of "pattern production" (details in complementary strategy sections below), but for a limited product range with minimal flexibility in quantities and no flexibility in SKUs. An alternative to rate-based production would be a K_{max}-K_{min} scheme (see Chapter 5) where the trigger point would signal immediate replenishment at a quantity based on EOQ (dependent on changeover times). The difference in the straight rate-based production versus the K_{max}-K_{min} scheme is that the rate-based produces at a continuous set rate and quantity, whereas with the K_{max}-K_{min} scheme, production only occurs when a replenishment trigger is released.

For the Repeaters ("B"s), these products are medium volume and should be produced on a kanban-replenishment scheme, and depending on product mix, changeover times, etc., the scheme may require integration of a Heijunka or CONWIP enabler (details in complementary strategy sections below) due to potential capacity constraints.

For the Strangers ("C"s), these are low-volume products with unpredictable, erratic demand patterns. These items should be cautiously produced to a forecast, and most likely will likewise require integration of a Heijunka or CONWIP enabler (details in complementary strategy sections below) due to potential capacity constraints. Because these items reflect unpredictable, erratic demand patterns, you must be cautious to prevent producing excess and potentially obsolete inventory. The Strangers are high-risk inventory items and must be produced accordingly.

In my opinion, the Outsiders ("D"s) are products that are questionably being retained within a company's active product portfolio. But they are probably being retained for "business reasons," usually at the request of the Sales folks. Companies must really look at the disruptions that these "outsiders" make to their production flow; these production-disruptions inadvertently increase the operating costs of all products, including the Repeaters and Strangers, and possibly the High Runners. The Outsiders interject extra waste into the manufacturing operations (e.g., more WIP, more transportation, longer queues, more changeovers).

As previously alluded to, differentiated manufacturing incorporates many of the manufacturing strategies to be discussed in further details in the following sections of this book. Differentiated manufacturing requires a company to make further decisions on which strategy to utilize based on historical demand and the subsequent A-B-C stratification.

Pull-Manufacturing System

A pull-manufacturing system is a system that synchronizes manufacturing quantity with customer demand. Customer demands "pull" manufacturing requirements.

A prerequisite for a fully optimal pull-manufacturing system would be cellular manufacturing; you could implement a pull-manufacturing system (and get some benefits) without cellular manufacturing, but you would certainly lose some of the effectiveness of the system. Cellular manufacturing provides optimized material handling, maximum inventory control, real-time quality feedback, self-scheduling, optimum line-staffing, etc.

Depending on the variations between upstream and downstream operations, most pull-manufacturing systems would incorporate a supermarket concept. A supermarket is a stocking location where standard-inventory supplies downstream processes, and as its name implies, it functions much the same as your common, everyday supermarket (e.g., grocery store) The supermarket decouples the upstream operations from the downstream, as the supermarket holds the upstream inventory at a predetermined quantity and most likely, a predetermined safety stock or buffer stock, which makes the downstream operations nondependent on the process cycle times of the upstream operations. The inventory amount compensates for any lead time discrepancies between the upstream and downstream. And the safety stock or buffer stock compensates for any demand volatility, upstream equipment losses, etc. (See Figure 5.9 for an example of a supermarket system.)

And the item that links production to demand is the kanban (see Figure 5.8).

So, a pull-manufacturing system is that simple; a customer demand initiates a withdrawal signal to a supermarket and then the supermarket issues a production signal and production then replenishes the supermarket.

To keep the supermarket inventory low, the production process lead times must be short, which means minimal-to-zero waste, especially work-in-process.

Pattern-Manufacturing System

A pattern-manufacturing system can also be called a rhythm wheel or production wheel; the principle of this manufacturing system is a fixed sequence or pattern of production that is continually repeated. However, the actual amount and type of product produced each time in the cycle may be unfixed and vary according to customers' needs. The definition of the "pattern" is another potential application of A-B-C stratification. In my past experiences, I would establish a pattern of x-hours/production-day for "A"s, y-hours/production-day for "B"s, and z-hours/production-day for "C"s. So over a short time period, I would have manufactured all "A" items; and a portion of "B," and a portion of "C." And this pattern would repeat until all "B" and "C" had been manufactured, thus completing one cycle. And during this one cycle, it's likely that most (probably all) "A"s and possibly some "B"s have been manufactured more than once. See Figure 6.6 for an example of rhythm-production cycle.

Figure 6.7 shows a pattern-production scheme for a fabrication shop based on a 12-day cycle. And, equally, it's an EPEI scheme, as all parts will be fabricated during the 12-day cycle.

And there are a few techniques to assist in scheduling the individual "A, B, and C"s. They are:

■ *Heijunka Box*: A box (or board) for leveling the type and quantity of production over a fixed time. This enables production to efficiently meet customer demands while avoiding batching and at a minimal operating expense and shortest production lead time. See Figure 6.8.

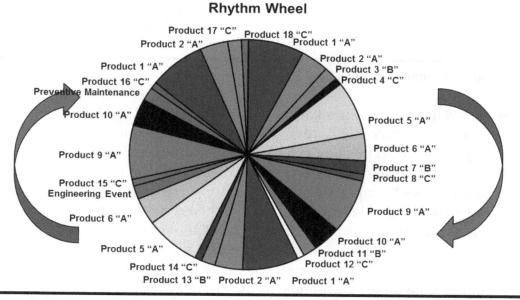

Rhythm Wheel

Figure 6.6   Example Pattern Production/Rhythm Wheel.

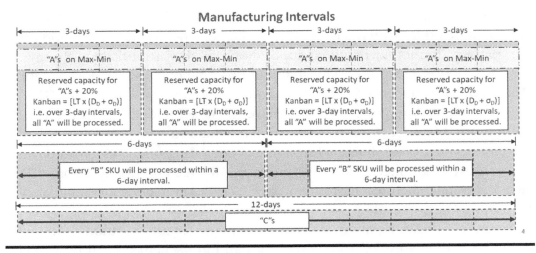

Figure 6.7   12-Day Pattern Production/EPEI.

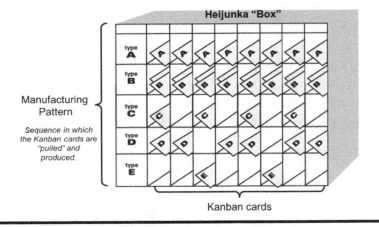

Figure 6.8   Example Heijunka Box.

■ CONWIP: CONWIP is a kanban system that's based on the premise of "constant-work-in-progress." The system is geared toward a high-mix, low-to-medium volume manufacturing environment, where you have a finite capacity and you manufacture to true customer demand, but because of limited capacity, sequencing of the customers' orders is required based on a priority scheme. See Chapter 5 and Figure 5.11 for the basic mechanics of the CONWIP system.

One strategy that can be adopted within the CONWIP system is to maintain the larger inventory levels closer to the customer, which will improve the ultimate lead time to the customer. This strategy is based on the basic concept of the CONWIP system, i.e., the sequencing of

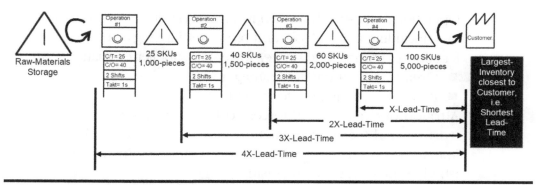

Figure 6.9 CONWIP Mini-Supermarket.

kanbans based on prioritization of customers' demand; thus the WIP inventory (kanbans) serves as a mini-supermarket that can quickly react to customer demand (see Figure 6.9).

Manufacturing Outsourcing – Offshore

I'm thinking that many companies have already outsourced or are thinking about outsourcing overseas. And I have extensive experience in this, so I'll share my perspective of some key do's and don'ts.

Here are a few steps to assist you in your outsourcing endeavors:

1. *Define clear objectives and expectations (qualitative and quantitative).* A successful offshore outsourcing strategy begins with clearly defined objectives, expectations, and measurable goals. Objectives state the reasons for the offshore outsourcing initiative, quantifies its business value, and provides an analytical framework for supplier selection, risk assessment, etc., determines which outsourcing model to use, what projects to outsource, and what levels of risk to assume. Outsourcing offshore should only be undertaken if fully meets all anticipated objectives and expectations.

2. *Total Cost of Ownership.* Manufacturing outsourcing is a strategy that many companies are opting for, usually as a cost-savings initiative. And my first immediate warning, think Total Cost of Ownership (see Chapter 4).

   When considering outsourcing, the costs that you must be very diligent in evaluating and monitoring are:
   – Start-up Operational and Administrative Costs:
     • Supplier selection: Expect this to take several man-months for a cross-functional-team.

- Operational start-up: Transition inventory, productivity loss and quality loss (including material loss and product scrapping), knowledge-transfer support (remote and onsite), lower-tier supplier evaluations, etc.
  - Organizational change-management.
  - Redundant activities (for months!).
- Attrition of existing workforce: Costs associated with removing existing staff (severance, etc.).
- Managing an offshore contract: The costs of maintaining a finished contract can be surprisingly high.
- Dealing with cultural differences (business and social): Invest in cultural training, e.g., "no problem" means that you are probably going to have a problem. Personally, having worked and lived overseas for 20 years, and off-and-on for another ten years, underestimating the impact of cultural (and language) differences can lead to catastrophic failure.
  - It's best to create a "personal-business relationship" whenever possible. Although the advice to maintain a degree of separation between onshore and offshore resource teams may seem reasonable, it's not. In a process-intensive activity, such as offshore outsourcing, it's easy to lose sight of the personal aspects of offshore engagements. While processes (FMEA, etc.) are useful to constrain risks and ensure consistency in performance, ultimately it is the people that make an engagement successful. The greater the extent to which personal relationships are fostered among onshore and offshore team members, the more chances you have for success.
    - When engagements face difficult times, as they certainly all do, it's unlikely that teams will dig deep, make personal sacrifices, and find additional motivation out of loyalty to a process. But personal relationships that are built upon mutual trust and respect can warrant the needed loyalty, especially if all parties are personally committed to the same goals with mutual expectations.
  - Absorption costs – Some companies fail to properly understand the impact outsourcing has on the remaining absorption costs at the "sending-sites"; absorption loss can have a major impact on the profit margins of retained self-manufactured products.
  - Shipping costs – A supplier's location has a major impact on shipping cost, as costs and complexity typically increase as the distance between

the supplier and the receiving point increases. And if the supplier in on a different continent, there's the multimodal transportation factor that creates a far greater degree of costs and complexity. Additionally, you must plan for agent and brokerage fees, as required. And if you're planning on ocean shipments, then you might as well budget a few expedited air shipments a year. In today's political environment, potential tariff increases make import costs an unstable financial variable.

- Shipping Times – Shipping times can be a substantial time variable for imported items, as you must account for documentation creation, customs clearance, etc. Ocean transport times can easily range from two to eight weeks or more, depending on the country's location and infrastructure. Inventory buffers must be sized appropriately to accommodate for shipping-time variability.

- Inventory – In addition to traditional cycle-stock inventory levels, buffer inventory must be held to accommodate for shipping-time variability and to hedge against a potential supply interruption due to political unrest, natural disasters, etc. These costs should include the buffered inventory value plus preservation and storage costs, financing costs, and risk of obsolesce.

- Supplier Management Costs (including travel costs for supplier governance) – These costs are often overlooked, but provisions should be made for costs incurred for traveling to build and strengthen relationships, to provide technical and production support, and to resolve any unforeseen supply-chain disruptions or quality issues.

- Foreign Currency Fluctuation – Potential foreign currency fluctuations if paying in foreign currency.

- Intellectual Property Protection costs. This is very country-dependent, as some countries have no intellectual property protection laws; thoroughly research any country that you're potentially outsourcing to. Proceed with extreme caution if intellectual property protection is a major concern for your products.

- Financial/Commercial Obligations – Payment terms, administrative and banking fees, etc.

Experience reveals that hidden costs can range from 15–60% of the outsourcing contract itself. But these costs can be minimized with meticulous, proactive management and relentless diligence. I suggest that you conduct a comprehensive total cost of ownership assessment throughout the entirety of the outsourcing initiative, with quarterly joint reviews.

3. *Understand and actively manage the risks* – A successful outsourcing/ offshore strategy requires an aggressive, robust risk-mitigation strategy. Your risk-mitigation plan will need to be multipronged:
   - Business Continuity is #1 – You must have a solid business-continuity plan. I always strongly suggest maintaining (a.k.a. retaining) capability (including engineering revision changes) at the sending site; if that's not possible, then a "sister" inter-corporation site or a second external supplier (preferably in a different geographic-region or at a minimum, a different country). Develop this redundant capability at the outset of your initiative.
     - Additionally, I would require my outsourcing supplier to develop a business-continuity plan for all material required to manufacture the outsourced products. And I would require the plan to include inbound and outbound logistics.
   - Failure Mode and Effect Analysis (FMEA) – The FMEA is a very powerful tool. The FMEA, by definition, is a methodology aimed at allowing organizations to anticipate failure during the design stage by identifying all of the possible failures in a design or manufacturing process. And that definition, as standard and acceptable as it is, to me, is an injustice to the FMEA's applicability. I have often utilized a Reverse-FMEA as a great problem-solving tool and/or methodology. So to de-risk an offshore outsourcing initiative, I would utilize an FMEA as:
     - Project Management – I'd use the FMEA as a guide to go through every phase of the outsourcing initiative and identify every possible failure point; and then brainstorm appropriate countermeasures. I would apply "Murphy's Law" throughout the project and list every possible failure mode and the appropriate prevention or detection activities. I would also utilize the Reverse-FMEA to identify potential project-failure modes and identify where they could possibly occur during the outsourcing initiative and take appropriate action.
     - Process FMEA (PFMEA) – I would require a joint PFMEA by the receiving and sending teams for every outsourced product, and these documents would be a critical management tool in monitoring the progress of the initiative.

   The risks to your offshore outsourcing initiative may occur in many forms; here are some of the more notable risks that can surface and derail the initiative:
   - Poor communication can create debilitating morale. A company's outsourcing plans must be clearly articulated to all parties in a

timely manner (i.e., before any activity commences). The lack of honest and truthful communication can do damage far beyond the outsourcing initiative itself.

- Failing to adequately calculate the total cost of outsourcing could mislead decision makers and create undesirable results.
- Failing to exert uncompromising effort and unrelenting due diligence in finding the right outsourcing partner.
- Overlooking capacity-requirements; while ensuring quality expectations are fully understood when outsourcing, it's equally important to choose a supplier (partner) with the capability to scale production seamlessly in response to unexpected demand increases.
- Creating a communication gap with the chosen supplier by failing to provide thoroughly detailed and documented specifications. All product details must be completely and flawlessly documented and articulated to the outsourced manufacturing operations to ensure world-class quality and errorless production.
- Underestimating the required onsite support required by all parties and unwillingness to continue support far past the initial learning curve.
- Not proactively monitoring the supplier's, and their lower-tier suppliers', compliance with relevant global environmental, health and safety concerns

Case-in-Point 6.1: EPEI – Assisted by SMED

A medical-device manufacturer had model changeover times >40-hours. So they were purposely planning very large production-run cycles, i.e., Every-Product-Every-Interval (EPEI) of four weeks, which resulted in large amounts of overproduced inventory (approximately six weeks of inventory). And this overproduced inventory created significant levels of excess and obsolete products, resulting in large annual write-offs of "C" products (high-mix, low-volume products). A major SMED initiative reduced the changeover times by 60% and thus reduced the EPEI to less than two weeks. Average Finished-Goods Inventory (FGI) was reduced from six weeks to two weeks (including statistically sized safety stock). With the reduced EPEI, increased demand flexibility resulted in On-Time-In-Full (OTIF) service level increasing from the 93–96% range to >98% for "A" products.

Case-in-Point 6.2: Manufacturing Execution Strategy

Company: Fortune Global 500 health service provider.
Background: This case story involves a medical-device manufacturer that produced medical gloves. The gloves were produced on a continuous flow dipping line, called a dipline. And a dipline could be equipped with approximately 4,000 to 10,000 molds per side; there's a left-hand

side and a right-hand side. Typically, there were eight sizes from 5½ to 9 per product, so the manufacturer needed capability for producing all eight sizes. And this required numerous setups, with each setup (i.e., size changeover) requiring up to 48 hours.

Assessment: An A-B-C stratification of the eight sizes would reveal that the smallest and the largest sizes would be the lowest-demand "C" types, the second-smallest and largest sizes being "B"s, and the middle four sizes being "A"s. The A-B-C stratification doesn't follow your normal 80–20 distribution because of the small population (eight), but the four middle sizes are approximately 80% of the customers' demand.

The traditional manufacturing execution strategy was to run one size at a time and to have very long process runs, as the dipline changeover was extremely long and laborious. This one-size strategy would create large inventories of the four outlying (small and large) sizes.

Solution: After much experimentation and some equipment modifications, it was determined that four sizes could be run concurrently – typically, two "A" s, one "B," and one "C" on each side of the dipping line. The percent of molds dedicated the "B"s and "C"s would be very small. The ratio of the four sizes would closely follow the ratio of customer demand.

So the manufacturing execution strategy changed from loading basically one size at a time to concurrently processing four sizes at a time; this would reduce four changeovers for four sizes to no changeovers for four sizes, and excess inventory would basically be eliminated. To run eight sizes, it would still require a changeover, but to run the full range of eight sizes would require one changeover versus eight changeovers for the original, traditional strategy.

Case-in-Point 6.3: Rhythm Wheel in Wafer-Fab (Semiconductor Wafer-Fab)

This case story involves a semiconductor wafer-fab operation of a diversified global integrated-semiconductor company. The site for this case story produced a large portfolio of semiconductor wafers. A typical high-demand wafer went through 22 major process (equipment) steps with a total average process lead time of 14.2 days. All of the wafers had varying process cycle times and shared many pieces of processing equipment.

It was determined that setting up a Rhythm Wheel with a 7-day wafer launch repeating cycle could reduce the process lead time from 14.2 days to an average of 6.5 days. A "virtual" cell was created by dedicating 40% of the site's equipment to its highest-running product group.

To assess the overall process flow of this wafer group, a detailed Routing-by-Walking-Around[1] (RBWA) was conducted. The RBWA revealed that a typical wafer took a total of 1,977 steps (total tasks, not just

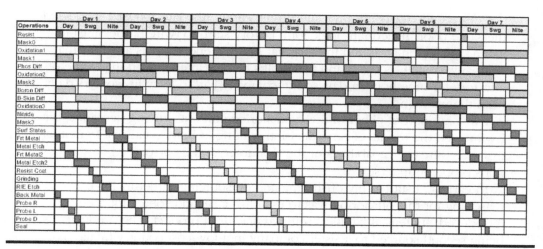

Figure 6.10 Representative Example – 7-Day Pattern Production.

equipment process steps) to complete, and the value-added number of steps was a very respectable 12%. With the implementation of the virtual cells, the total number of process steps (tasks) was reduced to 1,028, a 48% reduction. The value-added content was improved from 12% to 23%, a 92% improvement.

Figure 6.10 is a representative structuring of a 7-Day Rhythm Wheel cycle; launching a new lot (batch) of wafers daily on a repetitive A-B-C pattern.

Case-in-Point 6.4: Offshore Outsourcing (Making It Personal?)

I got my first taste of offshore outsourcing in 1978 when I was supporting a wire-harnessing operation in Port-au-Prince, Haiti. The decision to outsource was made before I arrived at my employer, and the purpose of outsourcing was strictly cost, although almost 100% of all harnesses required some type of rework. Many cable assemblies got damaged in customs operations in Haiti and the US, but most likely in Haiti, as the infrastructure in Haiti was truly undeveloped. That assessment can be validated by my rental car, a 1960s Simca, and the five flat tires that I encountered during my week there. We provided all the tools, harness-layout boards, etc., and Haiti only provided the labor. And, while the labor was much cheaper than in the US, their workmanship was no better than in the States (I guess fishing villagers were supposedly good at making fishing nets, so why not complex computer mainframe wire harnesses? – an incorrect assumption). But once the items were outsourced, it was thought that it was better to leave the items offshore rather than expending money to onshore them back.

Coincidently (or comically), later in my career (the late 1980s), I witnessed the same poor "fisherman" logic for a factory start-up (wire harnessing) in a fishing village on an island in Malaysia. But that ended up as a fail for that company as well, as the island fisherfolks had no interest working inside of a factory for nine hours a day, so the company had to ferry in workers daily from the mainland.

I was not part of either of these offshoring and outsourcing decisions, but I witnessed the results of poor decision making in both instances. In neither instance were the capabilities of the workforce at the outsourced destinations properly understood.

In earnest, I started my offshoring and outsourcing career in 1984. The reasoning for this offshoring was to establish a second source for a newly introduced, strategically critical self-manufactured product. The product was being second sourced to a sister company in a low-cost country (Malaysia). This was a single SKU to be produced at a relatively small quantity, but again the real priority was to develop a second source as a business-continuity solution for a strategic-product. The receiving company sent four engineers to North America for six months (one remained for 12 months) so that they could fully understand every element of the manufacturing process for this single SKU; and when the product was to commence manufacturing offshore, I went to their site for two weeks to assist and oversee their manufacturing start-up. The bottom line is that this was an extremely successful project; there was never a single cost, quality, or delivery issue due to the extensive effort upfront in preparing, training, and planning the project. And I did create strong personal relationships with the whole outsourcing team, and I strongly believe that these personal relationships were significant in the ultimately very successful offshoring project. Over more than the next six years, we used this same project management blueprint for outsourcing of a wide array of complex products (hundreds of SKUs) to multiple sites in Malaysia and Thailand. Over more than a ten-year period, there was never a serious quality issue and never a premium freight shipment due to a delivery issue. All-in-all, there were many years of trouble-free offshoring with zero negative impact and never any hidden costs, etc. The key success factors were the mutual commitment by both teams to be successful (leveraged by the personal relationships) and the extensive, meticulous training and planning prior to any product or equipment transferred, as well as the extensive ongoing remote and onsite support by the "sending" site.

After these extremely successful knowledge transfers to a sister company, I used the same recipe for offshoring/outsourcing to matrix-manage successful projects of offshoring a completely new product platform and an existing product platform to European supply partners. In all instances, personal relationships of varying degrees were a success factor.

On a larger scale, I matrix-managed a greenfield manufacturing start-up in rural China. I spent two years during the planning and preparation stages prior to starting manufacturing in China. I interviewed and site-visited multiple potential supply partners (primary equipment and service providers and a few critical components) in China, Hong Kong, and a few other Asian locales before selecting any suppliers for our new supply chain. Extensive due diligence went into the selection of suppliers, and personal relationships had begun to form with all the chosen suppliers.

In my later years, I have supported many of my employers' offshore supply partners (contract manufacturers), and in all cases there were personal relationships built (some stronger than others). I provided extensive Lean Six Sigma training at these suppliers at no charge and mentored them in projects, thus creating strong, win–win business relationships. These were all fully transparent business relationships built on mutual respect and trust.

Once, I was exposed to an offshore outsourcing initiative that was primarily negotiated at the corporate level with minimal site-training or support by either side and virtually no personal relationships in play. Upon learning of the situation, I immediately predicted major issues would develop. A couple of months later, a major quality bust occurred that resulted in large financial losses by all parties, which further strained the business relationship. And this business relationship has been beset by hidden costs, continuous premium freight, adversarial-negotiations, etc., from the outset, i.e., they didn't address or uncover the full range of potential risks before undertaking this offshoring-initiative. To make matters worse, the company that they chose had a workforce (70%) that was migrant foreign workers (potentially subjected to human rights issues). This fact was unknown to the company, as they never asked about the workforce because they were mainly ignorant of the business culture of the country to which they were outsourcing a critical, single-source product. I befriended one of the supplier's staff and learned this in a matter of minutes; actually, I just validated my thinking, as I knew the business culture of the region already.

In conclusion, developing personal relationships with outsourcing partners is important; you don't have to become best friends forever (BFFs), but a strong mutual personal respect for each other is important and will assist in overcoming many minor issues and circumvent many others.

End Note

1. An RBWA is a methodology that is easily defined by its name, i.e., Routing-by-Walking-Around. It's a methodology that is executed by "going-to-the-gemba" and "walking-the-process," and observing and gathering data throughout the process. See Chapter 8 for a full explanation of the methodology and its application.

Chapter 7

Risk or Crisis Management

Introduction

Everything from natural disasters and geopolitical conflicts to material price spikes and labor shortages can now impact entire supply chains, domestic and international (see Figure 7.1).

The growth in outsourcing, offshoring, etc., has made the world smaller and increased the risks to your supply chain.

Having spent a large portion of my career living and working in underdeveloped countries, I've witnessed firsthand the effects of a factory fire, political unrest (riots, port and road closures, etc.), natural disasters, the SARS-epidemic outbreak, Gulf War travel restrictions, etc., on the supply chain. So I understand the need to create and maintain a robust, executable business-continuity/risk-mitigation plan. But these supply or manufacturing disruptions are not limited to underdeveloped or developing countries. Although the infrastructure in such countries may be more fragile than that of the strong, industrialized countries, all countries and businesses have risks that they must identify and prepare for. And there can be attractive commercial and strategic reasons to venture offshore, so you just need a plan to mitigate potential risks.

Let's start with a couple of definitions to ensure that we're all on the same page:

- *Business continuity* is the capability of the organization to continue delivery of products or services at acceptable predefined levels following a disruptive incident.

Figure 7.1   Potential Business-Continuity Risks Come from Many Sources.

- *Risk mitigation* is the implementation of measures to deter specific threats to the continuity of business operations, and the ability to respond to any occurrence of such threats in a timely and appropriate manner.

There are typically four levels of supply-chain disruptions:

1. *Variability* is the normal range of activity that routinely occurs in your supply chain and somewhat controllable with normal practices.
2. *Uncertainty* has wider variations and typically is less predictable than "variability," and requires preventative and corrective actions.
3. *Risks* can be identified in advance, but the timing and magnitude is uncertain, e.g., political unrest, tariffs, labor strikes,
4. *Crises* are low-probability but potentially higher-impacting events such as major natural disasters (earthquakes, floods, tsunamis, tornadoes, etc.), factory fires, trade embargoes.

In this chapter, I will address several approaches to identify potential supply-chain disruptions and methods to ensure supply continuity; most approaches that I'll discuss are probably at a more grassroots level than you may be accustomed to, as I think the key is being knowledgeable of the potential risks and then applying business common sense to mitigate them. But regardless of the approach that you take; companies must be proactive in risk and crisis management.

There are many approaches to crisis management relative to your supply chain, but they all basically include:

■ Assessing supply chain's crisis vulnerabilities.
■ Strategically planning for mitigating any potential vulnerabilities.
■ Addressing a crisis when it occurs.
■ Learning from any crises resolved.

SWOT

One tool that is often overlooked when contingency planning for uninterrupted business continuity is the SWOT analysis. A SWOT analysis is used to identify a company's strengths, weaknesses, opportunities, and threats. And I'll cover the traditional applications for SWOT in Chapter 8. To utilize SWOT for crisis or risk management, you align your company's corresponding strengths, weaknesses, opportunities, and/or threats with potential crises.

Figure 7.2 shows an example of the alignment of your company's corresponding strengths, weaknesses, opportunities, and threats with potential vulnerabilities.

The strength of many companies may be their lean-manufacturing/ operational-excellence capabilities, but along with the benefits of getting the maximum value out of the minimal resources come some legitimate vulnerabilities that you must plan or prepare for, e.g., statistically sized safety or buffer inventory, flexible capacity, cross-sourcing, etc.

Companies' weaknesses can vary, but companies that aren't outsourcing to create some redundant capabilities expose their businesses to high risk for self-manufacturing disruptions by risks (or crises) such as factory fires or any structural damage to a factory that minimizes or eliminates its manufacturing capabilities.

A company's opportunities for growing its business can be vulnerable to internal and/or external supply disruptions caused by a multitude of risks or crises.

And the largest threat to any company is the myriad of risks or crises that could disrupt the supply from any single-sourced material or service, or catastrophic events that may disable multiple sources in the same geographic region, such as earthquakes, severe weather, political unrest, wars, etc.

Strengths *(internal)*		Weaknesses *(internal)*	
Strengths	**Vulnerability**	**Weaknesses**	**Vulnerability**
1. Lean Manufacturing	1. Minimal Inventory	1. Too much inspection	1. False confidence
2. Just-in-Time	2. No buffers	2. Minimal equipment	2. Breakdown
3. No Incoming Inspection	3. Supplier quality-busts	3. No outsourcing	3. Factory-fire

Opportunities *(external)*		Threats *(external)*	
Opportunities	**Vulnerability**	**Threats**	**Vulnerability**
1. Increased Demand	1. Capacity & Resource constraints	1. Natural Disaster / Severe Weather	1. Lost of facilities / lengthy supply-delays
2. Offshore outsourcing	2. Distance & transit-unknowns	2. Political unrest	2. Port-closures / Riots / Strikes
3. Multiple-sourcing	3. Effort to establish & manage	3. War or threat of war	3. Restricted-travel / embargoes

Figure 7.2 Example – SWOT Risk Analysis.

And there are economic risks that must be managed, as they may not disrupt a company's capability to supply its customers but may cause significant financial losses for a company. These include tariffs, foreign currency fluctuations, market crashing, supplier bankruptcy, etc.

Cause-and-Effect Diagram (a.k.a. Fishbone Diagram)

Another approach to assessing risks to your supply chain can be the old reliable cause-and-effect diagram (a.k.a. fishbone diagram), and this is one of the simplest approaches, but when performed with a cross-functional team can be as effective as any other method.

In Figure 7.3, I've constructed what a sample fishbone may look like for assessing the risk to an American self-manufacturing site.

I've construed that the three highest probability risks would be:

1. Single-source suppliers (see Case-in-Point 7.1).
2. Factory fire (per the Insurance Information Institute in 2017, there were slightly less than half a million structural fires in the US).
3. Cyberattacks.

In Figure 7.4, I've constructed a sample fishbone for assessing the risk of a hypothetical single-source offshore supplier.

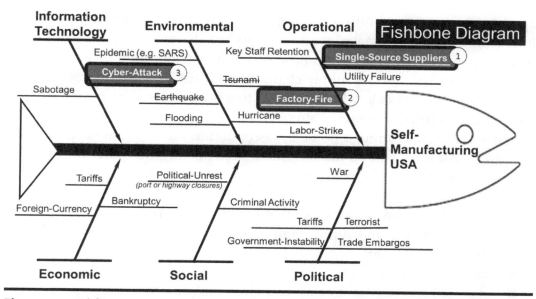

Figure 7.3   Risk Assessment Fishbone – Self-Manufacturing.

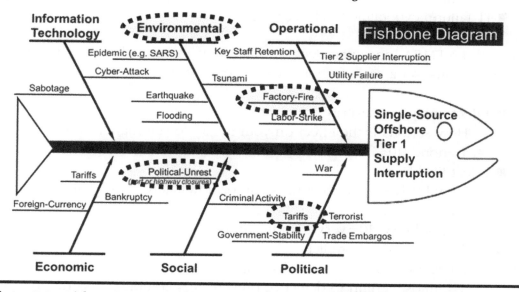

Figure 7.4   Risk Assessment Fishbone – Single-Source Offshore Supplier.

And the fishbone could lead directly into doing an FMEA on the consensus top three risks.

Failure Modes and Effects Analysis (FMEA)

The Failure Modes and Effects Analysis (FMEA) can be a very effective tool for assessing the risks to your supply chain and can assist in identifying appropriate corrective and preventive action. The FMEA is a tool created for assessing the risks associated with new product designs, system development, process development, and process improvement, but it can also be utilized to assess risks to the supply chain (i.e., the risk to business continuity).

First, you must decide what you want to assess, i.e., self-manufacturing risks, logistics risks, or material-supply risks.

For self-manufacturing; a possible disruption to the external supply could be a high-risk area, and I'll discuss that independently, but other factors that you'd want to analyze for self-manufacturing may include:

■ Factory fire or any other crisis that could disable your ability to self-manufacture and supply your customers, such as severe weather, a natural disaster, etc.
■ Labor strike or loss of key staff.
■ Catastrophic equipment or infrastructure failure.
■ Litigation risks.
■ IT failure, cyberattack, sabotage, etc.

So with an FMEA, once you decide what you want to analyze as a potential risk; you must set a scale for your assessment, such as:

■ Effect impact or severity
  – How serious is the effect on your ability to self-manufacture?
  – 1=none, 10=fully disabled.
■ Effect likelihood
  – How likely is this effect to occur, or how likely is the criterion is to fail?
  – 1=not likely, 10=very high likelihood.
■ Ability to detect or predict
  – Likelihood to detect before it happens.
  – 1=almost certain to detect or prevent, 10=complete uncertainty.

Then you would analyze each factor in a typical FMEA approach; see Figure 7.5 for an example for a self-manufacture facility.

For external suppliers, there are countless factors that you must consider when you analyze the potential risks (and many are country or region biased):

■ Factory fire or any other crisis that could disable your suppliers' ability to supply your material, such as severe weather, a natural disaster, etc.

Risk	Failure Mode	Potential Cause	Potential Effect	Detection Method	Severity	Likelihood	Detection	Composite Score
Loss Capability to Self-Manufacture	Factory-Fire	Electrical-fault	Facility destroyed	Safety-Walks	10	3	5	150
	Hurricane	Weather	Facility damaged	Weather-forecast	9	2	8	144
	Cyber-Attack	Sabotage	IT system corrupted	System Protection	9	1	9	81

Figure 7.5   Example Self-Manufacturing/FMEA Business-Continuity Analysis.

- Natural disasters; the potential damage and rebuilding (severe destruction from tsunamis, earthquakes, floods).
- Political unrest, e.g., labor strikes that close seaports, highways, airports, customs processing (government agencies), etc.
- Catastrophic equipment or infrastructure failure.
- Litigation risk.
- Financial (e.g., bankruptcy, etc.)
- IT failure, cyberattack, sabotage, etc.
- Lower-tier suppliers' disruptions from any of the above factors.

See Figures 7.6 and 7.7 for international and domestic supplier examples.

Risk	Failure Mode	Potential Cause	Potential Effect	Detection Method	Severity	Likelihood	Detection	Composite Score
Critical Supplier (SE Asia)	Factory-Fire	Poor Standards	Facility destroyed	Safety-Walks	10	4	9	360
	Port Unavailable	Political Strike	Port inaccessible	News Warnings	10	5	8	400
	Factory Disabled	Natural Disaster	Facility damaged	Weather Reports	10	5	10	500
	Price Increase	Tariff	Lower Margins	Government	6	8	10	480

Figure 7.6   Example Raw Material Supplier (International)/FMEA Business-Continuity Analysis.

Risk	Failure Mode	Potential Cause	Potential Effect	Detection Method	Severity	Likelihood	Detection	Composite Score
Critical Supplier (North America)	Factory-Fire	Wiring Fault	Facility destroyed	Safety-Walks	10	3	6	180
	Raw Material Supply	Tier 2 Supplier	Missed Shipments	Advance Warning	10	5	10	500
	Factory Disabled	Natural Disaster	Facility damaged	Weather Reports	5	2	8	80

Figure 7.7   Example Raw Material Supplier (Domestic)/FMEA Business-Continuity Analysis.

Calculating Your Tolerance Level

Many companies are reverting to a quantitative approach to understand their supply-chain tolerance level, i.e., to understand impact and recovery, such as:

- Identifying and understanding the most critical items of your supply chain, the impact of each, and the worst-/best-case time frame for resumption following an unscheduled interruption.
- Determining the maximum tolerable outage for each element.
- Defining potential recovery (or contingency) strategies for each element.
- Outlining dependencies and/or barriers that exist both internally and externally that impact the potential recovery (or contingency) strategies.

And there's been a complete metric created to assist your company in understanding its tolerance level:

- *Time-to-Recovery (TTR):* This is defined as the time it takes a facility (i.e., a self-manufacturing or supplier's facility, or a warehouse or distribution-hub, etc.) in the supply chain to recover after a disruption.
- *Time-to-Survive (TTS):* This metric indicates that if there is a disruption in a specific facility, the length of time the company can keep matching demand.

A company may want to start by calculating their Time-to-Survive (TTS), as it helps identify the challenges and threats within their supply chain based on:

- How long would current inventory levels along the supply chain allow your company to survive?
- Is there a viable second source that could be ramped up?
- A company can simulate removing or disrupting facilities to determine how long the supply chain can meet the historic customer demand with the remaining supply options.

Time-to-Recovery (TTR) measures how long it would take to fully recover from a disruption, i.e., rebuild or repair a facility, source and qualify a new supplier, replenish loss inventory, etc.

And to really survive, a company's TTS must be higher than its TTR.

Whether you actually calculate these numbers (TTS and TTR) or not; it's the model that every company must contemplate, i.e., given your current supply chain and potential risks that you've identified; for each type of risk, you must consider how long you can survive and how long will it take to recover. Then you'll be able to quantify the impact of each risk.

Case-in-Point 7.1: Supplier Rationalization for Single-Sourcing, My Personal View

Many companies are trending toward single-sourcing, but I'm not sure that's a great strategy.

There are obvious benefits to single-sourcing such as:

1. Single-sourcing means less effort to qualify a single versus multiple sources; there is less administrative effort (e.g., less paperwork) in dealing with only one supplier.
2. Potentially better quality.
3. Potential for better supplier innovations.
4. Giving all your volume to one source maximizes your leverage based on the "economies of scale" rationale and provides the opportunity to emphasize this during negotiations, etc.
5. Potential to leverage long-term contracts (although suppliers may have concerns of committing too many resources to a single major customer, thus shrinking their customer base which could be risky for them)
6. The supplier should feel a special obligation to help the buyer in terms of availability, etc. Again, in the process of awarding this business to the supplier, the fact that the buyer's company is relying on the supplier for material availability should be made clear.

But there are significant risks that I think outweigh the benefits of single-sourcing, such as:

1. *Business continuity is the largest risk* in my opinion; you're basically at the "supplier's mercy"; but there's also the risk that the supplier has a catastrophic event (fire, weather, political, etc.), has financial problems, gets acquired by a competitor, etc.
2. In periods of tight supply, the company may be at a disadvantage in being able to ask other suppliers to accept orders. The company has become dependent on that single source.
3. Other suppliers may lose interest in trying to compete for the business if they see that a sole source situation is likely to persist, i.e., shrinking supplier base and losing some economic competition

Personally, I'm not a fan of single-sourcing, as I have witnessed single-source supplies being disrupted by fire, labor strikes, political unrest, flooding, port closures, tsunamis, etc., and even suppliers making their own business decisions to discontinue a product or service. I think you must treat suppliers like life, i.e., be prepared for "Murphy's Law"[1].

What I am a fan of is dual suppliers with some SKU overlap, i.e., cross-sourcing.

Dual-sourcing is the supply-chain management practice of using two suppliers for a given component, raw material, product, or service. Cross-sourcing includes overlapping the purchases from two suppliers. Cross-sourcing is a method of expanding the supplier base without increasing the number of suppliers.

For an example of cross-sourcing, let's consider a scenario of two suppliers, "X" and "Y"; "X" is the single source for five items, and "Y" is the single source for five other items. "X" has the manufacturing capability to produce some (i.e., not all) of the items that "Y" can produce. "Y" has the capability to produce some of the items currently being manufactured by "X." Thus, a buyer may move items among the suppliers fully or partially. Thus, the opportunity exists to keep the supplier base intact while moving items to ensure the continuity and/or adequacy of supply.

The challenge for the buying company is the supplier qualification and selection process. In addition to product quality, two important factors are the supplier's ability to produce a number of different products (or families of products) and the flexibility of its manufacturing system. The overall objective is the selection of suppliers that can be flexible partners in meeting the company's requirements.

When dealing with the suppliers, it must be a win–win situation. Given the fact that two sources have the capability to produce the same items, the company's risks have been reduced by cross-sourcing. Cross-sourcing can also be done at the corporation with dual suppliers supplying multiple sites with a larger array of items supplied. The capability of having dual sources within the existing supplier network can be activated by altering the mix of products at either supplier. Risks are reduced, and a win–win environment is the result. I worked for one company that leveraged this concept extremely effectively. They spread their outsourced products across three suppliers, and even had a couple more with their process "pre-certified," so if demand rose sharply or something happened to the other three, there was a contingency plan in place. And the three prime active suppliers were fully aware of the multiple-supplier/cross-sourcing scheme being deployed by the company, as everything was as transparent as possible. The suppliers had facilities across two countries. During my few years associated with this company, the outsourced products were *effectively* moved about to at least six suppliers. And it should be noted that originally, these low-margin outsourced products were self-manufactured, but since there were so many viable outsourcing options, the self-manufacturing facility was sold, which resulted in a major reduction in overhead. And with these being low-margin commoditized products, the elimination of overhead and reduction in operating expenses was potentially a major competitive advantage.

Another single-source type of scenario involved a self-manufacturing pharmaceutical company that had a major dilemma, as they needed to create some manufacturing redundancy but didn't want to expand their business, as there were labor unions, community issues, etc., that made expansion highly undesirable. And there were no realistic suppliers or regional manufacturers to outsource the items to, but to have any potential risk-mitigation opportunities, they urgently needed multiple sources. The solution was that the company had to develop new sources, which they did by creating a couple of new business entities which had their own facilities, management teams, etc. These new sources (i.e., suppliers) were basically an "extension" of the manufacturer's operations but operated in different regions of the country with non-unionized facilities as independent business entities. Often under special situations, manufacturers are required to develop their own sources, such as this scenario, and often it's just components or items with limited sourcing options, so to ensure business continuity, they must be developed with the creation of redundant viable sources (i.e., risk-mitigation options) being a higher priority than price/cost.

See Figures 7.8 and 7.9 for examples of utilization of the Fishbone and the FMEA (Failure Modes and Effects Analysis) for single-source international supplier.

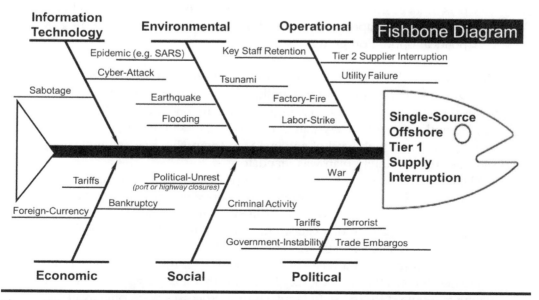

Figure 7.8   Risk Assessment Fishbone – Single-Source Offshore Supplier.

Risk	Failure Mode	Potential Cause	Potential Effect	Detection Method	Severity	Likelihood	Detection	Composite Score
Critical Supplier (SE Asia)	Factory-Fire	Poor Standards	Facility destroyed	Safety-Walks	10	4	9	360
	Port Unavailable	Political Strike	Port inaccessible	News Warnings	10	5	8	400
	Factory Disabled	Mother Nature	Facility damaged	Weather Reports	10	5	10	500
	Price Increase	Tariff	Lower Margins	Government	6	8	10	480

Figure 7.9 Example Supplier (International)/FMEA Business-Continuity Analysis.

Case-in-Point 7.2: Risk-Mitigation and Business-Continuity Planning

Company: US Fortune 50 healthcare service company

Scope: The scope of this case-in-point is this company's largest self-manufacturing site, which is the company's largest revenue-generating site with profit margins that generally exceed 60%. It's a "cash-cow." It's the single source for this product portfolio. And this site is in a country known for political unrest and torrential flooding. So robust risk-mitigation and business-continuity planning were essential, as the location of this site was a constant concern for the company's board of directors and shareholders.

Background: During a recent three-year period, this site had to annually deal with seasonal flooding that isolated many regions of the country for months, cutting off the supply routes of many of its local suppliers, thus crippling the site's ability to manufacture and ship finished products to its customers. And multiple times during this same period all of the country's seaports were closed due to ad-hoc rioting/protesting by political opposition groups.

The country had become infamous for political unrest and having a fragile infrastructure that was unable to handle natural disasters. Additionally, the political rioting gave the country an unjustified reputation for being a "dangerous" and unlawful society that put the company's board of directors and shareholders on a high level of anxiety. So a comprehensive risk-mitigation and business-continuity plan was mandatory.

The company's core self-manufacturing process required customized equipment, including tens of thousands of proprietary molds/forms, which constituted a multi-million-dollar investment; none of which could be easily replicated in the case of a catastrophic loss of the self-manufacturing facility. It would take years to reestablish capabilities from scratch. Thus, it was very important that a reliable second source for the self-manufacturing capabilities be established. Another issue was that a large portion of the raw materials required for the self-manufacturing processes were only available in a few southeast Asian countries, so any potential "self-manufacturing" second source had to be located accordingly. So, the options for establishing self-manufacturing capabilities within a second source would be challenging and limited.

Many options were evaluated, but the only viable economic second-source option was to establish a toll-manufacturing relationship in an adjacent country. With toll manufacturing, most equipment, proprietary molds, and proprietary formulation would remain under the management of the product owners; the toll-manufacturing contractor would provide a suitable fully fitted facility and management of the labor; thus, a second manufacturing source was established.

So with a second source established; there were still the other supply-chain risks that must be addressed.

Some of the key risks to be addressed were:

- Labor was a risk in two areas; government intervention was causing the minimum wage to rise sharply in many Asian countries, and the recruitment and retention of unskilled labor were becoming more difficult (demand was stronger than the supply).
  - Our mitigation plans were:
    • Automate labor where possible, but automation would be highly customized and expensive, and potentially a long-term solution at best.
    • Outsource the most commoditized, lowest proprietary-risk products to contract manufacturers to offset sporadic demand fluctuations.
- This was a very high volume with almost all customers in the US or Europe, so all shipments were by sea. Shipments had been delayed previously by months because of the ports being shut down by rebellious political activists. There were two major ports available in the country of origin, and both were a prime target of activists who wanted to cause major pain to the country's economy.
  - Our mitigation plans were:
    • Establish suitable ports in neighboring countries where products could be transferred by ground-transportation and then shipped by sea to end customers (a costly, time-consuming alternative, but the only option).
    • For the plan to be viable, periodic shipments were required through these points.
- There were specialty raw materials that were single-sourced, and alternate sources were scarce.
- The primary supplier of packaging material was in a highly vulnerable flood-plain area, so other sources needed to be developed locally and in a neighboring country.

Item	Current Status	Next Steps			
		Strategy	What	Who	When
Labor	Utilize contract labor to offset large demand fluctuations	• Minimize labor requirements through productivity improvements & selective automation.	Outsourcing of powdered, powder-free & synthetic gloves	yyyy	FY-??
Ports	Three available deep sea ports in Thailand	Collaborate with Global Trade to have a robust contingency plan established & validation thru proactive execution	Inbound: annual "testing" of validity of plan	xxxx	FY12
			Annual review/refresh with Global Trade	xxxx	Ongoing
Product X	Two qualified sources exist but neither is currently viable[1]	Outsource minimal volume (DIP & PKG) to develop capability	Supplier evaluation/selection	yyyy	FY-??
Critical Chemicals	Increase safety stock to 1-year (100% Complete)	Maintain safety-stock at 1-year. Selective (limited) 2nd sourcing.	2nd source: Biocide (PCMX)	xxxx	FY-??
Packaging Materials	Two sources for all items, two suppliers for most items	• Develop back-up suppliers • Develop suppliers' internal contingency plans	Develop two local suppliers - dispensers	xxxx	Complete

Figure 7.10   Example Risk-Mitigation/Business-Continuity Analysis Sheet.

The above is just a sampling of the risk-mitigation business-continuity plan; an example of an analysis sheet is shown by Figure 7.10.

End Note

1. Murphy's law is an adage that is stated as "Anything that can go wrong, will go wrong."

Chapter 8

Supply-Chain Optimization

Up to this point, we've covered the major components of the supply chain; now we're going to look at how to conduct a performance assessment of your supply chain to establish a baseline, and quantitatively and qualitatively assess the gaps in supply-chain optimization (see Figure 8.1).

Figure 8.2 shows the type of data that'll be collected during the data-based assessment. The data collected during the actual assessment may vary depending on the areas on which you want to focus.

Assessment Tools and Methodologies

There is a large toolbox of tools and methodologies that can assist you in creating the baseline for your Lean Transformation journey. I will provide you with some how-to advice on utilizing some of the most commonly used tools and methodologies (i.e., the ones that I most commonly use).

Figure 8.1   Elements of Supply-Chain Optimization.

Supplying	Producing	Distributing	Delivering
• # suppliers	• Demand synchronization	• Portfolio management	• Packaging
• # raw materials	• Manufacturing run strategy / Product mix	• # warehouses	• Order size
• Inventory levels	• Operation capacity	• Geographic rationalization	• Service levels
• Packaging requirements	• Labor & facility efficiency	• Shipping volume	• Region size
• Lead-time	• Yield	• Transportation modes	• Volume
	• Throughput / Cycle-time	• FG inventory levels	• Fleet capacity
	• WIP levels		• Product mix
	• Enabling technology		

Figure 8.2   Supply-Chain Operational Assessment.

But before you get too deep into the quantitative and qualitative analysis of your supply-chain operations; I suggest that you take a high-level view of your perceived strengths, weaknesses, opportunities, and threats to your current supply chain. And the tool for this analysis of your supply chain would be the SWOT matrix (see Figure 8.3).

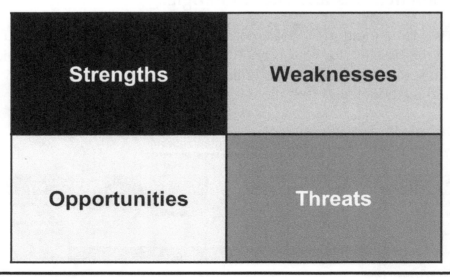

Strengths	Weaknesses
Opportunities	Threats

Figure 8.3   SWOT Matrix.

SWOT Your Supply Chain

A SWOT analysis is a study undertaken to identify the internal strengths and weaknesses, and the external opportunities and threats of an entity or process.

- *Strengths* describe the positive attributes of your organization that are within your control and can assist in exploiting external opportunities. And strengths should address a critical customer's, both internal and external, needs.
- *Weaknesses* are aspects of your business that detract from the value you offer or place you at a competitive disadvantage. And the failure to capitalize on external opportunities are usually the result of the company's weaknesses.
- *Opportunities* are positive external factors that should be exploited. Opportunities relate to positive or favorable current or future advantage or trend. Opportunities represent reasons your business is likely to prosper.
- *Threats* relate to an unfavorable situation, trend, or change. Threats are external factors beyond your control that could place your strategy, or the business itself, at risk. You have no control over these, but you may benefit by having contingency plans to address them.

So a SWOT should help you determine:

- How to sustain and/or maximize your strengths, i.e., accentuate your strengths.
- What the drivers of your weaknesses are, and how to eliminate or overcome your weaknesses.
- How to effectively maximize your opportunities.
- How to proactively minimize or avoid potential threats.

The structure of a generic SWOT is shown in Figure 8.4.

For the purposes of a supply-chain SWOT, it's important to consider the good and bad attributes of your own supply chain, along with your suppliers' attributes.

Use the SWOT analysis of the supply chain to identify opportunities to:

- Improve supply chain and/or manufacturing strategy.
- Optimize supply-chain processes.
- Improve availability of purchased items.
- Identify risk-mitigation needs.

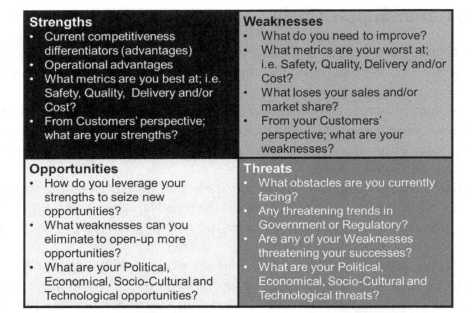

Figure 8.4 SWOT Matrix Structure.

Figure 8.5 highlights some potential questions to be addressed in terms of your supply chain during the SWOT analysis.

A good initial point to start the assessment would be Value Stream Mapping (VSM). The VSM has been mentioned numerous times already in this book, but now I'll get into the details of developing and analyzing a VSM.

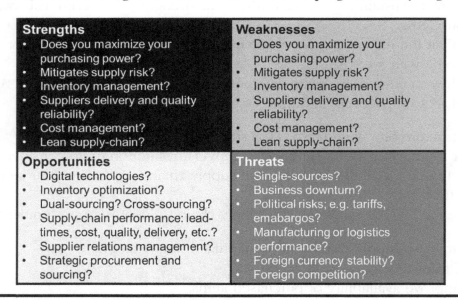

Figure 8.5 Supply-Chain SWOT Analysis.

Value Stream Mapping

Value Stream Mapping is the mapping (a.k.a. diagramming) of the flow of material, product, and information through each value stream. A value stream is a sequence of activities required to produce and supply a specific good or service.

One of the goals for supply-chain optimization is to create uninterrupted flow throughout the value stream, from external suppliers to external customers. Uninterrupted flow is achieved by minimizing work-in-process, minimizing waiting and queues, utilizing visual management to minimize the physical flow of information, while striving for one-piece product flow.

The steps for constructing a Value Stream Map, and subsequent analysis, are:

1. Create a SIPOC diagram. See Figure 8.6 and 8.7.
   - SIPOC is an acronym for Suppliers – Inputs – Process – Outputs – Customers. SIPOC is a tool that summarizes the inputs and outputs of one or more processes in a tabular form. A SIPOC can be deployed early in the assessment to help identify potential team members and/or stakeholders (e.g., Value Stream's processes' stakeholders), the outputs are the metrics which will be used to measure the project, the inputs allow the project team to consider various potential critical process drivers, and, of course, the process itself provides the stop-start barriers (i.e., the transformation's scope). A SIPOC helps define a complex project that may not be well scoped.

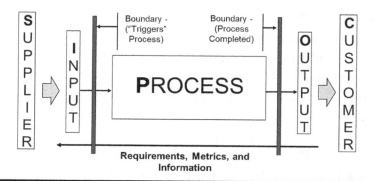

Figure 8.6 SIPOC Diagram.

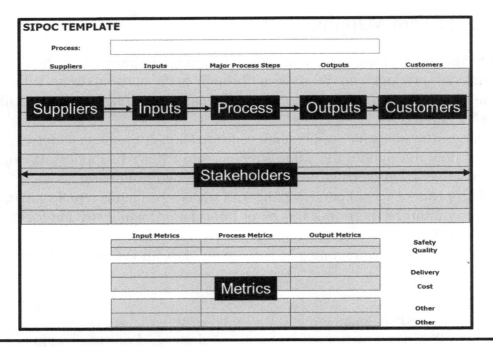

Figure 8.7   Example SIPOC Template.

SIPOC ensures that the correct stakeholders are involved in the Value Stream Mapping process.

2. Conduct Gemba Walk[1] to get a quick overview of the processes to be mapped.
3. Determine product and/or process family on Value Stream Map (VSM)
   – Determine Takt Time[2]
4. Create the Process Flow Map (see Figure 8.8).
   – Post-It notes
   – White Board/Brown Paper (butcher paper)
5. Add the Material Flow to the Process Flow Map
   – Inventory which is designated by a triangle of the Value Stream Map.
   – There are two accepted techniques to quantify the amount of inventory stored at each location.
     • *Technique #1:* This technique can be extracted from, supposedly, the VSM "bible," *Learning to See* by Mike Rother and John Shook; it is the first book that I read on the subject of Value

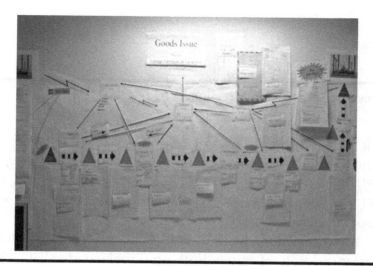

Figure 8.8 **"Brown" Paper and Post-It VSM Creation Technique (Current-State).**

Stream Mapping. In *Learning to See*, the amount of inventory (WIP) stated on the VSM is determined by the equivalent Process Lead Time (PLT), and it is calculated as shown in Figure 8.9.

It's assuming that inventory will be consumed equal to the takt time, which is a reasonable assumption, but the minor fallacy of this technique, in my opinion, is that there is no relationship with the consumption rate at the subsequent station, but if the cell/line is actually set to the takt time, then this method is fully valid. But if there are individual workstations or equipment, then the WIP may be consumed at a different rate than the takt time rate. If the WIP is 10,000 pieces and the takt time is 30 seconds, the PLT is approximately 10.4 days, and the inventory denoted on the VSM would be 10 days. The assumption is that the cell/line is properly balanced and that the inventory will be consumed in 10.4 days (i.e., the takt time).

- *Technique #2:* This calculation of PLT is based on Little's Law, because this technique is more realistic and more reflective of the VSM's current state. For this technique, the lead time is calculated as shown in Figure 8.10.

Using the same example above, if the WIP is 10,000 and cycle time at the station is 60 seconds, the lead time is 600,000 seconds

$$PLT = \frac{\text{Inventory (pieces)}}{\text{Takt-Time (time/piece)}}$$

Figure 8.9   Inventory Calculation: Technique #1.

or 10,000 minutes. Assuming a two-shift operation (21.5 hours), there would be approximately 1,290 minutes in a day, thus the PLT equates to approximately 7.8 days (10,000/1,290); thus, the PLT is calculated based on the consumption rate (i.e., subsequent operation's throughput (exit) rate).

My conclusion: Technique #1 is best if the cell/line is balanced to a takt time; if it's an unbalanced cell/line or single unlinked pieces of equipment, then technique #2 may be more accurate.

6. Add the Information Flow to the Process Flow Map (From/To).
   – Electronic flow (e.g., email, fax, MS Office file, ERP-message, etc.).
   – Hard copy (e.g., document, etc.).
7. Add and Populate the Process Data boxes.
   – A tip here: Don't be afraid to add ranges to the data; it doesn't have to be a finite number. You should convey the variability that exists in the current process. Showing the variability in an activity is important to generate discussions about the nature of the variability and potential countermeasures to reduce it.
   – The purpose of a current-state map is to depict what is actually happening, so if variability occurs it should be represented on the map.
8. Calculate the key VSM Metrics; Value-Added Ratio, Process Lead Time (PLT).
   – Process Lead Time (sum of all steps' cycle time plus inventory time).
   – Value-Added Ratio (value-added time divided by total PLT).
   See Figure 8.11 for an example of a Current-State VSM.

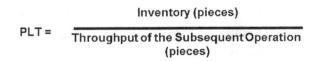

$$PLT = \frac{\text{Inventory (pieces)}}{\text{Throughput of the Subsequent Operation (pieces)}}$$

Figure 8.10   Inventory Calculation: Technique #2.

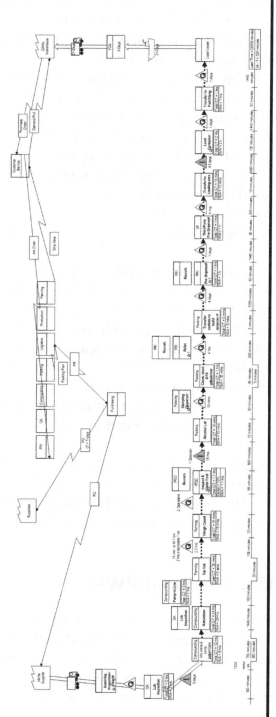

Figure 8.11   Current-State Value Stream Map.

9. Validate Current-State Map via Gemba Walk (see Step 2 above).
   – A crucial part of the validating of the current state is to "go-see-the process." Go to the process and watch the operator perform the task; see what the operators are doing.
   – And validate the Current-State map with as many stakeholders (upstream and downstream), as possible who were not a part of the VSM team. Gain as many perspectives as you can. And engagement beyond the immediate team is important to ensure greater commitment to the successful implementation of the future state. If the VSM team is not sufficiently involving others (outside the VSM sessions) in establishing that the current state is a common cause for failed future state implementations, there will likely be issues down the road.
10. Brainstorm "unconstrained" improvement opportunities (initiatives) for Current State.
    – Focus on opportunities not constrained by money or existing technologies. Identify improvement opportunities on the current-state VSM with "kaizen bursts." See Figure 8.12.
    – Create a B&E chart (Benefit versus Effort). See Figure 8.13 for chart. Figure 8.14 shows an example of a template that can be utilized to create the B&E chart.
    – Prioritize initiatives (management buy-in).
    – Identify initiatives to be completed within the next 12 months.
    – Create a Gantt chart for implementation initiatives < 12 months (a.k.a. Future-State VSM).
11. Create "Ideal" State Value Stream Map incorporating Kaizen Bursts with all reasonable improvement initiatives (i.e., all initiatives but bottom right area of B&E). The "Ideal" State is the starting point for backward planning, i.e., what shall be included in Future-State Rounds 1, 2, 3?

Routing-By-Walking-Around (RBWA)

As a Lean Practitioner, I am a big fan of Value Stream Mapping as a great tool for identifying waste and improvement opportunities, and I have mentored and coached hundreds of Lean Practitioners in leveraging Value Stream Mapping for identifying improvement opportunities.

But it does have its limitations in recognizing waste. Value Stream Mapping is great for identifying large buckets of waste such as Inventory, Transportation, possibly Waiting and maybe Overproduction (a.k.a.

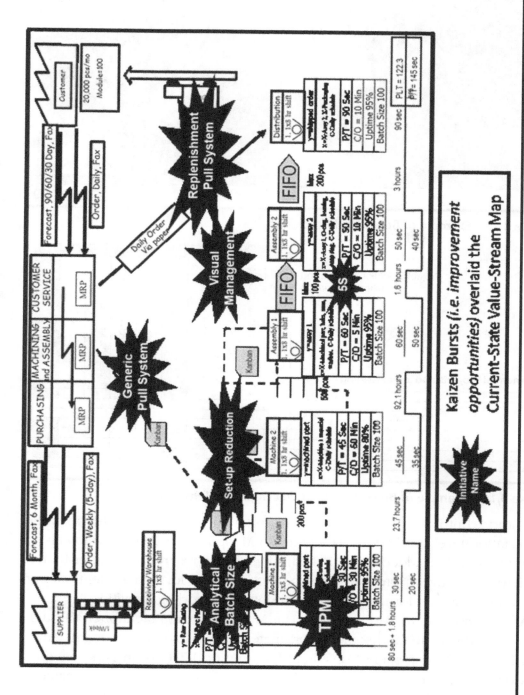

Figure 8.12   Example of Current-State Value Stream Map w/Kaizen Bursts.

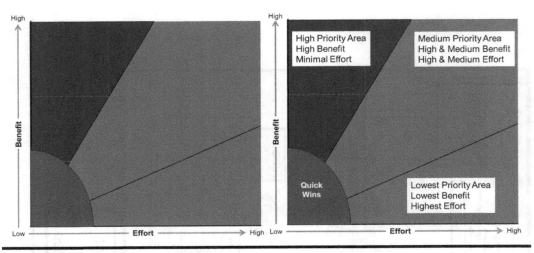

Figure 8.13   Example of Benefit & Effort Chart.

Potential Projects and Impact Rating			Cost Savings Impact 5 = $100k, 7 = $250k 10 =	Direct Links to Strategic Goals	Relates to Business / Process Objectives, e.g. Plant Goals	Customer Satisfaction impact / Improved Quality	Overall Benefit	Requires External Approval	Risk to Quality and/or Customer	Implementation Timeline 1 = ≤6-months, 5 =≤9-months	Cost to Implement	Overall Effort
		Significance Ratings	10	10	10	10		10	10	8	8	
Scoring : 10 = Very High, 1 = Low												
	Project	Savings										
1							$0					0
2							$0					0
3							$0					0
4							$0					0
5							$0					0

Figure 8.14   Example of Benefit & Effort Development Template.

Inventory). But it has definite limitations in identifying waste at the operator/ workstation level. And while Value Stream Mapping can allow you to calculate your Value-Added Ratio, it again does it at a macro-level rather than a micro-level. And macro will often be too high of a level in a relentless pursuit to eliminate all forms of waste and non-value-adding activities.

After a more than 20-year career as a Manufacturing Practitioner, through a series of fortunate (and some unfortunate) events, I started a second career as a Business Management Consultant focusing on JIT (Just-in-Time) manufacturing; obviously this was in the days before Lean or Six Sigma became common terminology. And this was years before Value Stream Mapping became a tool of choice for assessing and baselining an operation, so on day one of my consultancy career, I was introduced to the methodology of Routing-By-Walking-Around (RBWA).

And the RBWA methodology immediately converted me from a seasoned manufacturing guru to a business process consultant; it's the ultimate go-to-the-gemba tool for learning to see (i.e., learning to see waste).

An RBWA is a methodology that is easily defined by its name, i.e., Routing-by-Walking-Around. It's a methodology that is executed by "going-to-the-gemba" and "walking-the-process," and observing and gathering data throughout the process.

The basic objective of the RBWA methodology is the identification and elimination of non-value-adding activities and the identification of process improvements.

And by conducting an RBWA analysis, we would be able to:

- Establish the baseline ("as-is") for existing process flows and performance.
- Expose waste and hidden steps.
- Classify activities as either value-added or non-value-added.
- Identify all PLT contributors (workstation's cycle time, waiting, travel distances, WIP queues, equipment availability, etc.).
- Provide a strong basis for future "to-be" design.

The basic stages of conducting an RBWA analysis are:

1. Go to the Gemba and gather data.
2. Evaluate the current way of doing business.
3. Create an "As-Is" baseline of the current process flow and performance.
4. Develop a process redesign (a "To-Be" concept).

Data that are observed, extracted, and gathered during a typical RBWA, include:

- Hands-on observation of the process and all activities (you do it in the Gemba).
- Detailed sequence of process steps.
- Time study (observations) of all relevant activities.
- Distance traveled.
- Data for a spaghetti diagram.
- Waste observations and identification/categorization.

■ Uncovering hidden steps and/or activities.
■ Identifying non-value-adding steps and/or activities.

The RBWA Template

The first step of an RBWA must be to obtain or develop an analysis form (template). The template that I use has evolved over time, mainly with the addition of "auto-tabulating" and "auto-calculating" of the step-categories, time and distance. Excel has enabled our automating a lot of meticulous steps of the RBWA data analysis.

And the RBWA step-categories have changed over time as well. When I conducted my first RBWA analysis, the categories of Lean Waste had not yet been institutionalized. My first form was just based on "common knowledge and common sense," with a very simple objective: finding improvement opportunities in a process by identifying unnecessary steps.

The truth is that the RBWA form is not that significant; it's just a data-collection sheet. I have, many times, conducted an RBWA by taking a blank sheet of paper and followed the process while taking detailed notes of what I saw. The important thing was that I followed the methodology but without the ease of a formatted data-collection sheet.

So you can use the example in Figure 8.15 to develop (and customize) your own RBWA form.

The RBWA template is a data-collection form; the data entry points are shown in Figure 8.16 and defined thereafter.

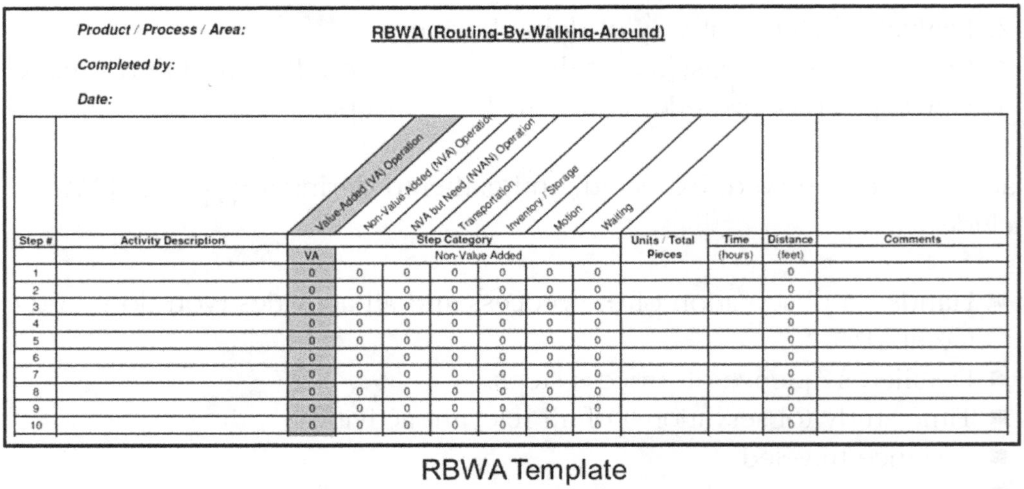

RBWA Template

Figure 8.15   Routing-By-Walking-Around (RBWA) Analysis Template.

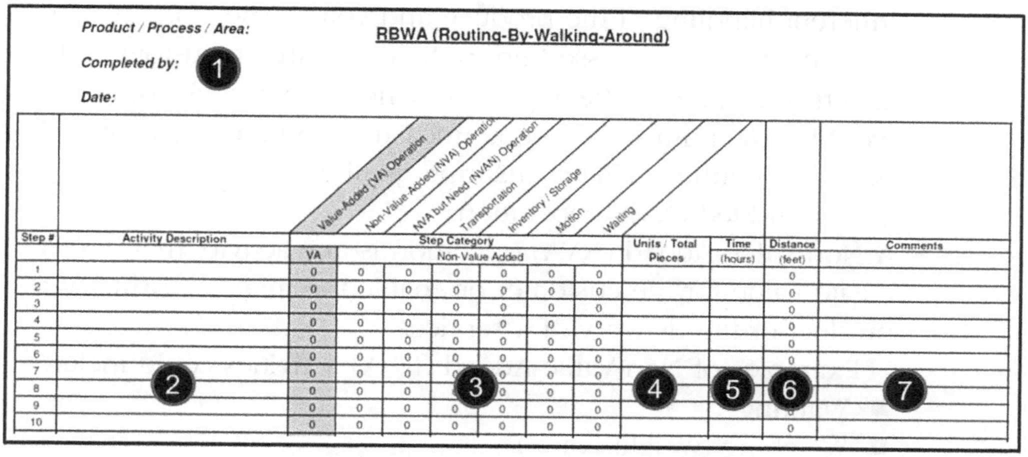

RBWA Template – Data Entry Areas

Figure 8.16   Routing-By-Walking-Around (RBWA) – Data Entry.

1. *Title Box*: Basic details about the specific RBWA being constructed.
2. *Activity Description*: In this area, you would describe the activity being performed at this step of the process. Start your activity description with a verb and break your activities into the smallest distinguishable steps or elements as possible. The number of steps that you have has no relevance, but being able to break activities into small elements where you can clearly segregate (distinguish) value-added versus non-value-added elements will greatly increase the overall power of your RBWA analysis. It's important that you don't miss any elements, as every distinct work or job element must be captured.
3. *Step Category*: This is the area where we'll tabulate the various steps within the following categories:
   – Value-Added (VA) Operation
     • A Value-Added (VA) operation is a step that changes the form, fit, or function of the product. A VA step can also be defined as an activity that the customer would be willing to pay for, i.e., it's seen by the customer as adding value to the product.
     • Internal Inspection is an operation that could be debated as value-adding or not. Internal Inspection is defined as the inspection of your own work. Some folks will say any type of inspection is non-value-added, as your process should produce perfect products every time. But I take a different view, as no process is 100% perfect; there's always going to be variations. So my perspective is that if you incorporate inspection of your own work into your

inherent handling of the product, and your inspection ensures that no defects are passed on to the downstream/customer, then significant value has been created. And this internal inspection would allow immediate countermeasures to be implemented if an issue is identified. This is ensuring quality at the source.

– Non-Value-Added (NVA) Operation
  • A Non-Value-Added (NVA) operation is any activity that doesn't create value for the customer or enable the manufacturing of a product or the delivery of a service.
    Examples of Non-Value-Added (NVA) activities could include:
    ■ Walking.
    ■ Weighing (weight-count).
    ■ Stirring, mixing, pouring, etc.
    ■ Verifying.
    ■ Getting tooling or fixturing.
    ■ Issuing a report or other information.
    ■ Collecting data.
  • An NVA operation is pure waste, so there is some overlapping with the Transportation and Motion categories. But the reason for segregating Transportation and Motion from a generic NVA category is that these two types of waste typically are highly prevalent within a process. Thus, we want to segregate and address them separately.
    ■ Transportation (pure waste; non-value-added):
      – Any transporting (movement) of material or product.
    ■ Inventory/Storage (pure waste; non-value-added):
      – The inventory within a process is referred to as Work-In-Process (WIP) or Raw-In-Process (RIP). "Raw" refers to raw material stored in the production line, and can also be used to classify subassemblies, etc., stored within the production. WIP refers to the items that's being produced (transformed) throughout the various stages of production; not its components (i.e., raw material). And the focus is (should be) mostly on the WIP, as the amount of WIP directly affects the Process Lead Time (PLT), i.e., Little's Law. And Little's Law is represented by this equation: PLT = WIP/Exit Rate. Exit Rate is the number of units exiting the production area, i.e., the rate that a product is completed and sent to the subsequent operations area.

- Motion (pure waste; non-value-added):
  - Motion is the movement (handling) of a product, material, etc., by an operator or machine during the product transformation process. Motion is movement within the workstation or work area, not the transporting of material, etc., to/from workstations, areas, etc.
- Waiting (pure waste; non-value-added):
  - To wait or queue represents a disruption in the flow of the product.
- Non-Value-Added but Needed (NVAN) Operation
  - Operational Step Non-Value-Added-Needed is non-value-added activities that are wasteful but are required to enable the manufacturing of a product or the delivery of a service. So they are Non-Value-Added but Needed (NVAN).
    - There are a couple of differentiating factors between an operation being NVA or NVAN.
    - To be an NVAN Operation:
      - It must be an activity that creates no value but is required to get the product out the door, *and* which cannot be eliminated based on the current state of thinking or technology.
      - It's an activity that is required by regulatory, legal, or mandated by the customer.
      - It's necessary due to the non-robustness of a process (e.g., inspection, testing, auditing).

    Examples of Non-Value-Added but Needed (NVAN) activities could include:
    - Inspecting (external).
    - Monitor process chemicals (pH, viscosity, etc.).
    - Auditing or monitoring of online quality, product attributes, etc.
    - Testing or reporting regulatory.
    - Deciding (i.e., no obvious next step).
    - Invoicing customer.
    - Issuing a purchase order.

4. *Units/Total Pieces*: Denote the number of units at the workstation, queueing and staging areas, etc. The units could be lots, bins, cartons, reels, etc. Additionally, in the comment column (or somewhere), you must denote the number of pieces per unit.
5. *Time.* The time required to complete an activity (or step). This should be obtained by timing the activity with a stopwatch.

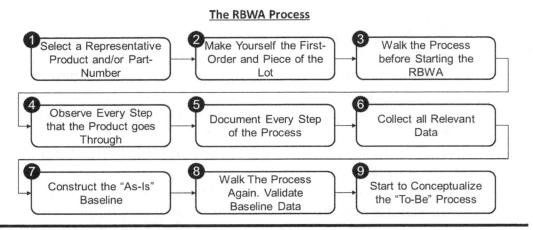

The RBWA Process

1. Select a Representative Product and/or Part-Number
2. Make Yourself the First-Order and Piece of the Lot
3. Walk the Process before Starting the RBWA
4. Observe Every Step that the Product goes Through
5. Document Every Step of the Process
6. Collect all Relevant Data
7. Construct the "As-Is" Baseline
8. Walk The Process Again. Validate Baseline Data
9. Start to Conceptualize the "To-Be" Process

Figure 8.17   The Routing-By-Walking-Around (RBWA) Process.

In determining the time for inventory or waiting, I would typically utilize Little's Law. Little's Law states that the Process Lead Time (PLT) would be equal to WIP (Work-in-Process) divided by its Exit Rate. The exit rate would be the cycle time of the next operation.

6. *Distance:* The distance that the product traveled in accomplishing this activity (step) is measured and recorded. The walking distance by a person not transporting product and/or material is ignored.
7. *Comments*: You can denote any special or relevant observations in this area or any comments from operators, engineers, supervisors, etc.

Now that you understand the RBWA template, let's look at the steps to construct an RBWA (see Figure 8.17).

The RBWA Process

1. Select a representative product group(s) and part number(s)
   - Typically, you'll want a high-volume product that has a process flow that's representative of the most common process flow. Remember *the Pareto Principle*; focus on the "critical-few" rather than the "trivial-many"; so, choose a product group and part number that represents the process flow of the "critical-few."

     But if there are a lot of variations between the "critical-few" products, then you'll want to construct multiple RBWA analysis to ensure the "critical-few" are covered.
2. *Make Yourself the First Order and Piece in the Lot*
   - The RBWA methodology is all about going to the Gemba and physically following the process.

- You are going to follow a product through its entire process, so you can "staple" yourself to an order (work order, lot card, traveler, or whatever) and follow that order through its end-to-end process.
- *Physically go everywhere the order/product goes; don't allow any open loops in the process.*

3. Walk the full process prior to starting your actual RBWA; become fully aware of all aspects of the process.

4. Observe every step that the product goes through from start to finish.
   - The starting point of your RBWA should be incoming receiving (or at a minimum, the raw material warehouse), and the ending point being the finished-goods warehouse or shipping container (depending on the process).

5. Document every step of the process:
   - List the steps in sequential order as the process progresses.
   - Categorize each step during walk-through.
   - Document every step that the order/product goes through from start to finish; *no step or activity is too small or insignificant.*
   - Document exact observations.
   - Be objective; don't assume anything.
   - Gather all relevant documentation (i.e., information), e.g., any and all forms, copies of logs, etc.

6. Collect all relevant data:
   - For each step, record how much time is required to complete each step:
     • Use a stopwatch to record times.
     • Existing time observations, engineering standards, or machine standards can be used, but you must confirm through observation.
   - Wait/Queue Times
     • Calculate wait/queue times based on Little's Law.
     • Conduct interviews with operators, technicians, and/or engineers to estimate wait/queue times. Validate flow through observations.
     • Observe queue quantities at a minimum of three different times to validate estimates.
   - Inventory and Storage Times:
     • Calculate inventory-storage times based on Little's Law.
     • Conduct interviews with operators, technicians, and/or engineers to estimate storage times. Validate flow through observations.
     • Observe inventory quantities at a minimum of three different times to validate estimates.

- Take note of any inventory preceding or following each step (i.e., Work-in-Process). Record the quantity of inventory and how much time it will take to typically process the inventory. **Note:** The RBWA is a snapshot in time, so record the inventory as it is when you are there; later you can adjust it based on inventory reports, etc. But for your RBWA activity, record exactly what you see on your "Walk-Around." Document the snapshot in time exactly as you witnessed it during your RBWA. And be honest. You're not trying to find fault; you're trying to identify opportunities for improvement.
  - Record any distance that the "base" material travels through the process, i.e., travel accomplished by human (walking), fork trucks, conveyors, automatic guided vehicles, etc. You can also add distance that the operator travels to get a tool, paperwork, etc., while the "base" is in the operator's workspace. Capture all travel distance of the base material and operators. Later, we can use this data/information to construct a spaghetti diagram.
  - Collect any available quality data, e.g., yields, scrap rates, defects-per-million, etc.
7. Construct the "As-Is" baseline
   a. Calculate the Process Lead Time – The amount of time required to complete one order.
   b. Tabulate the number of steps within each category. Construct a graph of results.
   c. Calculate the percentages of Value-Added and Non-Value-Added steps.
   d. Tabulate the process time by categories. Construct a graph of results.
   e. Calculate the percentages of Value-Added and Non-Value-Added time.
   f. Sketch a spaghetti diagram.
8. Walk the process flow several times to make sure that the RBWA data is accurate and complete. Validate the As-Is baseline.
9. Start to conceptualize the "To-Be" process
   - As you walk the process, think about how the process should flow; conceptually, start mentally creating your "To-Be" design:
     - Where can waste be eliminated?
     - Which Non-Value-Added activities can be eliminated?
     - Is the layout optimized? Can travel distances be reduced?
     - How to reduce the wait/queue steps and time?
     - How to reduce inventory and storage?

Constructing the "As-Is" Baseline

■ Process Lead Time (PLT) is the sum of all the cycle times for each process step. And this is your most important baseline metric, as any improvements that are made in reducing waste, eliminating non-value-added activities, and reducing inventory will result in a reduction in the baseline's PLT.
■ Categorizing the steps and comparing value-added and non-value-added.
  − We must calculate the number of steps and process time for each category. And then we can plot the sums for each category in a simple bar graph.

And that concludes the data-collection portion of the RBWA; now let's consider the analytical steps.

Steps Description

■ Standardized use of "Action" verbs to describe steps:
  − Move/Issue.
  − Wait.
  − Setup.
  − Load/Unload.
  − Test/Count/Record/Label.
  − Assemble/Machine/Glue (per the operation).
■ Focus on Detail, Too Many Steps is Better Than Not Enough!!

Process Data

■ Number of machines, lots, etc... used/available for this step.
■ Number of people, hand-offs, etc.
■ Distance traveled.
■ Time at this step or process rate.

Comments

■ More detailed description of the step characteristics.
■ Record what is necessary to describe how the step is done.

■ Record various inventory quantities.
■ Capture important quality information for each step.

Summarize the RBWA Data

Current Process Evaluation

■ Convert detailed documentation into usable information.
■ Establish the baseline for existing process flows and performance measures.
■ Quantify waste and hidden steps.
■ Quantify value-added versus non-value-added steps and time.
■ Quantify specific cycle-time contributors, e.g., process time, waiting time (queue, dwell-time, etc.), distance traveled, inventory levels (WIP), etc.
■ Use as basis for developing targets for conceptual designs.

Figure 8.18 shows an example of a graphical summary of collected RBWA data. The next step is to identify improvement opportunities. And always be focused on eliminating or minimizing the seven operational-wastes (see Figure 8.19 as a refresher).

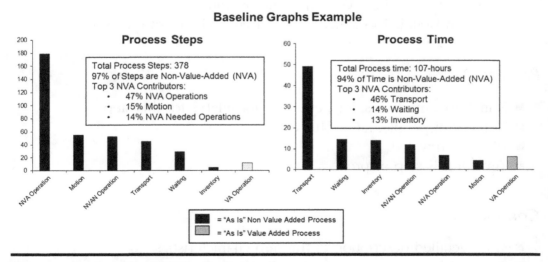

Figure 8.18   Example: RBWA - Data Graph.

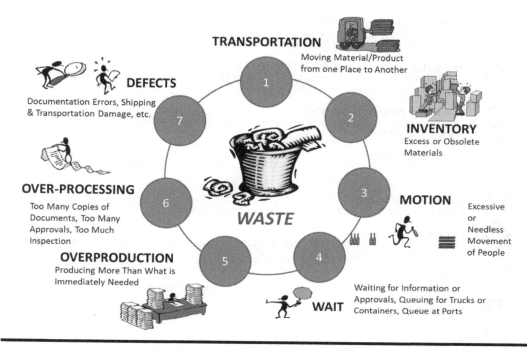

Figure 8.19   Seven Operational-Wastes (T-I-M-W-O-O-D).

Process Mapping

A process map is a tool to visually illustrate the flow of the product/service. The purpose of process mapping is to obtain a better understanding of the process. It involves the gathering and organizing of facts about the work (data can be extracted from related RBWA) and displaying them so that they can be questioned and improved by the stakeholders.

The RBWA is one technique for creating a process map and the most thorough, but a process map can be constructed in many ways. The objective of process mapping is to visually document the steps of the process, preferably utilizing some "industry-standard" symbols.

Figure 8.20 shows the common symbols used in process mapping.

Figure 8.21 shows a representative sample of a process-mapping diagram. The objective is to improve the process flow by eliminating/minimizing waste (i.e., non-value-adding activities), in the following ways:

- Minimizing non-value-added steps.
- Eliminating inspection.
- Minimizing storage, inventory, queues, etc.
- Minimizing transports/moves

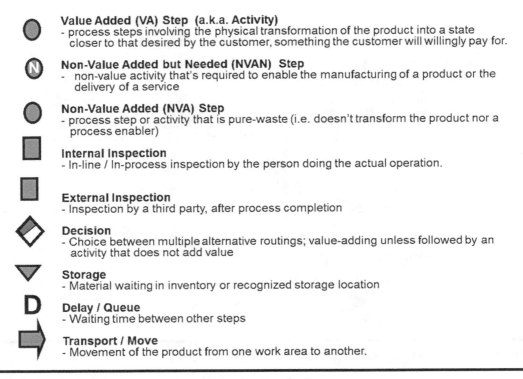

Value Added (VA) Step (a.k.a. Activity)
- process steps involving the physical transformation of the product into a state closer to that desired by the customer, something the customer will willingly pay for.

Non-Value Added but Needed (NVAN) Step
- non-value activity that's required to enable the manufacturing of a product or the delivery of a service

Non-Value Added (NVA) Step
- process step or activity that is pure-waste (i.e. doesn't transform the product nor a process enabler)

Internal Inspection
- In-line / In-process inspection by the person doing the actual operation.

External Inspection
- Inspection by a third party, after process completion

Decision
- Choice between multiple alternative routings; value-adding unless followed by an activity that does not add value

Storage
- Material waiting in inventory or recognized storage location

Delay / Queue
- Waiting time between other steps

Transport / Move
- Movement of the product from one work area to another.

Figure 8.20 "Common" Process-Mapping Symbols.

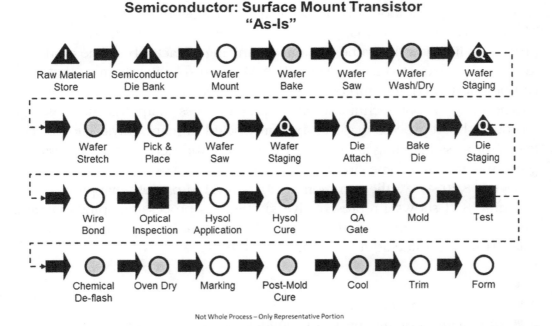

Not Whole Process – Only Representative Portion

Figure 8.21 Example: Process-Mapping with Symbols.

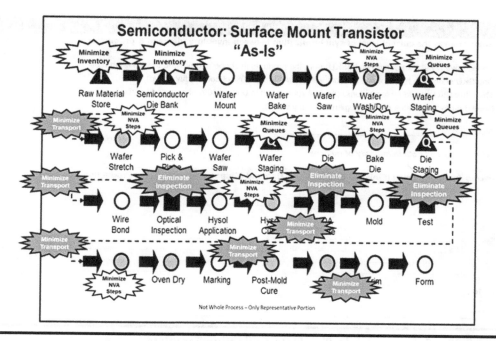

Figure 8.22   Example: Potential Improvements Identified.

Figure 8.22 reflects the process after improvements have been identified.

Triple-Play Chart

An analysis tool that may not be as common as some of the other assessment tools is the "Triple-Play Chart." As the name implies, it's a comparison of three variables on one chart, i.e., Production, Shipments (a.k.a. Customer Demand), and Finished-Goods Inventory. And the objective is to assess the synchronization of those three variables.

And in an effective "pull system," those three variables should be synchronized.

Figure 8.23 shows an example triple-play data-collection template.

Figure 8.24 shows a plot of a triple-play diagram with a couple of analytical comments:

1. Demand-shipment and actual production quantities are well synchronized; showing a semblance of production quantities being produced (pulled) by the amount of product being consumed by the customers.
2. Finished-goods inventory seems to be managed (pushed) independently of the customers' consumption.

Triple Play Chart			
Goal: Analyze the current level of synchronization between inventory, demand & production.			

Choose two (2) stock keeping units(SKU) from the products in scope and provide the following data.

One SKU should be high-volume (Annual volume within top 10% of commodity group).

The other SKU should be low-volume (Annual volume within bottom 10% of commodity group).

Need data for a 52-week period (beginning at any week).

SKU: _____

Report all data in quantity of devices

Weeks	Inventory Level (Finished Goods)	Demand (Shipments)	Production Run Rate
1			
2			
3			
4			
5			
6			
7			
8			
9			
10			
11			
12			

Figure 8.23   Example: Triple-Play Data-Collection Template.

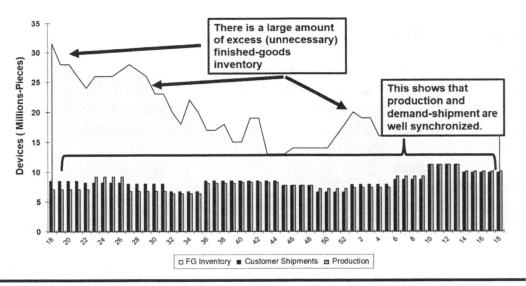

Figure 8.24   Triple-Play Chart.

Financial Analysis

Materials		Direct Labor		Staff & Indirect Labor		Overhead	
Please indicate sub-totals by major material families		Include only wages and benefits. Please indicate sub-totals by department.		Include only wages and benefits. Please indicate sub-totals by department or function, including:		All other cost, including:	
Description	Value	Description	Value	Description	Value	Description	Value
				Sales & Marketing		Occupancy*	
				Engineering		Process Utilities (Energy, Water, Waste Processing)	
				Planning & Production Control		Equipment Depreciation	
				Supervision		Financing	
				Material Handling (Including Warehouse & Receiving)			
				Shipping			
				Maintenance			
				After Sales Service			
				Quality Assurance & Control			
				Document Reproduction			

Figure 8.25   Financial Analysis Template.

Financial Analysis

In the initial analysis of a company's supply-chain optimization initiative, it's important to get a snapshot of the company's financials by taking a quick look at the company's Profit & Loss statement and its Balance Sheet. For this snapshot, you're not doing an in-depth financial analysis, but you're trying to identify large buckets of cost or expenditures (i.e., financial opportunities).

Figure 8.25 shows a financial-analysis data-collection template.

Case-in-Point 8.1: SWOT Example

We had a client that was a highly diversified US Fortune 100 company, and we were asked to assess one of their major divisions, their Semiconductor Product Group. So an initial step was to assess what were their perceived (and actual) internal strengths and weaknesses, and what positive and/or negative external factors they must be prepared to take advantage of or to have contingencies to offset (see Figure 8.26). (Note: This SWOT was created circa 1999, so, the opportunities and threats have probably changed.)

This SWOT analysis assisted (i.e., supported) improvement initiatives such as:

- Implementation of cellular manufacturing to reduce overall lead time and operations' cycle times through an optimized layout. *Total process lead time was reduced from 10 days to 1.3 days.*
  - Shorter process times aided improvements in quality, i.e., less handling, less storage (e.g., queues, waiting).
  - Lot sizes were reduced by 67%.
  - Created more flexibility and responsiveness to market and customer changes.

Strengths	Weaknesses
• Management support & overall leadership • TPM program • Quality & yield – incoming wafer • Quality & yield of backend assembly & test process • Short order fulfillment lead-times (large buffer inventories) • Integrated device manufacturer (own wafer, assembly, test & OEM)	• Layout constraints (centralized molding) • Long Manufacturing Process Lead-Time • Poor data management / ERP system • Large lot sizes • Wafer fab in US; long transit times and inventories
Opportunities	**Threats**
• Customer demand management – too much volatility • Customer demanding shorter lead-times • Mobile phone market is exponentially growing	• Competition – devices are mainly commodity (easy market entry) • Most devices are not leading-edge technology (no competitive advantage) • Wafer foundry landscape shifting from US to Taiwan and Korea • Fabless & pure-foundry options

Figure 8.26 SWOT Matrix for a Supply-Chain Assessment of a US Manufacturer.

■ Information-technology capabilities expanded to improve data management and enhance demand management, thus smoothing demand requirements to be more consumption based rather than forecast based.
■ Commodity portfolio rationalization with more emphasis on emerging technologies.

Case-in-Point 8.2: SIPOC Examples

The purpose of this case-in-point is to share a couple of examples of typical SIPOC applications.

Example #1

Company: A US OEM industrial equipment manufacturer

Figure 8.27 is a simple SIPOC for a subassembly operation of a metal-fabricated part assembly. This SIPOC was used to establish the scope and identify the stakeholders for a project to improve the Process Lead Time (PLT).

Example #2

Figure 8.28 is a SIPOC for an order-fulfillment process from a medical-glove manufacturer to a US customer. This SIPOC was used to establish the scope and identify the stakeholders for a project to improve the Order

SIPOC Diagram

Subassembly "X": weld & assembly

Suppliers	Inputs	Process	Outputs	Customers
Material Control	Work Order Tag	Laser Cut Sheets	Subassembly "X"	Product "X" Final Assembly Workstation
		Press Brake		
Metal Fab Shop / Kanban	Fabricated Parts	Stud – Tack Weld		
		Robot Assembly Weld		
External Suppliers / Kanban	Purchased Parts	Hardware Attach		
External Suppliers / Kanban	Sheet Metal	Leak Test		
		Polish / Paint		

Figure 8.27   Example SIPOC for Metal-Fabricated Subassembly.

SIPOC   **Process: Medical Glove Manufacturing**

Suppliers	Inputs	Major Process Steps	Outputs	Customers
Supplier "A" - Thailand	Nitrile (Latex)	Compounding	Nitrile Compound	
Supplier "B" - Malaysia	Glove Molds	Forming	Finished Glove	
	Finished Glove	Storage - Supermarket		
Supplier "G" - Malaysia	Glove Dispenser Box	Packaging	Gloves in Dispenser in Cardboard Carton	
Supplier "C" - Malaysia	Cardboard Cartons			
Supplier "D" - Malaysia	Shipping Container	Container Loading	Shipping Bill-of-Lading	
Supplier "D" - Malaysia	3rd Party Trucker	Trucking to Port		
	Shipping Bill-of-Lading			
Supplier "E" - Malaysia	3rd Party Container Ship	Sea-ship to USA	Shipping Bill-of-Lading	
	Container	FDA Inspection		
Supplier "F" - USA	3rd Party Trucker	Ground transport to Customer Warehouse	Invoice	Customer "A"
	Malaysian Manufacturer		Medical Gloves	

Input Metrics	Process Metrics	Output Metrics	
	First Aid / Lost-Time		Safety
	Defects per Million Gloves	FDA Acceptance Rate	Quality
	Process Lead-time		Delivery
Nitrile Cost/Kg (wet)	Cost-to-Manufacture	Average Selling Price	Cost
Packaging Cost	Manufacturing Variance	Gross Margins	Cost
	Shipping Cost		Other

Figure 8.28   SIPOC for Order-Fulfillment Process.

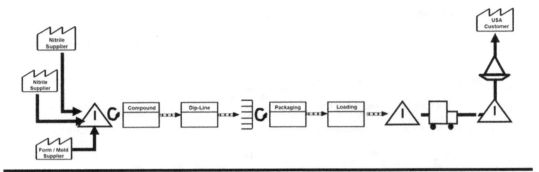

Figure 8.29   Simplified Value Stream Map.

Fulfillment Process Lead Time (PLT). Additionally, it identified the key metrics so that a data-collection plan (a.k.a. measurement plan) could be created and the data-collection process initiated.

The information from the SIPOC allowed us to construct a simplified VSM (see Figure 8.29).

This completed project resulted in a 15% reduction the Order-Fulfillment PLT from 59.2 days to 50.3 days. And after a full assessment of all the operating-cost factors, the gross margins were improved by 30% (from 10% to 13%).

Case-in-Point 8.3: Results of a Lean Transformation

This case story is about a Japanese white-goods (household appliances) manufacturing site in Southeast Asia. The scenario was that the company was facing very strong cost competition from many Chinese appliance manufacturers. So we were contracted as consultants to lead a Lean Transformation to improve their overall competitiveness.

I led the initial steps of the project, which encompassed a full assessment of their current ways of doing business. This was a complex vertically integrated facility with fragmented manufacturing departments (warehousing, metal fabrication, plastic molding, electronics, etc.) spread out throughout the site.

After the full assessment was completed and the performance gaps validated, the client prioritized what initiatives they wanted to undertake as Phase 1 of their transformation journey, and they contracted our consulting services to assist them.

I led Phase 1 of the transformation implementation, which included the following initiatives:

■ Process flow modeling: Identify and minimize non-value-added activities. Redesigned several manufacturing cells, improving material and product flow at the shop floor.

- Implemented robust process controls (statistical and visual) and quality improvements initiatives: Led an "attack" to identify and validate root causes of yield and scrap issues, and established process controls (poke-yoke) to prevent defects at the source.
- Machine setup time improvement (SMED): Introduced parallel activities while the machine is running, and initiated some fixture and equipment design changes to reduce setup time and increase production flexibility
- Manufacturing run strategy: Categorized the product groups to create a manufacturing build schedule of daily and weekly buckets, and optimized equipment and cell changeovers. CONWIP system utilized in certain areas to sequence kanbans based on priorities (see Figure 8.30).
- Bottleneck optimization: Identified bottleneck operation and optimize loading sequencing of products to meet demand.
- Capacity and line balancing, and resource allocation: Allocated products to machines and cells to optimize the balancing of operational capacity per demand (Takt-Rate).
- Kanban implementation: Implemented kanbans to control inventory and synchronize production to actual demand. Implemented supermarkets to decouple the fragmented functional departments (see Figures 8.30 and 8.31).

The results obtained were:

- Setup time reduction of 97%.
- Improved labor cost-per-unit by 20%.
- Increased production capacity by 60%.
- Annualized overtime reduction of US $200 k in savings.

There were another two phases of transformation activities which the company took on with the use of a full-time consulting team, but we did provide ongoing advisory assistance whenever requested.

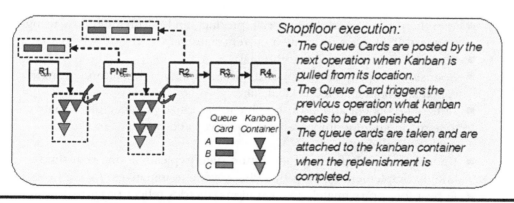

Figure 8.30   CONWIP System.

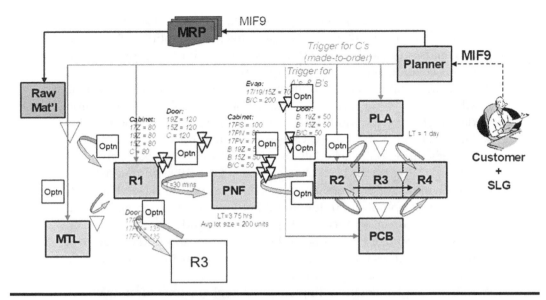

Figure 8.31   Reflects the "To-Be" of Production Pull System.

The company has subsequently survived the onslaught of Chinese competition and has stabilized its market share, so mission accomplished.

Case-in-Point 8.4: Transformation via Value Stream Mapping

Company: A US manufacturer.

Background: The company had a very strong Lean culture and utilized VSM as the center of its continuous improvement activities. The company followed a rule of thumb that you would proceed through five iterations of current state to future state before potentially obtaining its theoretical ideal state. The value stream maps were inclusive of the entire supply chain, i.e., suppliers to customers.

Process: This company basically followed the standard VSM creation process:

- Map the process, and the material, product, and information flow using standard VSM icons to create a current-state map.
- Walk the Gemba to validate the map.
- Brainstorm improvement opportunities, thinking of breakthrough projects that would lead to an ideal state.
- Utilize the benefit and effort graphic to prioritize projects (use x-matrix to assist in aligning improvement initiatives and priorities to site's goals/objectives).
- Undertake next iteration of the future state (typically a one-year timeline) by implementing prioritized improvement initiatives.
- Repeat for approximately five iterations (metrics reflect progress toward an ideal state).

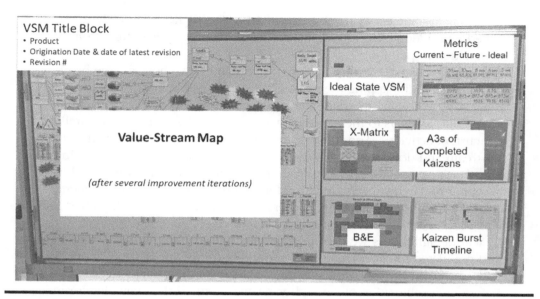

Figure 8.32   Example of a VSM Communication Board.

Items	Current-State	Future-State*	Ideal-State Target
Value-Added Ratio	10%	14%	19%
Process Lead-Time	10-days	6-days	5-days

* Future-State represents approximately 3-itrerations.

Figure 8.33   Snapshot of Improvement Progress.

And the company was very successful in its VSM initiatives.

Figure 8.32 reflects an example of a VSM communication board.

The focus of the VSM in Figure 8.32 was to reduce overall Process Lead Time (PLT) and increase Value-Added Ratio (i.e., ratio of value-added time versus total PLT).

Figure 8.33 reflects a snapshot of the progress that had been made to reaching its ideal state through approximately three iterations.

Case-in-Point 8.5: Transformation via Value Stream Mapping

Company: Oil and Gas
Scope: Upstream Operations – Offshore Oil Delivery

This was one of my first attempts at VSM.

This was a consulting client in an industry in which I had no experience. I had just arrived at the client's site (the night before), and I wanted to learn more about their process, so there's no better or faster methodology for understanding a process than to value stream map the process with a team of the client's Subject Matter Experts (SMEs). The client had already established a problem to be solved, i.e., reducing the process lead time from well completion to pumping oil.

After the customary introductions, we immediately chose a large blank wall and started mapping the process utilizing Post-it notes. Post-it notes quickly proved to be the right medium, as there was considerable debate among the SMEs as to the exact sequence of activities, particularly parallel concurrent activities. And the debates (discussions) between the SMEs and upstream and downstream stakeholders were very important to garnering everyone's perspective. As the collaborative team proceeded through the VS mapping process, we captured all information discrepancies and challenges, issues, improvement thoughts, barriers, etc., in a "Parking Lot" flip-chart for later investigations, validations, and discussions.

Within eight hours we had fully mapped the offshore oil delivery process and populated multiple pages of "Parking Lot" notes, all of which would be addressed over the following few days. Utilizing a digital camera (this was before the proliferation of smartphones), we captured the manually created Post-it note process as our "draft" baseline. It would remain a "draft" until all parking-lot items were resolved. (A recreation of the manually created Current-State VSM is shown in Figure 8.34.)

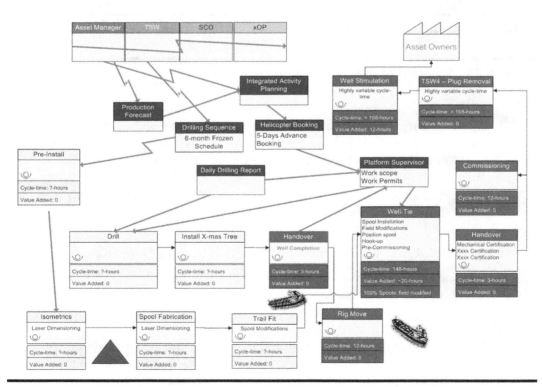

Figure 8.34 Current-State Value Stream Map.

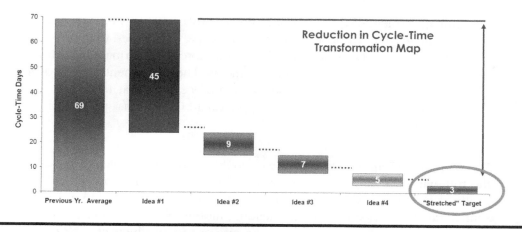

Figure 8.35   Waterfall Chart – Targeted PLT.

We had thus established a VSM Process Lead Time (PLT), and on the following day the same group would start brainstorming improvement opportunities. We started with a current-state VSM with a PLT above 20 days, but the historical data showed a past 12-month average of 69 days, so the cycle times given for the VSM were what they thought they should be, not what was exactly happening. We spent several hours of unconstrained brainstorming of improvement opportunities with a goal to theoretically reduce the PLT to as low as possible. We collected all brainstormed improvement ideas on Post-it notes. We created over 50 potential improvement ideas and then utilized Affinity Diagraming as a method to organize the ideas into groups. After affinitizing the ideas, we created four groups of related ideas (>50 ideas to four groups). And we utilized a waterfall chart (see Figure 8.35) to show the proposed future PLT target of three days.

This was not exactly the traditional VSM approach, as we used the current-state VSM to establish a current-state theoretical PLT which was less than a third of the actual average, so we were able to use the VSM to identify the differences between theoretical and actual, and that gave us immediate improvements to go after; we then brainstormed what the ideal state would be, i.e., three days.

So this VSM exercise was very effective in identifying discrepancies between "doing what-you're-supposed-to-do" versus what they were actually doing, i.e., a great revelation for some of the stakeholders.

Case-in-Point 8.6: RBWA/Triple-Play/Spaghetti Diagram

Company: Fortune 50 Integrated-Semiconductor Manufacturer
Background: The consultancy firm that employed me had been contracted by this company's Global President of Operations to do a

full assessment of their order-fulfillment process. This was a division of a huge American conglomerate; our scope was limited to their Semiconductor Division but still covered more than ten manufacturing sites in four countries on three continents. The assessment would cover the full supply chain and all supporting processes; I was the Lead-Consultant/Team-Lead for the "Supply-Chain Operations" portion of the assessment.

We used the "T" approach, where we would get basic information on the full manufacturing portfolio but then "drill-down" on a couple of products. My initial RBWA would be constructed for a high-volume semiconductor device used by the leading mobile phone manufacturer (at that time). So I would drill-down on one or two products at each of their ten manufacturing sites, and I would conduct at least one RBWA at each facility.

The starting point for each RBWA will be the incoming material receiving area. And as we follow a wafer through the process, we record:

■ Description of activity that transformation and/or movement of the "wafer" (or the wafers' by-product, i.e., a die), while breaking down the activities into work elements which later will be categorized as value-added or non-value-added elements.
■ The amount of time to complete the activity or work element. This is not a detailed time study, but we want to capture a reasonable estimate of how much time it takes to complete the tasks.
■ The amount of inventory at the workstations or inventory buffers between workstations. The inventory to be counted is Work-in-Process only, not raw materials or offline built subassemblies. Important Notes: (1) We are tracking the wafer and/or its by-product, so offline, etc., subassemblies are not counted, (2) This is a snapshot in time, so we count (estimate) how much inventory (WIP) is present at the time of our RBWA, (3) The amount of inventory should be recorded as the amount of time (days, hours, minutes, or seconds) required to process the inventory.
■ The distance traveled by the wafer/die and travel distance by the operator required to transform the wafer/die into a product.
■ The "Analysis of Time" classification of time as value-added or non-value-added activities or elements.

RBWA Scope: This example will focus on the front end of the supply chain for a specialty[3] semiconductor device from wafer foundry to die-prep to final assembly and test.

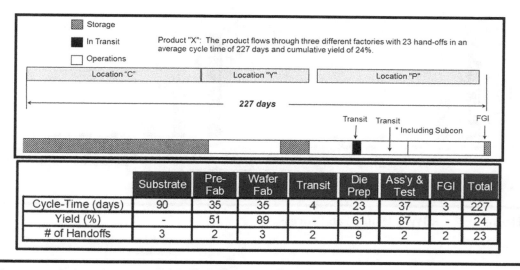

Figure 8.36   Product "X" Average Process Lead Time.

Approach: We conducted RBWA analysis at three facilities in three countries and two continents. Figure 8.36 shows the process flow across the three facilities. And Figure 8.36 shows a cumulative average process lead time of 227 days with a roll-through yield of only 24%, and a total of 23 hand-offs[4] for the total. This data is based on transactional-history and stocking targets for each site's full product portfolio.

The first RBWA was conducted on Product "X"'s wafer-fab process at location "Y."

- The total process time of the Product "X" wafer-fab process at Location "Y" is 19 days, of which only 8.4% add value.
- Storage and queue steps account for 66% of the total process time.
- The process consists of 1,567 steps, of which only 12.5% add value.
- Delays account for 48.8% of total process steps.

Figure 8.37 shows a graphical summary.

The second RBWA was conducted on Product "X"'s die-prep process at location "S."

- Total cycle time of Product "X" wafer-fab process at Location "S" is 15.1 days, of which only 10.7% is value-added.
- Storage and queue steps account for 62.3% of the total process time.
- Total process was 2,077 steps, of which only 5.3% are value-added.
- Delays account for 54.1% of total process steps.

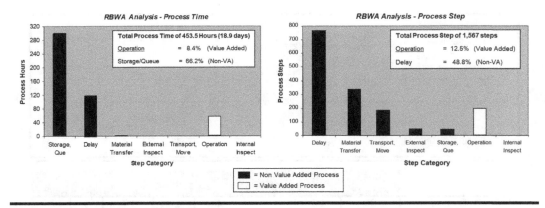

Figure 8.37   RBWA: Wafer-Fab Process.

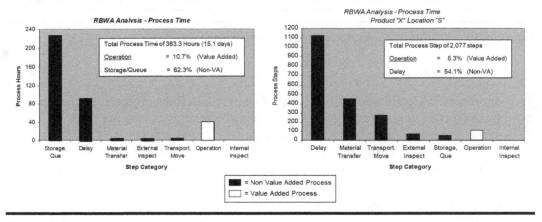

Figure 8.38   RBWA: Die-Prep Process.

Figure 8.38 shows a graphical summary.

The RBWA allows us to create a spaghetti diagram[5] of the flow through die-prep at location "S." The device travels over two kilometers from receiving to packing. The devices are staged in a desiccator between operations.

Figure 8.39 is a spaghetti diagram of the flow through the die-prep process.

The final RBWA was conducted on Product "X"'s assembly and test at location "P."

- Total cycle time for assembly and test was 7.8 days, of which only 2% is value-added.
- Storage and queue steps account for 93.8% of the total process time.
- Total process was 100 steps, of which only 3% are value-added.
- Storage and queue steps account for 91% of total process steps.

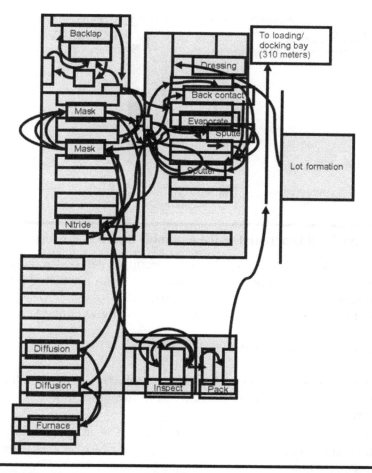

Figure 8.39   Spaghetti Diagram: Die-Prep Process.

Figure 8.40 shows a graphical summary.

We also did a Triple-Play analysis of the relationship between the inventory and production (i.e., assembly and test) and customer demand.

Figure 8.41 shows a graphical comparison of the finished-goods inventory levels against new production and customer demand. The graph shows a strong synchronization between production and customer demand, but a major disconnect with FGI management.

Figure 8.42 shows the same graphical comparison of the finished goods inventory levels against new production and customer demand as Figure 8.41 but with the die-prep inventory overlaid. Again, the graph shows a strong synchronization between production and customer demand but a major disconnect with FGI management, and a huge (monstrous) disconnect with the die-prep inventory. The die-prep inventory is approximately 25-to-40 times greater than the average customer demand.

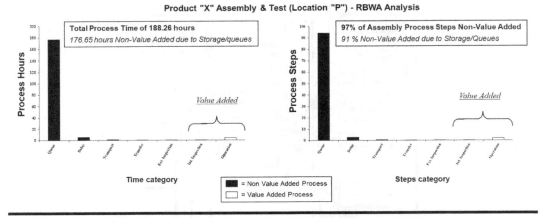

Figure 8.40 Spaghetti Diagram: Device Assembly and Test Process.

The next RBWA that I'll include in this example will be for the assembly and test operations at location "P," as this is an area on which the company's improvement efforts would be concentrated.

Scope: RBWA was for Assembly and Test of a High-Volume Semiconductor Surface-Mount Transistor.

The RBWA analysis revealed:

■ Total process lead time was 12 days, of which only 4% is value-added.
■ The major process-time categories were Inventory (84%) and Waiting (10%).
■ Total process was 355 steps, of which only 7% are value-added.
■ The major process steps were Waiting (50%), Motion (21%), and Transport (15%).

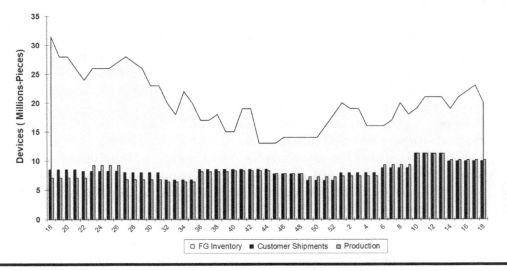

Figure 8.41 Triple-Play (FGI – Customer-Demand – Production).

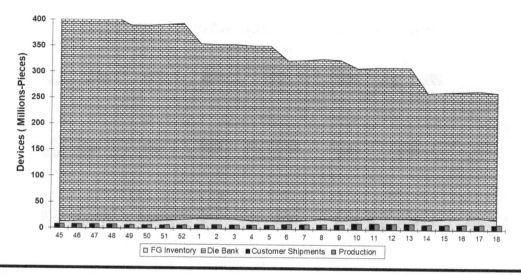

Figure 8.42   Triple-Play (FGI – Customer-Demand – Production – Die-Inventory).

Figure 8.43 shows a graphical summary.

The RBWA data allowed us to create a detailed process map of the assembly and test operation for this transistor. A portion of this process map is shown in Figure 8.44.

The total distance that this device traveled through assembly and test was 2,411 feet (approaching a half-mile).

So this RBWA gave us a great snapshot of the process performance for this device and identified my priorities for process improvement.

Additionally, because we gathered this data at the gemba, we were also able to make key observations of the activities being performed.

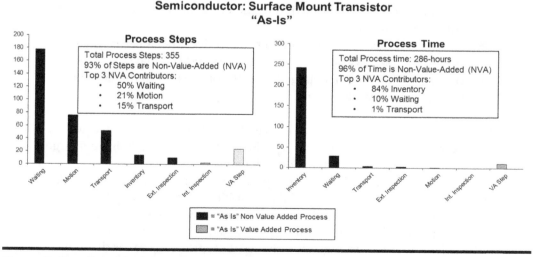

Figure 8.43   Graphical Summary RBWA.

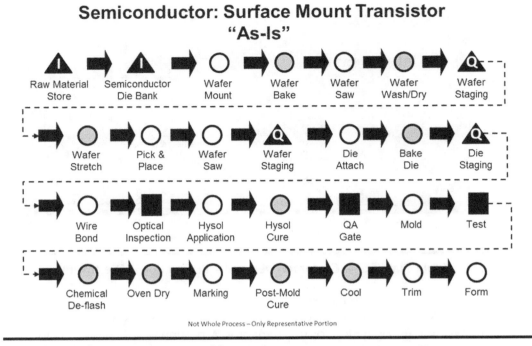

Figure 8.44   Process Map: Assembly & Test.

Based on the data and our observations, the immediate improvement opportunities were:

■ Too much WIP inventory consumed 84% of their PLT, so the WIP is equivalent to more than 10 days of inventory.
■ The layout was a process village concept, as equipment was laid out in groups based on the function of the equipment, not the flow of the product or material.
■ There was no dedicated equipment, which led to extensive waiting (50% of the process steps involved queues and/or delays).
■ Lot sizes are too big. The large lot sizes contributed to the Waiting steps and the Inventory time.

The Solution: An immediate solution, which was very apparent, was to implement cellular manufacturing. A cellular layout would eliminate a large portion of the "as-is" non-value-added elements.

The one challenge with implementing cellular manufacturing in this situation was the molding operation. All the molders were centrally located in a walled area within a clean room manufacturing environment, and the costs for any major reconfiguration of that area would have been astronomical. So the solution was to arrange all activities (except molding) for this device into manufacturing cells and to link the molding activities into the cells as a virtual cell. Minimum modifications to the molding area were needed to accommodate multiple entry/exit points for lots in/out of the molding area while maintaining the integrity of the clean room and having dedicated molding equipment for select devices. All non-molding equipment would be rearranged to create several efficient manufacturing cells which would allow end-to-end continuous flow through the full manufacturing process and eliminate the waiting steps by 10%.

We were contracted by this company to facilitate the full implementation of the manufacturing improvements. The major improvements that we implemented were:

- Cellular manufacturing: Minimize material handling, continuous product flow, etc.
- Kanban-pull system: Synchronize production with demand and minimize inventory except for safety and buffer stock.
- Process flow simplification: Minimized non-value-added activities; e.g., minimize visual inspections, reduce cure times, reduce plating times, etc.
- Enhance process controls and problem-solving techniques: Focus on root causes and prevent defects.
- Reduce equipment setup times: Implement SMED techniques.
- Manufacturing run strategy: Utilize an A-B-C production wheel (rhythm wheel).
- Traceability and administrative support: Minimize non-value-added activities.

Final results validated:

- Reduced total Process Lead Time from 10 days to one shift (10-hours)
- Customers' orders were shipped per consumption not forecasted ("A"s product daily).
- Reduced inventory by US $20 million.
- Annualized operational cost savings of >US $2 million.

Case-in-Point 8.7: RBWA Example – A Pharmaceutical Manufacturer

Company: An Asian privately owned pharmaceutical manufacturer.
Scope: The company had a large portfolio of prescription and over-the-counter products. We chose to complete an assessment of the top seven product families, and the initial (and primary) assessment methodology would be the RBWA. For the case-in-point example, I am using a high-volume, over-the-counter pharmaceutical product. The process scope will start at "raw material withdrawal" and conclude with "product transport to distribution center." *The "As-Is" RBWA:* As I stated earlier, the RBWA template was a tool that we

continuously improved (or at least modified). The next figure is a snapshot of an excerpt from the template that was utilized for this client. We had modified the template to do all of the numerical accumulations and resulting math for us, and to automatically create all graphs, etc. The data-collection method for this template is basically the same as any other template, but this was a tabulation time-saver, especially if you're doing RBWAs for multiple products and their processes consist of many steps. So you can use the figure below to develop (and customize) your own RBWA form, or you can send me an email at rbwatemplate@gmail.com to receive this free Excel version (see Figure 8.45).

The RBWA data characterized the process as:

- The total process steps were 169-steps:
  - 29% of the steps involved inventory (a.k.a. storage).
  - 28% is transporting.
  - 14.7% was categorized as value-adding.
- Total Process Lead Time equals 34.6 days.
  - 77% of the time involved inventory (a.k.a. storage).

Figure 8.46 is a graphical summary of the RBWA data.

Figure 8.47 is another example of graphically displaying and summarizing the RBWA data.

Figure 8.48 shows a spaghetti diagram created from the RBWA data.

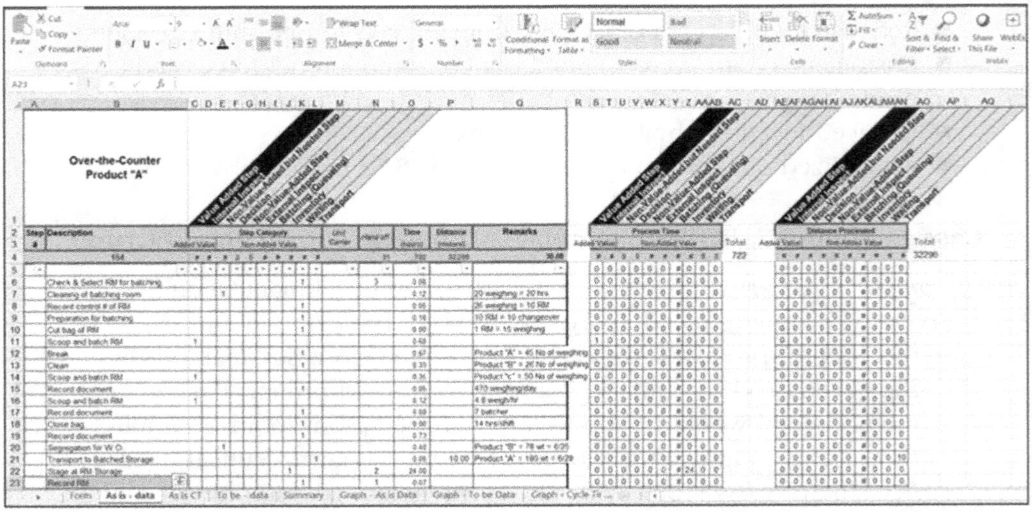

Figure 8.45 Excel RBWA Template.

"As-Is" RBWA: Over-the-Counter Pharmaceutical

Category	As Is Steps
VA Step	25
Internal Inspection	0
NVAN Step	27
Decision	2
Waiting	12
Transport	48
Inventory	49
NVA Step	5
External Inspection	1
Total	**169**

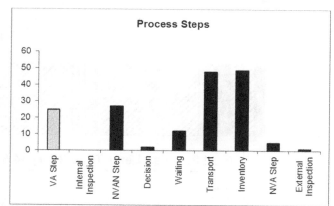

Category	As Is Time
VA Step	62.2
Internal Inspection	-
NVAN Step	9.3
Decision	0.0
Waiting	6.2
Transport	28.0
Inventory	638.0
NVA Step	5.4
External Inspection	0.0
Total	**749.2**

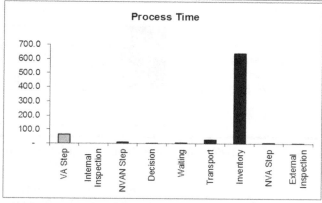

Figure 8.46 RBWA Summary.

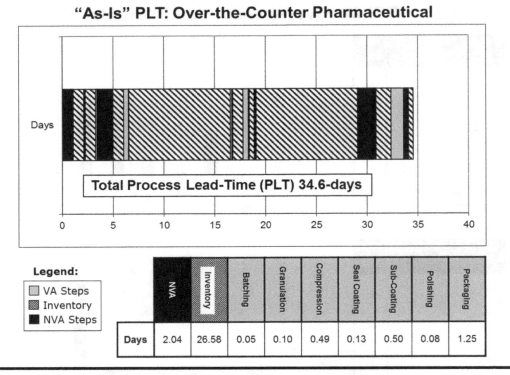

Figure 8.47   RBWA Summary: Process Lead-Time Analysis.

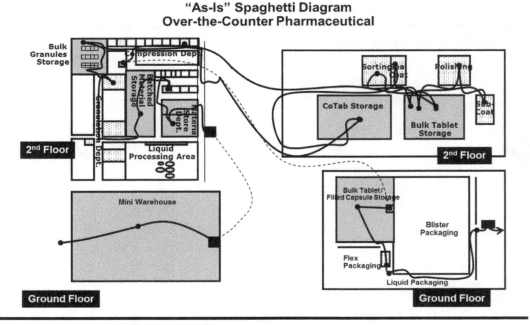

Figure 8.48   RBWA Summary: Spaghetti Diagram.

Case-in-Point 8.8: RBWA Example – Semiconductor Device Manufacturer

Company: German semiconductor assembly and test operations in Asia.
Approach: Routing-By-Walking-Around (RBWA) of a Semiconductor Device.

I am limiting this case-in-point example to reflecting the results of a standard RBWA.

As we do in all RBWA analysis, we break the data down to "Steps" (activities) and "Time" (hours). Figure 8.49 shows a composite summary of the RBWA results, a comparison of current and proposed states for the "steps' and "time" analysis, and the benefits to be obtained.

Figure 8.50 displays the current-state RBWA data for "Steps."
Figure 8.51 displays the current-state RBWA data for "Time."
Figure 8.52 displays the proposed-state RBWA data for "Steps."
Figure 8.53 displays the proposed-state RBWA data for "Time."

Activity	Symbols	Actual				Proposed				Benefits			
		No. of Steps	%	Cycle Time	%	No. of Steps	%	Cycle Time	%	No. of Steps	%	Cycle Time	%
Value Adding Operation	●	11	4%	8	3%	11	0	8	55%	0	0%	0	0%
Internal Inspect	■	0	0%	0	0%	0	0	0	0%	0	0%	0	0%
Support Operation	Ⓢ	3	1%	0	0%	2	0	0	0%	1	1%	0	0%
Decision	◇	3	1%	0	0%	0	0	0	0%	3	2%	0	0%
Motion	○	6	2%	25	9%	3	0	0	3%	3	2%	24	9%
External Inspect	□	5	2%	2	1%	0	0	0	0%	5	3%	2	1%
Storage / Inventory	▽	1	0%	219	77%	0	0	0	0%	1	1%	219	81%
Wait:	D	204	69%	30	11%	107	1	6	42%	97	57%	24	9%
Transport	⇨	62	21%	1	0%	3	0	0	0%	59	35%	1	0%
Total		295		285		126		14		169	57%	271	95%
Number of hand-offs													
Number of documents													
Total number of copies distributed													
Distance travelled		933				39				894			
First Pass Yield													

Figure 8.49 Current-/Proposed-State RBWA Summary.

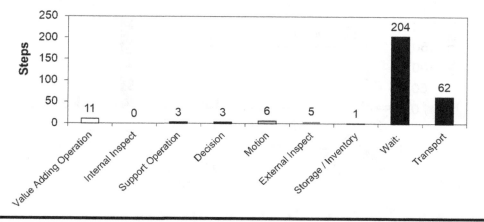

Figure 8.50 Current-State RBWA: Steps.

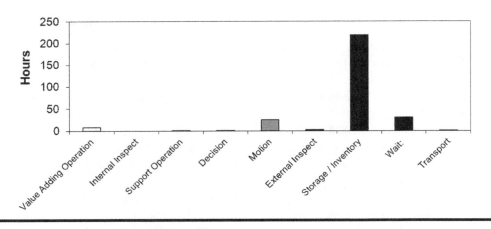

Figure 8.51   Current-State RBWA: Time.

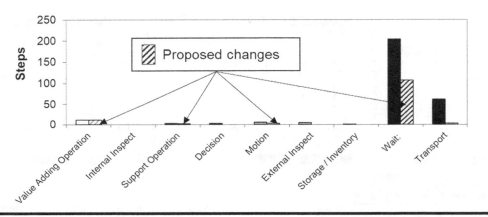

Figure 8.52   Proposed-State RBWA: Steps.

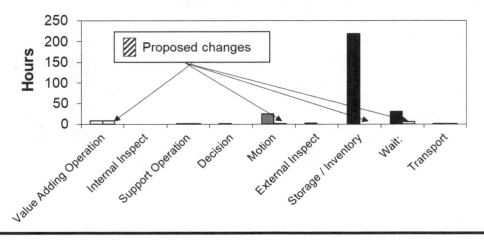

Figure 8.53   Proposed-State RBWA: Time.

Case-in-Point 8.9: Productivity Improvement via RBWA and Yamazumi.

Company: Electronic component manufacturer.
Objective: Improve productivity and reduce process lead time.

This improvement initiative started by constructing a VSM of the product's supply chain and then the brainstorming of kaizen improvement opportunities. See Figure 8.54 for the current-state VSM with improvement kaizens identified by bursts.

And Figure 8.55 reflects the ideal-state VSM.

The ideal state is expected after five iterations of improvement initiatives, with each iteration lasting six months to one year, with a new idea-generating kaizen prior to the commencement of each iteration.

The current-state mapping exercise revealed that there was an opportunity for a productivity initiative; with the next step of the productivity-improvement initiative being a detailed process mapping utilizing the routing-by-walking-around (RBWA) methodology.

Figure 8.56 is an example of the RBWA data on an alternate form for collecting the RBWA data, and my latest revision.

Our observation while conducting the RBWA was that the operations were not balanced, with many operations having substantial idle time, so instead of proceeding with my standard RBWA graphing/analysis, I decided to construct a Yamazumi[6] chart.

Figure 8.57 shows the current-state Yamazumi chart. The chart shows that they're currently using 18 operators, and when you plot each operator's cycle time against the takt time,[7] you see a lot of "white-space" between the operators' stacks and the takt timeline.

The productivity-improvement initiative's objective was to eliminate or minimize non-value-added and non-value-added-but-needed work elements from each operator and then to balance the operators.

Figure 8.58 shows the Yamzumi chart after the non-value activities have been eliminated and minimized, and then the operator's cycle time will be balanced.

The result is that the number of operators has been reduced from 18 to ten; that's an improvement of the headcount by eight and 55%. And that's an incredible improvement.

Figure 8.59 shows the before and after layouts; again, they were created from the RBWA data.

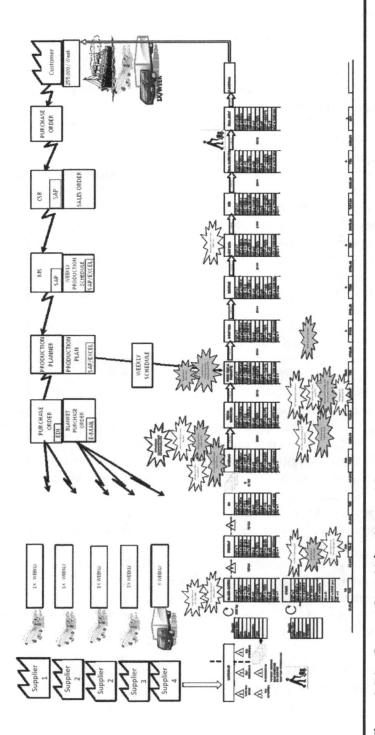

Figure 8.54   Current-State Value Stream Map.

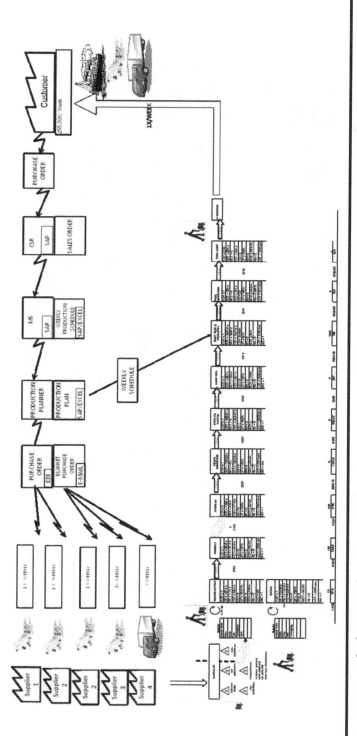

Figure 8.55   Ideal-State Value Stream Map.

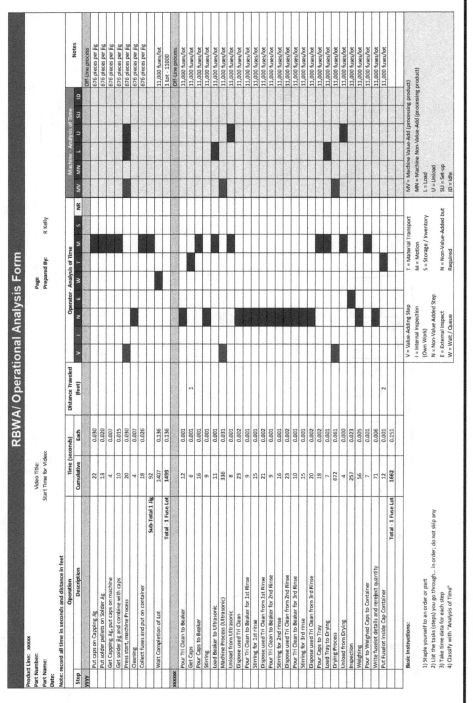

Figure 8.56 RBWA Operational Analysis Form.

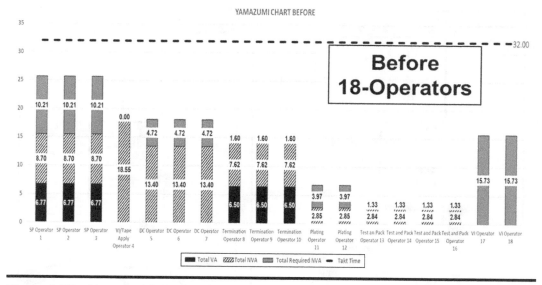

Figure 8.57 Yamazumi Current-State.

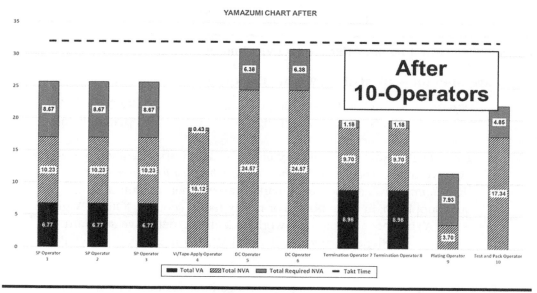

Figure 8.58 Yamazumi Future State.

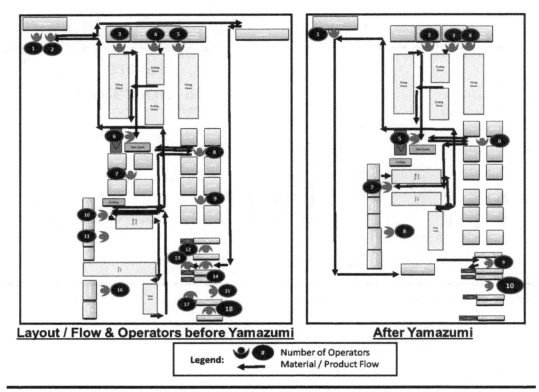

Layout / Flow & Operators before Yamazumi   **After Yamazumi**

Legend: 🐦 ⬤# Number of Operators
⬅ Material / Product Flow

Figure 8.59   Layout Before/After Productivity Improvement.

Case-in-Point 8.10: "Oliver Wight" Operational Excellence

Company: Fortune 600 Fast-Moving Consumer Goods (FMCG).
Objective: Optimize its Manufacturing and Supply-Chain operations in East Asia (seven countries).
Approach: This was a consultancy client, and they specifically requested that we utilize *The Oliver Wight Class A Checklist for Business Excellence* (OW) as the benchmark to assess their manufacturing and supply-chain operations. For nearly half a century, "Oliver Wight Class A" has been recognized worldwide as the definitive standard for business excellence, especially within FMCG companies, so it would provide a solid base for our assessment.

This assessment was more strategic and procedural than operational- and performance-oriented.

The areas that we assessed were:

1. *Centralized Sales and Operations Planning (S&OP)* – There are seven countries being assessed; they all have in-country warehousing and distribution but manufacturing in four countries only. We were to assess the benefits of one central S&OP process.

2. Centralized raw material and strategic finished-goods inventory – Same scenario as #1; seven sales, warehousing, and distribution centers and four manufacturing sites.
3. Auto-replenishment of Finished-Goods Inventory (FGI) – Implement pull system between warehouses and manufacturing.
4. Optimized warehousing and logistics-strategy – Optimize operating expenses by strategically utilizing warehouses and distribution systems.
5. Delayed-Differentiation – There were "base" manufactured materials that were transformed into various end-products within the production process by the addition of additives (flavoring, nutritionals, etc.); and, additionally, multiple packaging offerings further differentiated end-products. The "base" material was produced at multiple sites and quickly distinguished into the wide variety of end-products. Thus, the opportunity to centralize based-material production and strategically locate end-product differentiating activities would allow the delaying of end-product identification until the final stages of the production processes, thereby allowing maximum standardization along the production process.
6. Optimize supply-chain inventory.
7. Rationalize product portfolio and master database cleanup – Multilanguage packaging will greatly reduce product portfolio.
8. Rationalization Manufacturing Networking – Manufacture what – where?
9. Improve Information-Technology utilization.
10. Standardized nomenclature, bill-of-materials, etc.
11. Educate supply-chain users.

The approach that we took was to visit all seven sites, collect data, and interview key staff from multiple supply-chain functions and different staffing levels, including associates, supervisors, managers, directors, and a few vice-presidents.

And we had each interviewee rate themselves against selected areas of the OW checklist.

Figure 8.60 is a composite example of their self-assessment versus the consultants' (my team and me), and this information was used to create a gap of "where-they-are" versus "where-they-want-to-be."

Our consultancy firm also had a maturity profile that we utilize to gauge a company's current ways of working versus industry best practices. Figure 8.61 reflects our evaluation against the maturity profiles.

Figure 8.62 shows the supply-chain landscape for the region being assessed.

Based on the Oliver Wight Checklist, our maturity profiles and our site visits (interviews, data collection, and observation), we identified an array of improvement opportunities. Collaborating with the client's leadership team

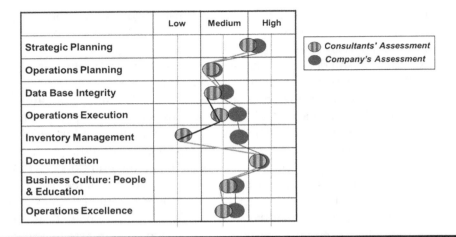

	Low	Medium	High
Strategic Planning			
Operations Planning			
Data Base Integrity			
Operations Execution			
Inventory Management			
Documentation			
Business Culture: People & Education			
Operations Excellence			

Consultants' Assessment
Company's Assessment

Figure 8.60   Consultants' & Company's Assessment versus Oliver Wight Checklist.

from all sites, we created the benefit and effort diagram and initiative prioritization shown in Figure 8.63.

Below is a summary of the improvement initiatives to be implemented within the next 12 months.

1. *Auto-Replenishment/Inventory and Warehousing Optimization:*
These were all high-benefit and low-to-medium effort items, so, we'd addressed these first. We developed a pull system (a max–min scheme) primarily for the "A" items, which would be pulled from centralized distribution centers by the customers, and that would send replenishment signals back to the manufacturing sites and subsequently back

Consultancy's Firm Maturity Profiles based on Industry Best Practices

	Innocence	Awareness	Understanding	Competence	Excellence
Order Capture					
Order Management					
Sales Forecasts					
Sales & Operations Planning - Process					
Sales & Operations Planning - Maser Scheduling					
Service Level Measurement					
Material Planning					
Raw Material Management					
Supplier Management					
Supplier Scheduling					
Material Call-Off					
Execute Manufacturing					
Production Planning & Conformance to Schedule					
Finished Goods Inventory Management					
Quality Management					
Product Phase Out					

Figure 8.61   Consultants' Maturity Assessment versus Industry Best Practices.

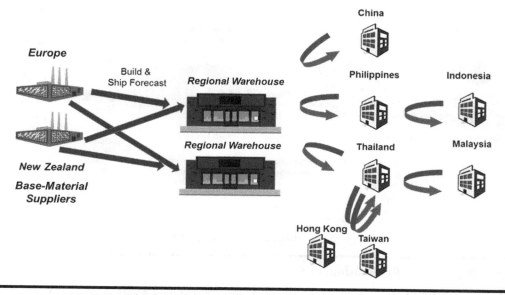

Figure 8.62   Current Supply-Chain Landscape.

to the base-material suppliers. "A" SKUs will be strategically held at centralized distribution centers.

Figure 8.64 shows a conceptual design of the planned supply network.

Many of the "B" and "C's are for the smaller market areas and many are packaged in single-use packaging (sachets; popular in Asia; low cost), so a third-party packing facility will be used for this as part of the late-differentiation plan. Full-scale late-differentiation was seen as a major

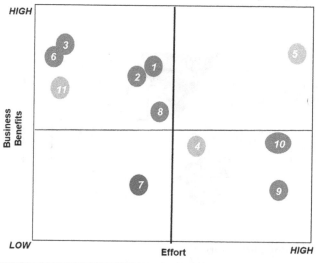

Improvement Initiatives

1. *Centralized SOP Process*
2. *Centralized Base Materials and Strategic FGI*
3. *Auto Replenishment of FG*
4. *Optimize warehousing strategy*
5. *Delayed Differentiation*
6. *Optimize Inventory*
7. *Rationalize Product Portfolio and Database Cleanup*
8. *Rationalize Manufacturing Networking*
9. *Improve BPCS Utilization*
10. *Standardize Nomenclatures, BOM, etc*
11. *Educate Supply Chain Users*

Figure 8.63   Improvement Prioritization with Benefit & Effort.

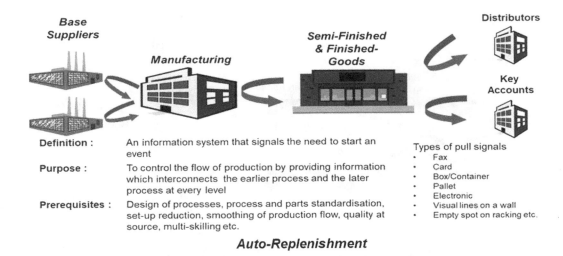

Definition : An information system that signals the need to start an event

Purpose : To control the flow of production by providing information which interconnects the earlier process and the later process at every level

Prerequisites : Design of processes, process and parts standardisation, set-up reduction, smoothing of production flow, quality at source, multi-skilling etc.

Types of pull signals
- Fax
- Card
- Box/Container
- Pallet
- Electronic
- Visual lines on a wall
- Empty spot on racking etc.

Auto-Replenishment

Figure 8.64   Auto-Replenishment Scheme.

benefit but medium-high effort initiative, but delayed-differentiation for packaging will be implemented for some items, and all sachet-packaging will be centralized at a third-party packing facility. Figure 8.65 shows a delayed-differentiating concept for some of "A"s, also.

2. *Centralized Sales and Operations Planning (S&OP)*: We assisted in defining and documenting a robust S&OP process that would be centralized to better utilize the resources within the region. Figure 8.66 shows the basics of the proposed system.

Figure 8.67 shows the final supply-chain model proposed for the region.

The final metrics to be obtained across all sites (estimates not fully validated):

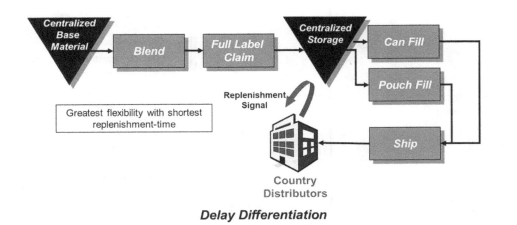

Delay Differentiation

Figure 8.65   Delayed-Differentiation Concept.

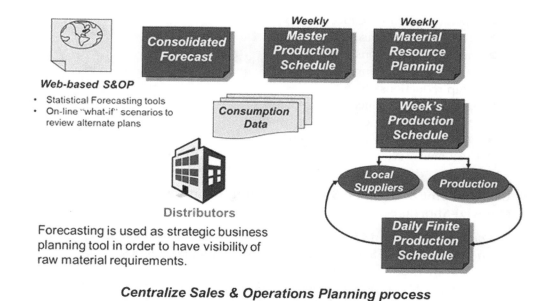

Centralize Sales & Operations Planning process

Figure 8.66   Proposed S&OP Model.

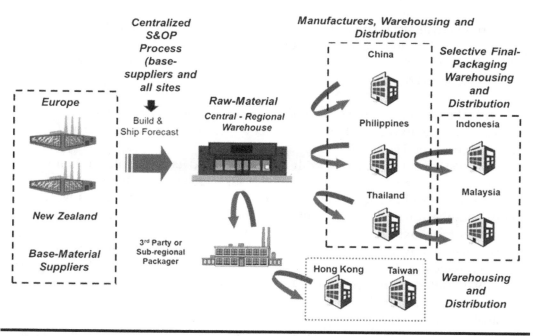

Figure 8.67   Proposed S&OP Model.

- Operational costs reduced by 13–40%.
- Productivity increase of 20–100%.
- Inventory reductions, 25–73%.
- Setup time reductions, 50–97%.
- Scrap reductions, 30–50%.
- Space utilized reduced by 30–50%.
- Quality improvements (yields), 50–90%.
- Order-to-Delivery lead time reduction, 30–87%.
- Customer Service (On-Time-In-Full) improved by 20–40%.

Case-in-Point 8.11: Value Stream Mapping Identifies Material-Shortages Issues

Company: American OEM commercial-equipment manufacturer.
Background: Use VSM to identify improvement opportunities.

Current-state VSM is shown in Figure 8.68 with numerous improvement opportunities highlighted by kaizen bursts.

The value stream analysis revealed that the assembly line's performance is hindered by parts shortages (a.k.a. stockouts). The value stream map shows that there's a large mixture of internal and external supply streams:

- Internal: Metal fabrication, wire-fabrication, computer and electronics assembly, and metal-fabrication assemblies
- External: Wide variety of domestic and imported commodities being supplied dock-to-stock, consignment, and bulk-supplies.

So to dig deeper into the source of the material shortages, we instructed the assembly line to collect shortage data for a month, i.e., part numbers and frequency (see Figure 8.69).

The stockout data, along with line-stoppage data, was collected and further affinitized into supply-source groupings, etc. (see Figure 8.70). And when looking at all line-stoppage occurrences; quality issues were the number-one occurrence, although the cumulative stockout occurrences (approximately 15 per month) exceeded quality stoppages (approximately 10 per month). Figure 8.71 shows a Pareto of all stoppage issues.

We wanted to analyze the causes of the stockouts, so we dug deeper into the ordering and replenishing processes. Figures 8.72 thru 8.75 show the analysis of the order and replenishments triggers, the issues and opportunities, and the recommended countermeasures.

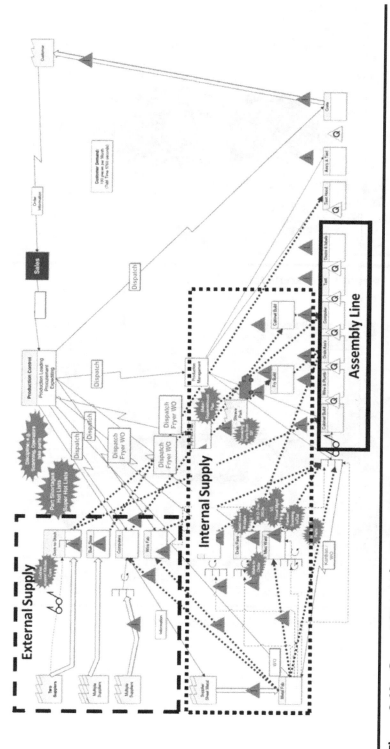

Figure 8.68   Current-State Value Stream Map.

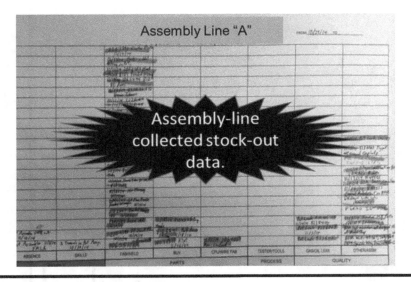

Figure 8.69   Assembly Stockout Data Collection.

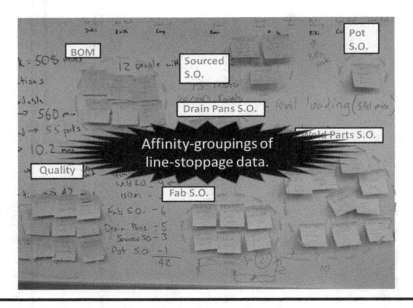

Figure 8.70   Affinity Groupings of Line-Stoppage Data.

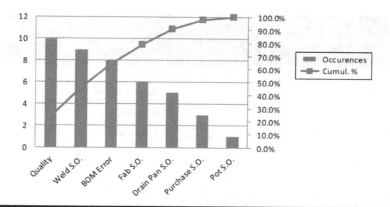

Figure 8.71   Pareto Chart of Line-Stoppage Data.

Area	Defined Order / Replenishment Trigger	Current-State Order / Replenishment Trigger	Issues & Opportunities	Potential Actions
Overall Material Management System: **Kanban Replenishment** **Demand-Driven**	Kanban Cards Non-Move Parts Demand based on equipment orders	Shortage Lists Hot / Super Hot Parts Production management required to expedite parts on a daily basis	• Bill-of-Material accuracy & completeness • Too many models • System execution is poor • Lack of accountability • Kanban system not synchronized with non-kanban items. Fragmented trigger/order points. • "Lead-times" not being met by production departments	Need to review exiting kanban system for improvement opportunities, e.g.: • Kanban sizing & safety stock analysis • K_{max}-K_{min} feasibility • Max-Min scheme for non-move • Kanban boards at select work centers; e.g. drain pans, misc. weld, fry pots, etc.
Dock-to-Stock	Vendor Managed Inventory	Poor execution by suppliers. Requires intervention by Production Control	• Suppliers doing more job of managing inventory • Service request depleted stock causing shortages on Dean line	• Eliminate Dock-to-Stock, have Production Control manage parts

Bulk Storage	Kanban triggered purchased parts	Kanban triggered purchased parts	• Poor delivery by suppliers, most notably:
			  – Burners
			  – Transformers
			  – Gas Valves
			  – Modules
			  – Knobs
			  – Steel
				• Need to increase manpower; i.e. Material Handlers
				• Second sourcing
				• Domestic sourcing
				• Inventory at domestic distributors

Figure 8.72   Order & Replenishment Analysis: Material Management

Area	Defined Order / Replenishment Trigger	Current-State Order / Replenishment Trigger	Issues & Opportunities	Potential Actions
Computers / Electronics	Kanbans Allocations	Kanbans Allocations with 2-days lead-time	• Occasional shortage of Interface Boards	• n/a
Wire Fab	Kanbans	Shortage Lists Hot Parts Assembly required to expedite parts on a daily basis	• BOM accuracy • Poor flow • Poor layout • Lead-time reliability	• Improve layout & flow
Drain Pans	Demand	Production provides list to Drain Pan dept. & expedites parts	• Shortage of welders • Too many models with minimal differences • Impacted by Kitchen Care	• Component kanban sizing review
Door Assemblies	Kanban Non-move parts	Kanban Non-move parts	• Components in storage vs a Supermarket • Overall layout & process flow	• Kaizen to explore opportunities
Fry Pots	Demand from "other-site"	Production required to expedite & "hunt" from pots Transport from "other-site" is unreliable	• Overall Safety is a concern • Need racks to transport pots from "other-site" to assembly line	• Kaizen required – Safety – Overall process from "other-site" to assembly line – Integrate "racks" into process – Consider impact of future relocation from "other-site" to Line Ave

Figure 8.73 Order & Replenishment Analysis: Off-Line Component Assembly Area #1.

Area	Defined Order / Replenishment Trigger	Current-State Order / Replenishment Trigger	Issues & Opportunities	Potential Actions
Misc. Weld	Kanbans	Shortage Lists Hot Parts Assembly required to expedite parts on a daily basis	• Shortage of welders • Lack of an overall system to address component supply and weld output	• Kaizen required – System structure & processes – Overall layout – Material flow – ? Kanban boards for status visibility / Visual Management
Pumps	Demand	Production provides list & expedites parts	• No structure to process or department	• Kaizen to explore opportunities
Automated Equipment "S"	Kanban	Kanban	• Routers need to be changed to for "special" parts	• n/a In-Process
Metal Fab	Kanban Non-Move Parts	Shortage Lists Hot / Super Hot Parts Production management required to expedite parts on a daily basis	• Need to fill the Dean Line supermarket • Need to address "accountability" issues with Operators • Quality issues need addressing • Backlog at Shear	• Outsourcing strategy to be implemented including level-loading demand "spikes" • Complete move of designated parts to V5 • Need capacity analysis of Laser & Shear • Quality action register

Figure 8.74 Order & Replenishment Analysis: Off-Line Component Assembly Area #2.

Area	Defined Order / Replenishment Trigger	Current-State Order / Replenishment Trigger	Issues & Opportunities	Potential Actions

Assembly Line	Supermarket
	
	Kanbans
	Non-Move parts
		Shortage Lists
		Hot / Super Hot Parts
		
		Production management required to expedite parts on a daily basis
			• Overall synchronization of components/parts doesn't exist. Order/trigger points are fragmented
			• BOM accuracy & completeness
			• Too many models
			• Systems' equipment are being assembled without proper pre-verification by Engineering & Quality
			• Supermarket isn't functional (lacking parts) & vertical storage space is a concern
			• Management is expediting and not managing line & people
				• Full implementation of previous Kaizen in-process
				• Green Belt projects in process
				  – Costs / line productivity (J. Sawyer)
				  – Ramp-Up
				  – Non-Move parts
				  – Vertical Storage space (
				• Set-up Super Tester
				• Set-up Transformer Box tester
				• Address component/parts issues as identified in the previous slides

Figure 8.75 Order & Replenishment Analysis: Final Unit Assembly.

Process: **Equipment A**

Suppliers	Inputs	Priority	Major Process Steps	Outputs	Customers
Fab	Metal Frabicated Parts	5	X Sub Assembly	Finished Unit	QC test hood
Misc. Weld	Welded Parts	4	Assembly I	Delivery	Customer order
Frypot	Fry Pots		Assembly II	Labor Performance	Upper Management
Misc. Weld	Drain Pans		Air Test		
Electronic	Computers/PCB's		Assemble Cabinet		
Wire Fab	Wire Fab Parts		Start Up		
Material Handlers	Purchased Parts	6	Sub Assemble Box A		
Material Handlers	Dock to Stock		Sub Assemble Box B		
Material Handlers	Bulk Storage		D Assembly		
HR/Agency	Manpower	1	Wire		
On the Job	Training	2	Cap Assembly		
	Standard Work-Instruct.	3	Test		
			Super test		

Input Metrics	Process Metrics	Output Metrics	
			Safety
			Quality
Part Shortages-No./day		Lead Time:12 to 10 days	Delivery
		55 unit count per day	Delivery
	x.x labor hours/unit		Cost
			Other

Figure 8.76 SIPOC Equipment-Level.

Case-in-Point 8.12: SIPOC and Value Stream-Driven Improvements: Deep-Dive Solutions

Company: American OEM commercial-equipment manufacturer.

Background: Use VSM to identify improvement opportunities.

Project Objective: Increase Line-Rate from 36.5 to 55 units/day and decrease the hours-per-unit from 5.9 hours to 4.4 hours.

Targeted Business Results: Increasing Line-Rate should result in additional sales that are estimated to increase profit by $5 M. Decreased cost per unit will result in $400 K annualized savings

Key Measure: Units-crated/day and hours/unit.

Baseline: 36.5 units/day and 5.9 hours/unit.

Goal: 55 units/day and 4.4 hours/unit.

We started the assessment process by creating a SIPOC (Supply – Input – Process – Outputs – Customers) diagram.

The SIPOC diagram was used to early-on identify and prioritize business-needs (see Figure 8.76).

Prioritize improvement opportunities:

1. Manpower.
   - Line balancing (Yamazumi chart).
2. Training.
   - Skills-Matrix.
   - 8-Step Method.
3. Standard Work Instruction.
4. Certified Skilled Tradesmen.
5. Internal Supply.
   - CONWIP system.
   - Supermarkets.
6. External Supply.
   - Pull-Replenishment system/kanban-sizing (see Figure 8.77).

The enterprise value stream revealed a total process lead time (PLT) of 10–12 days (about 3.5% value-added), and as stated above, the equipment-assembly cycle time is approximately 3.1 hours. The assembly line, which is a continuous-flow line, has a value-added percentage of approximately 83%.

The assembly line is fairly well balanced but it cannot meet the required takt-rate of 55 units/day or the cost-per-unit objective, so we must identify and eliminate waste and lower the cycle time for each operator. A kaizen was conducted, and a Yamazumi chart was created.

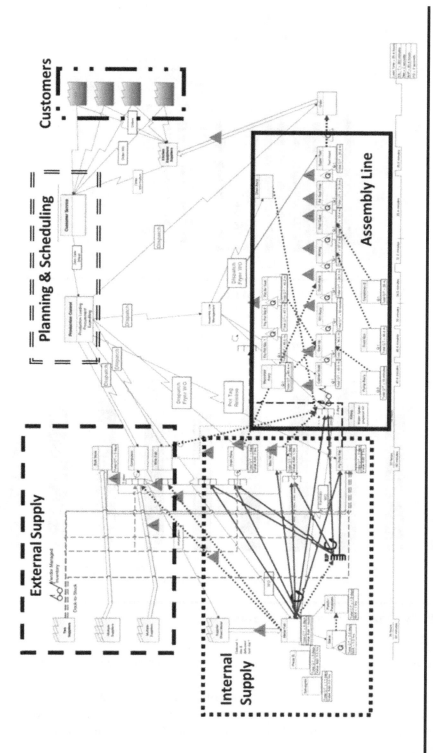

Figure 8.77 Supply-Chain Value Stream Map.

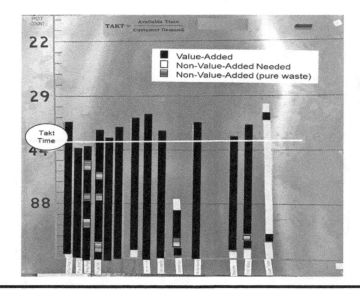

Figure 8.78   Yamazumi-Board Current State.

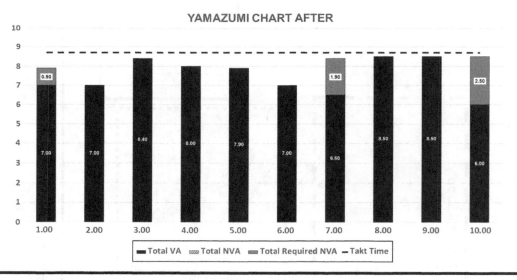

Figure 8.79   Yamazumi-Board Future State.

Figure 8.78 reflects the "working" Yamazumi chart that was created during the kaizen-event.

And during the kaizen-event, opportunities to remove waste and cycle-time reductions were identified. Figure 8.79 reflects the proposed future-state Yamazumi chart. And standard work (a.k.a. job instructions)

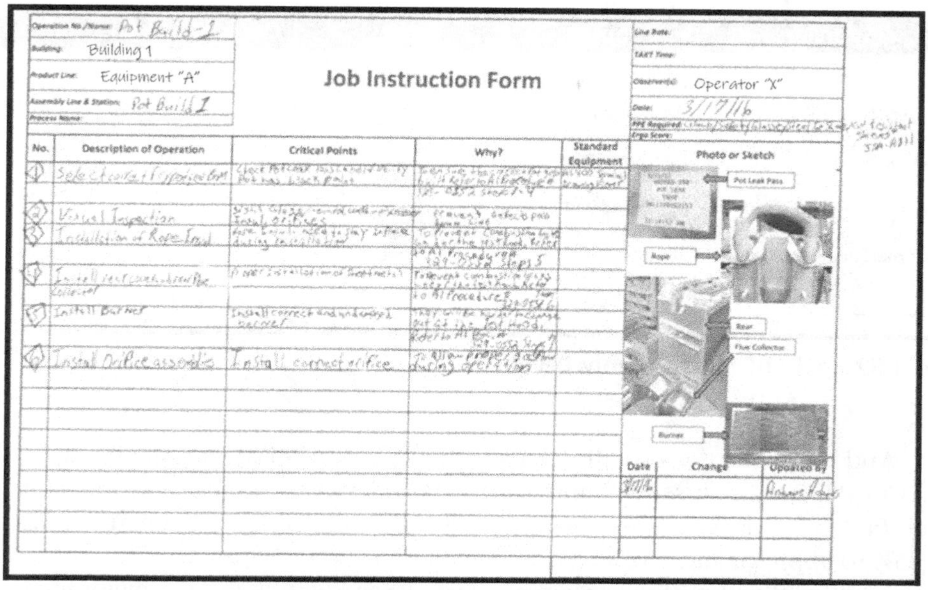

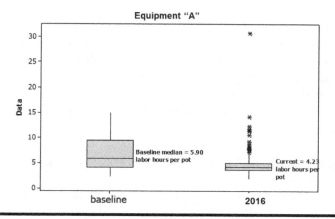

Figure 8.80 Standard Work Created and Validated during the Kaizen-Event.

Figure 8.81 12 Months Validated "New" Cost-per-Unit.

were created to document the new assembly methods; Figure 8.80 shows the standard work created and verified during the kaizen-event.

The future-state line balancing and productivity improvements will produce the desired results, i.e., 55 units/day and 4.4 hours/unit.

Figure 8.81 reflects the validation in reduction in hours-per-unit, showing a median of 4.23 hours, which resulted in a validated productivity savings of $346.7 k annually.

Suppliers	Inputs	Process	Outputs	Customers
		Laser		
Material Control	Work Order (Pot Tag)	Press Brake		
		Stud - Tack		
Fab / Kanban	Fabricated Parts	Robot	Unit	Assembly Workstation
External Suppliers / Kanban	Purchased Parts	Hardware		
External Suppliers / Kanban	Sheet Metal	Test		
		Polish / Paint		

Figure 8.82   SIPOC Subassembly Level.

And to reduce the overall enterprise PLT of 10–12-days, a pull system and a CONWIP kanban-sequencing scheme was developed, thus reducing overall PLT to 5.4 days and improving the overall value-added percentage from 3.5% to approximately 12%.

Additionally, the value stream analysis (VSA) identified that a major-issue is lineouts (i.e., assembly line stoppages due to material shortages). And the VSA identified that the lineouts were most often the result of material shortages due to the availability of a key subassembly. Figure 8.82 shows the SIPOC created for this key subassembly. And Figure 8.83 reflects the VSM for this subassembly.

To drive down into identifying the potential causes of the assembly lineouts due to the key subassembly, we created a fishbone diagram to brainstorm potential causes of the assembly lineouts (see Figure 8.84).

The consensus of the cross-functional team was that these are the top potential causes of subassembly lineouts attributable to the key subassembly:

1. Wrong demand-mix, i.e., scheduling and producing the wrong subassembly SKUs.
2. Operators don't follow first in first out (FIFO) processing of work orders.
3. Equipment downtime:
   - 2nd shift technical support.

The key countermeasures implemented:

- Rotating off-shift on-call technical support.
- Implemented a CONWIP scheme (via a heijunka board) for the subassembly that aligned pull signals and kanban-sequencing.
  - CONWIP forced FIFO, thus eliminating operators from "choosing" work orders for themselves.

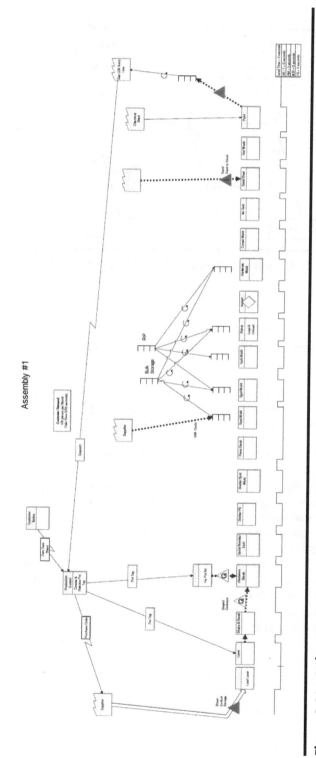

Figure 8.83   Value Stream Map Subassembly Level.

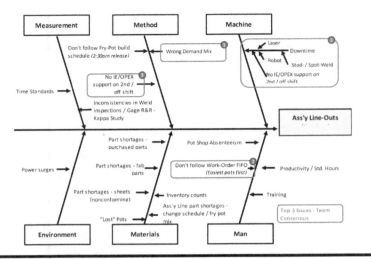

Figure 8.84   Assembly Lineouts: Subassembly Fishbone Analysis.

End Notes

1. Gemba Walk: Gemba is defined as "where the action takes place," e.g., factory floor, office area, etc. A Gemba Walk is referring to "go-see," i.e., to go to where the action is happening.
2. Takt Time: The available production time divided by the customer demand, which equates to the elapsed time between pieces exiting the end of the production line. A takt time of one second would mean that an item should exit the production line/cell every second.
3. High-margin special application device, extremely complex wafer-fab, and die-prep process with low yields.
4. A handoff is an official transfer from one department to another.
5. A spaghetti diagram is a line-based representation of the continuous flow of the device as it goes through some process.
6. Yamazumi is a Japanese word that roughly translates to "stacked-up." A Yamazumi chart is a stacked bar graph of each operator's work elements and cycle time. The Yamazumi chart is basically an operator balance chart, except that the Yamazumi's bars are broken into work elements and then classified as value-added, non-value-added, and non-value-added-but-needed.
7. Takt time is the available production time divided by customer demand, which equates to the amount of time that any single operator must complete his/her task.

Chapter 9

Case-in-Point Examples

In the previous chapters, I covered the key elements of the supply chain (including supply management and inventory-management), various strategies, and tools and techniques associated with optimizing a supply chain.

In this chapter, I have included six case-in-point examples of supply-chain transformation initiatives.

The case-in-point examples are:

- *9.1: Comprehensive Supply-Chain Assessment and Optimization*
  - *Company*: A multinational electronics OEM corporation.
  - *Project*: The Supply Chain Operational Optimization project was designed "to reduce cost and process lead times within the Manufacturing, Procurement, Planning, and Quality areas through the introduction of industry best practices, the simplification and standardization of processes, efficiency improvements, and a reduction in inventory levels."
- *9.2: Supply-Chain Transformation*
  - *Company*: Pharmaceutical manufacturer
  - *Project*: The assessment was conducted based on the Oliver Wight Business Excellence Checklist (a.k.a. MRP II Assessment) and complemented by a proven set of qualitative and quantifiable tools and methodologies.
- *9.3: Comprehensive Supply-Chain Assessment and Optimization*
  - *Company*: Pure-play Wafer Foundry.
  - The project's scope was to look at historical operational performance (full end-to-end supply- chain operations) and the alignment with past

business strategy and to develop a road map for operational and strategic improvements to decrease operational expenses and increase revenues.

■ *9.4: Supply-Chain Transformation – Medical Device*
  - *Company:* American Fortune 100 medical-device manufacturer.
  - The company was in a very competitive market space, but stakeholders were seeking larger profit margins while maintaining or growing the company's market share.

■ *9.5: Optimizing a Supply Chain in Heavy Industry*
  - *Company:* A heavy-industry (a.k.a. engineer-to-order) manufacturer/ builder; a subsidiary of a Fortune Global 500 conglomerate.
  - The company was planning to implement an enterprise-wide information-technology system to support its order-fulfillment processes, but prior to its implementation they wanted to assess and subsequently improve/optimize all of the order-fulfillment processes.

■ *9.6: Optimizing a Fast-Moving Consumer-Goods (FMCG) Supply Chain*
  - One of the company's manufacturing and distribution networks was performing at an unacceptable customer-service level. So the project was to assess the current supply chain and identify opportunities for improvement.

In each case-in-point example, I'll give a brief introduction to the background of the initiative and the problems and/or opportunities each company was facing. Within the case-examples, I'll cover the initiative's approach and include representative examples of the analytical tools and techniques utilized. And I'll conclude each example with the results achieved.

Case-in-Point 9.1: Comprehensive Supply-Chain Assessment and Optimization

Company: A Japanese multinational electronics OEM corporation.
Background: This was a consultancy client, and the stated objective of this Supply Chain Operational Optimization project was designed "to reduce cost and process lead times within the Manufacturing, Procurement, Planning, and Quality areas through the introduction of industry best practices, the simplification and standardization of processes, efficiency improvements, and a reduction in inventory levels."
Scope: The project scope would be limited to an OEM consumer product manufactured at several facilities in the state capital area of Malaysia. The product is manufactured for domestic consumption, although certain models would be exported to a few neighboring Asian countries.
Project Approach: The approach for this project is shown in Figure 9.1.

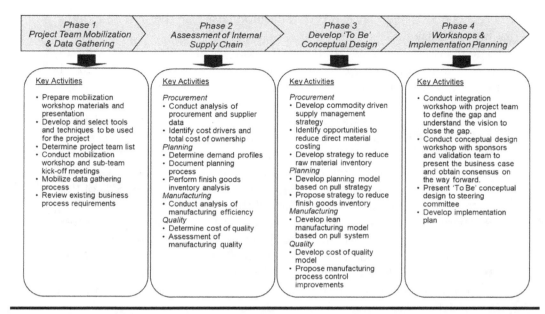

Figure 9.1   Case-in-Point's Project Approach.

The supply-chain assessment approach consisted of four phases:

1. Phase 1: Project Team Mobilization and Data Gathering
   – Establish what key data needs to be collected to construct a quantitative baseline "as-is" for the four areas of focus: Planning, Manufacturing, Quality, and Procurement.
2. Phase 2: Assessment of Internal Supply Chain
   – Analyze data across the four areas of focus: Planning, Manufacturing, Quality, and Procurement.
3. Phase 3: Develop "To-Be" Conceptual Design
   – Develop "to-be" designs for the four areas of focus: Planning, Manufacturing, Quality, and Procurement.
4. Phase 4: Workshops and Implementation Planning
   – Identify consensually achieved gap of "as-is" versus "to be."
   – Develop business case.
   – Develop implementation plan to close the "gap."

PLANNING ASSESSMENT FINDINGS:

Before weighing in too deeply in the Planning Assessment, let's start with a basic principle: We chose to conduct an A-B-C stratification of the product portfolio. We followed the methodology as described in Chapter 2 of this book.

The company's product portfolio identified a total of 1,066 active (saleable) product Stock Keeping Units (SKUs). So the next step was to stratify these 1,066 SKUs into an A-B-C classification based on the past 12 months of historical sales.

The results of the sales-based stratification revealed 50% of the company's revenue came from only 56 SKUs (i.e., less than 5% of the active SKUs). The full A-B-C stratification broke the classifications down as follows:

- 157 SKUs were classified as "A"s, which equated to about 15% of the total SKUs that accounted for 80% of the historical demand (a.k.a. revenue).
- 106 SKUs were classified as "B"s, which equated to about 10% of the total SKUs that accounted for 10% of the demand.
- 563 SKUs were classified as "C"s, which equated to about 53% of the total SKUs that accounted for 10% of the demand.
- There were 240 SKUs that are "active" but have no demand over the past 12 months, so we classified these as "D"s, and these 240 SKUs accounted for about 22% of the total SKUs but zero demand/revenue.
- We benchmarked a strong regional competitor and found that the competitor obtained approximately 80% of its revenue from only seven models, a vast contrast from our client.

Figure 9.2 is a graphical summary of the product portfolio stratification.

The next step of the Planning Assessment was to document the current (as-is) Planning Model. And we found that the current Planning Model can be characterized by:

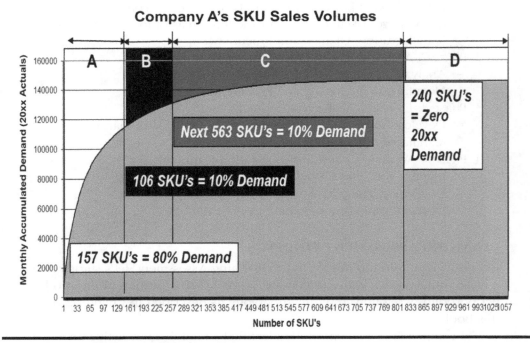

Figure 9.2   Product Portfolio Stratification.

- Planning actions driven by 3–4-month forecast
- Forecast accuracy over the past 12 months has had a range of approximately 30% to 53%.
- Requires approximately 100 days frozen-commitment time window from its internal Sales group.
- Total Order-Fulfillment Process Lead Time averages 123 days.
- Cash to Cash cycle is approximately 109 days.

See Figure 9.3 for the details of the Planning Model.

One of the key elements of the Planning Model's effectiveness is the synchronization of the demand with production, which is often reflected in the amount of Finished-Goods inventory retained. A key tool that we utilized to assess the synchronization of those three elements – shipments (demand), production, and finished-goods inventory – is the "Triple-Play Chart." This methodology allows the comparison of the inventory levels versus the weekly production versus the actual shipments (i.e., customer demand). And to get a fair assessment of the current model's effectiveness, we'll usually look at representative products from the various A-B-C classifications.

Figure 9.4 shows a Triple-Play Chart for one of Company A's high-volume products (a.k.a. an "A"). The huge "grey-mountain" shown in the Triple-Play Chart (see Figure 9.4) reflects the Finished-Goods Inventory level for the specified high-volume (a.k.a. high-demand) product. The black columns are the weekly demand and the white-patterned columns are the weekly

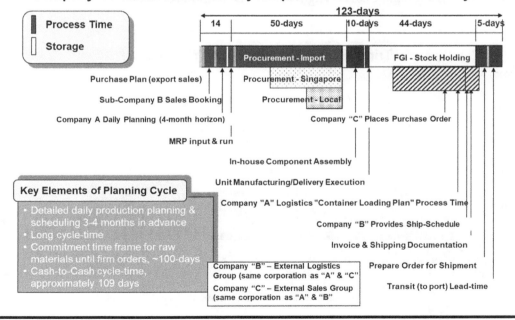

Figure 9.3   Planning Model.

production quantities. Simply, the Triple-Play Chart (see Figure 9.4) shows the lack of correlation between the production and inventory levels versus the actual demand, i.e., the current Planning Model is ineffective, and the level of Finished-Goods Inventory far exceeds any historical demand.

Figure 9.5 is a Triple-Play Chart for a different high-volume product, and the analysis substantiates the ineffectiveness of the current Planning Model.

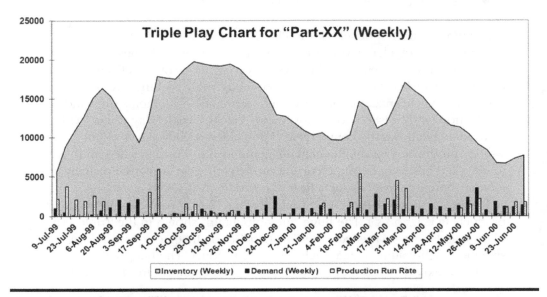

Figure 9.4   Triple-Play Chart – High-Volume/Demand Product #1.

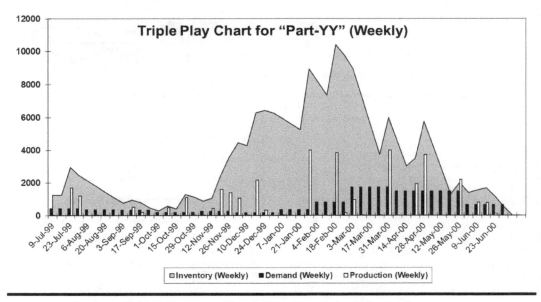

Figure 9.5   Triple-Play Chart – High-Volume/Demand Product #2.

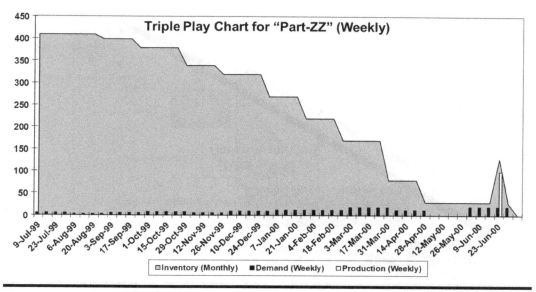

Figure 9.6 Triple-Play Chart – Low-Volume/Demand Product.

The Triple-Play Chart, Figure 9.6 is for a low-volume, low-demand product (a "B" or "C" part), and it reveals the same issues noted by the previous charts, but with it being a very slow-moving product, it highlights the risk of planning based primarily on a forecast rather than reacting to real demand signals.

It should be noted that the products selected to be displayed in these Triple-Play Charts were selected totally at random from a list of "representative" products.

Another reflection of the effectiveness (or ineffectiveness) of the current Planning Model is the amount of inventory across the supply chain. During the assessment, we take a snapshot of the amount of inventory currently within the supply chain (see Figure 9.7). The days of inventory are determined by the $-value of the inventory divided by the daily-historical (or forecasted) demand ($). Figure 9.7 shows that the supply chain had approximately 138 days of inventory. This would be considered excessive, as inventory doesn't come at no cost. And this reflects the cash to cash cycle, i.e., the length of time that money is "tied up" and not available for other use or investments. Inventory is classified as an asset, but it can often be thought of as of a liability, as it's susceptible to obsolescence and also at risk of damage. And this is not including the cost of holding and preserving the inventory, e.g., administrative and management activities, insurance, space, security, cost of money, etc.

For the case-in-point example, I'll stop with the assessment findings and finalize this section by identifying several potential improvement opportunities identified during the Planning Assessment, such as:

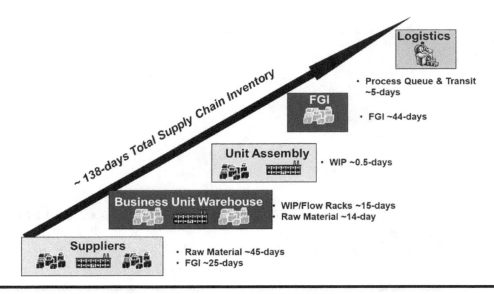

Figure 9.7   Company "A" Supply-Chain Inventory.

- Implementation of a finished-goods pull-replenishment scheme rather than relying heavily on forecasted demand.
- Potential to lower Finished-Goods Inventory via a push-replenishment scheme and statistical analysis of supply-and-demand variations.
- Simplified production planning/scheduling based on a pull system and cellular manufacturing, i.e., self-scheduling, flow-thru production.
- Utilize a Sales, and Operations Planning (S&OP) approach for long-term capacity and resource planning.
- Institutionalize an "A-B-C" stratification methodology to differentiate planning strategies.

MANUFACTURING ASSESSMENT FINDINGS:

One of the main assessment tools that we utilized for assessing manufacturing is the Routing-by-Walking-Around (RBWA) methodology. I cover that RBWA methodology in detail in Chapter 8 under the "Assessment Tools and Methodologies" section.

A simple definition of the RBWA is:

■ Walk the process "pretending" to be a single unit being processed.

The RBWA process is measuring the:

- Distance the unit traveled.
- Elapsed time of the end-to-end process.
- Process steps and activities.
- Work time (cycle time of individual workstations, activities, steps, etc.).

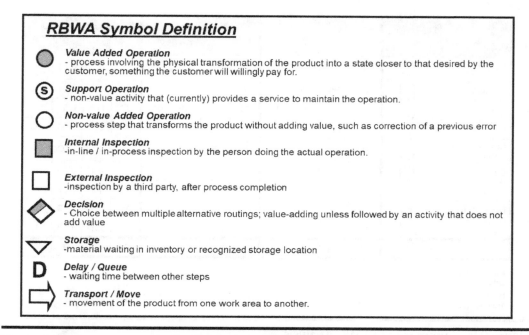

RBWA Symbol Definition

⬤ **Value Added Operation**
- process involving the physical transformation of the product into a state closer to that desired by the customer, something the customer will willingly pay for.

Ⓢ **Support Operation**
- non-value activity that (currently) provides a service to maintain the operation.

○ **Non-value Added Operation**
- process step that transforms the product without adding value, such as correction of a previous error

▣ **Internal Inspection**
-in-line / in-process inspection by the person doing the actual operation.

▢ **External Inspection**
-inspection by a third party, after process completion

◈ **Decision**
- Choice between multiple alternative routings; value-adding unless followed by an activity that does not add value

▽ **Storage**
-material waiting in inventory or recognized storage location

D **Delay / Queue**
- waiting time between other steps

⇨ **Transport / Move**
- movement of the product from one work area to another.

Figure 9.8   Summary & Definitions of RBWA Symbols.

Figure 9.8 provides a definition of the symbols utilized when conducting and analyzing the RBWA(s).

For our manufacturing assessment, we conducted an RBWA on three representative products. Figure 9.9 is a table summarizing the findings of the three RBWAs. The major cycle-time element for all three products was Storage (a.k.a. Inventory), totaling 96%, 92%, and 82%, respectively. Most of the number of steps for each product were involved with the execution of the following activities: Delays/Queues, Transport, and Transport, respectively. And the products traveled 138 meters, 238 meters, and 303 meters, respectively.

As part of the manufacturing assessment, we want to establish the ratio (percentage) of value-added activities versus non-value-added activities. The value-added percentages (based on time) of Products X, Y, and Z were 1%, 1%, and 3%, respectively. And although these numbers are low, they are typical for most manufacturing operations, as we typically expected the value-added time percentages to be less than 5%. The percentage of steps that are value-added is typically a higher percentage than cycle time; the value-added steps for Products X, Y, and Z were 7%, 19%, and 27%, respectively. The bottom line is that the RBWA assessment revealed multiple opportunities for improvement.

Another tool that we use while conducting a manufacturing assessment is the spaghetti diagram. The spaghetti diagram can be constructed from the RBWA data. Figure 9.10 shows a spaghetti diagram constructed for Product

Activity	Symbols	Product X				Product Y				Product Z			
		# of Steps	%	Cycle-Time	%	# of Steps	%	Cycle-Time	%	# of Steps	%	Cycle-Time	%
Value-Adding Operations	◯	4	7%	1.76	1%	29	15%	0.11	1%	51	24%	0.23	3%
Internal Inspect	▢	0	0%	0.00	0%	7	4%	0.04	0%	7	3%	0.01	0%
Support Operation	Ⓢ	4	7%	0.01	0%	23	12%	0.06	0%	23	11%	0.05	1%
Decision	◇	0	0%	0.00	0%	0	0%	0.00	0%	0	0%	0.00	0%
Non-Value-Adding Operations	◯	0	0%	0.00	0%	19	10%	0.05	0%	8	4%	0.02	0%
External Inspect	▢	4	7%	0.13	0%	19	10%	0.10	1%	12	6%	0.05	1%
Storage	▽	4	7%	172	96%	7	4%	15.8	92%	3	1%	7.37	82%
Delay / Queue	D	29	53%	2.41	1%	23	12%	0.05	0%	39	18%	0.10	1%
Transport	⇨	10	18%	3.46	2%	69	35%	1.05	6%	70	33%	1.16	13%
Total		**55**		**180**		**196**		**17**		**213**		**9**	
Number of Hand-Offs		8				7				3			
Distance Traveled (meters)		138				238				303			

Figure 9.9   Summary of RBWA Analysis.

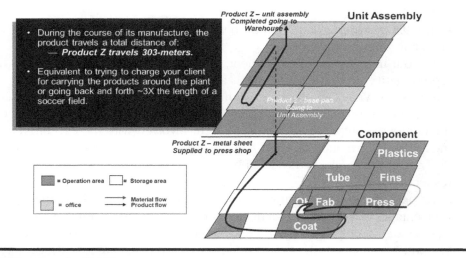

Figure 9.10   Spaghetti Diagram.

Z from the RBWA analysis shown in Figure 9.9. The distance traveled, 303 meters, on its own doesn't mean too much, but the importance of the number is that it establishes the baseline for improvement.

Another part of the manufacturing assessment is that we completed a simple space utilization analysis. Figure 9.11 shows the utilization calculation methodology and results. It was found that the manufacturing space was 94% underutilized.

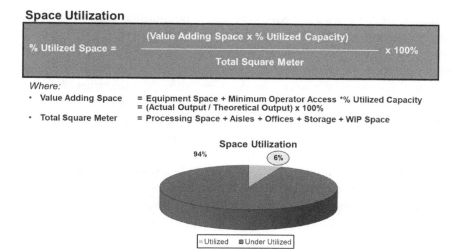

Figure 9.11   Space Utilization.

After determining the space utilization, we then focused on equipment utilization, and we calculated the utilization of key bottleneck equipment. The two pieces of key equipment that we analyzed had a capacity utilization of 46.7% and 13.7%, respectively (see Figure 9.12). Equipment "a" had 30% machine-time loss due to material shortages. Equipment "b" had 77% machine-time loss due to unscheduled time and an additional 9% due to material shortages. A large portion of the 77% loss was due to not manning a second or third shift, which was most likely a business decision, but the assessment wanted to point out the obvious in addressing the bottleneck. Sometimes it's difficult for companies to recognize and/or accept the obvious (i.e., can't-see-the-trees-for-the-forest). But the more critical finding was the machine loss due to material shortages, which is an unacceptable

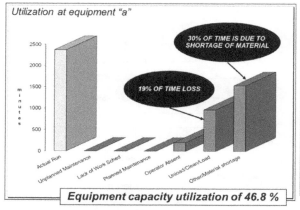 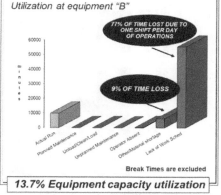

Figure 9.12   Equipment Utilization.

situation especially with the inventory levels being quite high. This problem must be addressed in the "future" state.

Another methodology that was utilized in this assessment was "Work Sampling." Work sampling is an analytical method to determine the details about the utilization of humans or machines through numerous observations taken at a random interval of time. This method helps to determine various categories like work, inspections, setting up a machine/cell, idleness, administrative, etc. And these results can be used to establish the utilization (productivity) of workers and machines, and the results will be utilized to improve efficiency, eliminate non-value-added activities, ensure work-balancing, and determine the applicable time allowances.

Figure 9.13 shows the Work Sampling results for Assembly Area "A." To summarize the sampling data:

- 44% of time doing work (transforming the product).
- 16% idle time or breaks.
- 12% performing inspection
- Machine setup/material changeovers only 4%.

Figure 9.14 shows the Work Sampling results for Assembly Area "B." To summarize the sampling data:

- 27% of time doing work (transforming the product).
- 27% idle time or breaks.
- 15% performing inspection.
- 8% administrative activities.
- 8% machine setup/material changeovers.

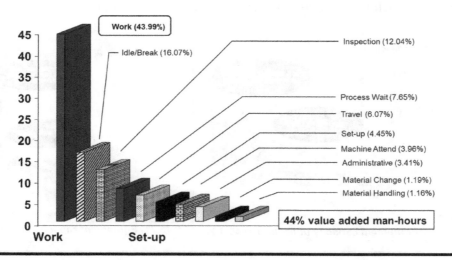

Figure 9.13   Work Sampling – Assembly Area "A".

Another area of manufacturing to be assessed is the model changeover process. The OEM product manufactured by this company contained a coolant system that must be charged with "gas," and the type of "gas" varied by the OEM-model. Figure 9.15 shows the breakdown of a typical model changeover. There's changeover optimization methodology known as SMED (Single-Minute-Exchange-Die) that we'll apply during the improvement phase of this project.

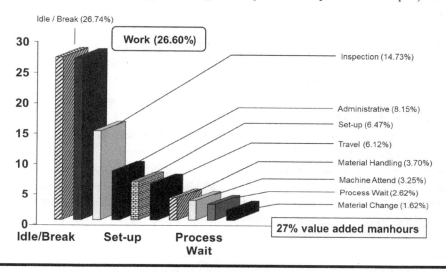

Figure 9.14 Work Sampling – Assembly Area "B".

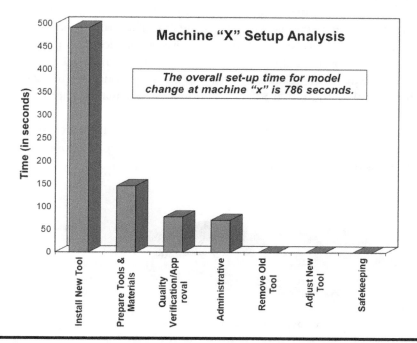

Figure 9.15   Model Changeover Analysis.

There were several potential improvement opportunities identified during the manufacturing assessment, such as:

- Process flow is not synchronized to demand.
- Excessive inventory at storage and buffers.
- Excessive inspections.
- Long manufacturing cycle times due to a large number of hand-offs, queues, WIP, etc.
- Potential deployment of cellular manufacturing to eliminate waste and non-value-added activities, and address space utilization.
- Need for setup/model changeover optimization.

QUALITY ASSESSMENT FINDINGS:

The manufacturing assessment uncovered that there was excessive inspection throughout the manufacturing areas. So, we started our Quality Assessment looking at the costs incurred by inspecting, and we uncovered inspection at incoming, subassembly, and all assembly areas, with much of the inspection in unit assembly being redundant. The annual cost for inspection in unit assembly is approximately $2.56 million, and the total for the facility is $3.8 million; thus, a huge opportunity for improvement existed (see Figure 9.16 for a breakdown of inspection cost).

And our Inspection Mapping confirmed that there are excessive and redundant inspections. In addition to the Process Quality Audit (PQA) inspections, there are five additional Quality Audit inspections. Figure 9.17 summarizes the inspections throughout the manufacturing process.

Our assessment also revealed that incoming inspection was ineffective. Incoming inspection averaged rejecting 2.4 lots per month, but production lines averaged 43.3 claims against suppliers for nonconforming parts, which resulted in an annual $180k additional claims against suppliers (see Figure 9.18).

And when we looked at the potential root causes of the incoming inspection issues, the consensus root cause was poor supplier development. Figure 9.19 shows a tree diagram of supplier development concerns.

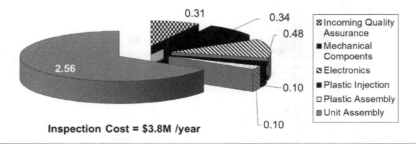

Figure 9.16   Inspection Cost Analysis.

Unit Assembly	Manufacturing Inspections					QA Inspections				
	Sub Leader	Line Inspector	Floor Inspector	PQA		QA Inspector	Block Assurance	Floor Inspection	Leader	QA Sampling
Chassis/ Fabrication	6	2			Gas Leak					
Unit	9	8	3	3	Gas Leak Appearance					
Inner	6	5	3	3	Appearance Insulation Run Performance					
Supply Line	3				Appearance Certificate Issue					
Final Packing	6	6			Appearance Check Inspection	125	6	6	6	
Warehouse					Construction Appearance					8
Function	4x/ day	100%	Model Change/ 4x/ day			100%	4x/ day	Model change / 4x/ day	4x/ day	1 set/ model/ day/ line

Actual inspection map shows multi-level inspection resources at QA and Manufacturing areas.

Figure 9.17   Inspection Mapping.

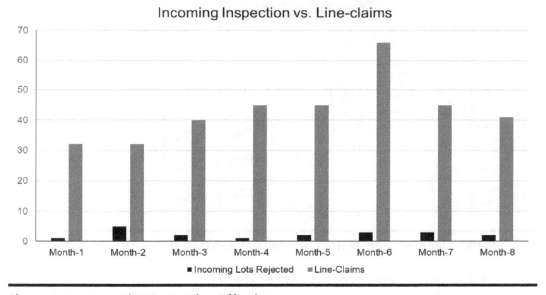

Figure 9.18   Incoming Inspection Effectiveness.

A further deep dive (see Figure 9.20) into nonconforming parts issues highlighted the following key concerns:

■ Too much "unnecessary" variation/complexity units and parts, e.g., similar parts creating misidentification/confusion, mixed parts, too many daily model changeovers (effective line purges).

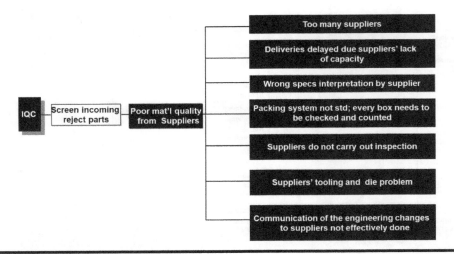

Figure 9.19 Tree Diagram Incoming Parts.

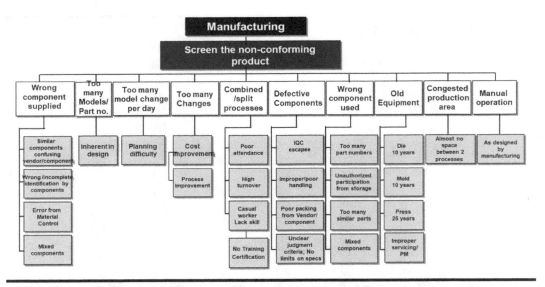

Figure 9.20 Manufacturing Non Conforming Material Issues.

- Defective components: For example, incoming inspection escapees, damaged by handling, poor-packaging/storage, poor-/unclear-specifications.
- Tooling and/or equipment life.
- Effective training and certification of suppliers.

Our summarized assessment of the company's Cost-of-Quality (a.k.a. Cost-of-Poor-Quality) revealed an annualized cost of $39.4 million, or approximately 32% of sales. But this amount excludes any potential "Loss of Sales"

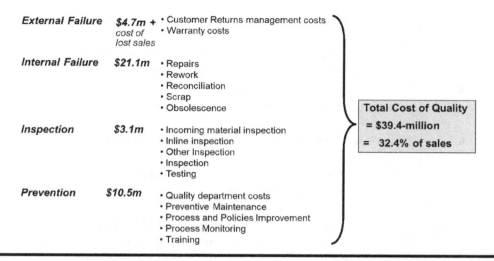

Figure 9.21   Cost-of-Quality.

resulting from External Failures. And a good benchmark for Cost-of-Quality is about 10–15% of sales (see Figure 9.21).

Quality Improvement Opportunities:

- Cost-of-Quality as a percent of Sales is too high. Primary drivers are:
- Too much inspection.
- Too much line lost (scrap, rework, reinspect, retest, etc.).
- Inventory obsolescence (push production versus pull, portfolio complexity, etc.).
- Too many staff linked to prevention instead of process simplification and process improvements.
- Too many procedures (i.e., need process simplification).
- Need to enhance employee training and skills certification.
- Closures of corrective actions at all areas not based on consistent effectiveness check. Lacking a closed-loop process.
- Visual inspection criteria are vague – tolerances not defined.

PROCUREMENT ASSESSMENT FINDINGS:

The last area of assessment is Procurement.

And to establish a baseline for Procurement, we started with a quantitative summary of current procurement practices:

- 460,000 Purchases Orders issued over the past 12 months, an astonishingly high number. For 365 days, that would be an average of 1,260/day.

- And 26,000 (6%) of the 460,000 purchase orders had to be revised or canceled.
- There are about 8,000 total purchased items, which equates to an average of more than 50 purchase orders per item per year
- There's no differentiated purchasing process for high- versus low-value items, so significant purchasing resources consumed buying low-value trivial items.
- There are 187 suppliers, again, a seemingly very high number.
  There are:
  - 30 suppliers for electrical/electronic components.
  - 27 suppliers for plastic components.
  - 15 suppliers for metal components.
- There's no consolidation of same commodity purchasing across multiple divisions, i.e., no attempt at economies of scale or reduction in administrative costs.

Figure 9.22 shows the number of purchase orders by commodity.

Figure 9.23 shows the number of suppliers by commodity. Figure 9.24 highlights the unconstrained complexity created by poor procurement practices.

Our next analysis is raw material inventory-management.

- The average amount of raw material inventory is $29.5 million,
- Inventory replenishment lead times are constrained by their internal processes, not the suppliers' manufacturing lead times (see Figure 9.25).

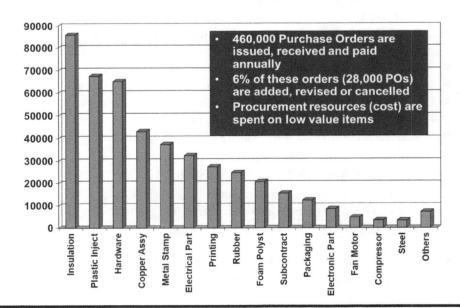

Figure 9.22   Number of Purchase Orders by Commodity.

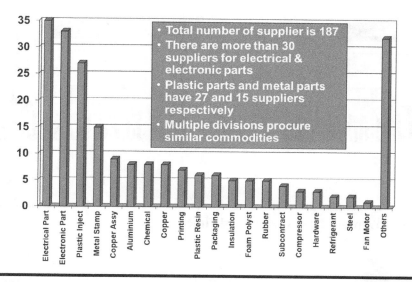

Figure 9.23   Number of Suppliers by Commodity.

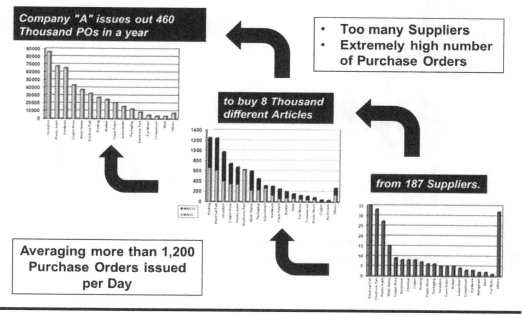

Figure 9.24   Poor Procurement Practices.

■ The highest area of inventory (days-on-hand) are:
  – Gases: 64 days.
  – Subcontractors: 57 days.
  – Rubber: 72 days.
  – Electrical/Electronic components: 38 days.
  – Others (miscellaneous): 44 days.

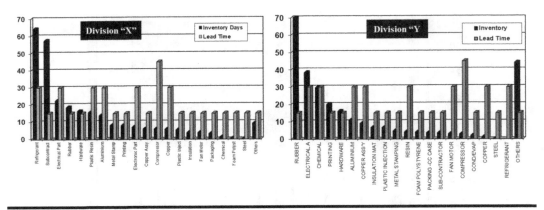

Figure 9.25   Inventory Days versus Lead Times.

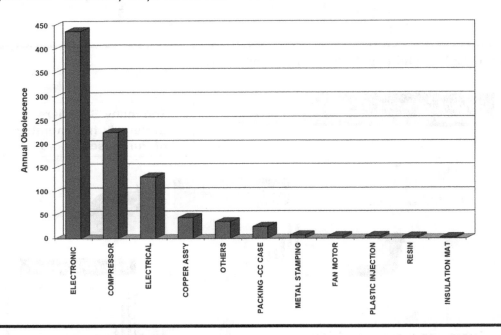

Figure 9.26   Inventory Obsolescence.

- There was $242k in obsolete raw materials (see Figure 9.26):
    - $145k (60%) in Electrical/Electronic components.
    - $59k (24%) in Subcontracted OEM Equipment.

Earlier, in the manufacturing assessment, we did a Routing-by-Walking-Around (RBWA) to assess the manufacturing processes, and we did a similar RBWA to assess portions of the planning and procurement processes.

Figure 9.27 shows the RBWA summary for "material planning to purchase order issued" process for an existing SKU from an established supplier. The process took eight days and it was characterized by:

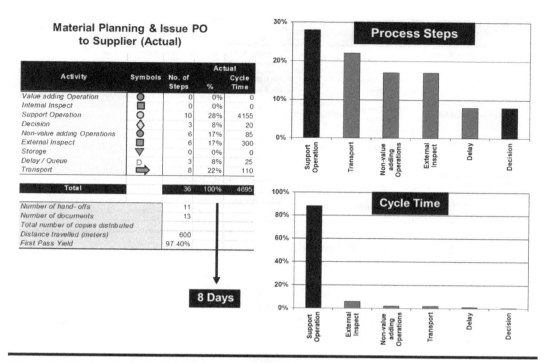

Figure 9.27   Routing-by-Walking-Around: Procurement.

- 100% non-value-added, as you would expect because the process doesn't actually change the form, fit, or function of a saleable product. But it is required process, although it's non-value-added.
- A total of 13 documents were required for a single part.
- And they went through 11 hands-offs and approvals.
- And the total distance that documents traveled was approximately 600 meters (0.37 miles).
- And 2.6% of the occurrences, there would be an error somewhere in the documents requiring rework (corrections) and rerouting, etc.

And since there's no differentiating the process based on the value of the item purchased, there would be significant administrative costs incurred to buy trivially commoditized items (e.g., office supplies, repetitive consumable items, etc.). The total administrative expense associated with the 460,000 purchase orders is $3.3 million, which equates to a measly $7.17/PO, but it's the sheer volume of purchase orders that creates the waste. And because there are 1,260 purchase orders being processed every day (365 days), that's a daily expense of $9,034 every day of the year.

Another assessment activity was to conduct a simple benchmarking versus similar companies in similar industries. Figure 9.28 shows actual performance versus the benchmarked companies. And there is a large gap, in all areas, of company A's performance versus the benchmarked standards.

Key Performance Indicator	Company A Actual	Benchmark	Comments
Raw Material Inventory Days	14 Days	5 Days	Company A is vertically integrated and should be holding minimal inventory.
Stock Accuracy	Measurement Incorrect	>99%	Stock measurement is by value instead of quantity. Surplus and deficit inventory is averaged out.
Supplier Reliability	Measurement Incorrect	Cumulative Performance > 99%	Delivery data entered not real time on-line. Incoming quality inspection not random. Paperwork accuracy should be included.
Material Downtime & Losses	No Consolidated Measurement	Zero	There is no consolidated information on production downtime due to material shortages or material quality problems; therefore not driving improvements.
Number of Suppliers by Commodity	9	between 1 - 4	Company A has 187 suppliers across 21 commodities.
Percentage of Strategic Suppliers	Not Measured	40%	Strategic suppliers: mutual planning & capacity reservation, demand driven, daily delivery, no incoming inspection.

Figure 9.28 Procurement Benchmarking.

Improvement Opportunities identified through the Procurement Assessment:

■ The data required to evaluate supply-management performance is not online and not centrally available, requiring significant investment in time and resources.

■ Company "A" does not consolidate and leverage its group direct materials requirements.

■ There are too many different articles within the same commodity with insignificant variations. There is also variability in raw material used.

■ DLM and article variability are driving procurement process complexity and non-value-added activities in Company "A" and at the supplier site.

■ Current subcontracting strategy of supplying parts and paying for value add is causing high indirect management cost.

■ There are many suppliers for certain commodities, e.g., plastic injection and metal stamping.

■ Significant opportunities to work with the distributor for electrical and electronic commodities, which have a high obsolescence amount.

■ Local suppliers lead time is long compared to actual process time. Lead time is driven by Company "A" planning.

TO-BE SUPPLY-CHAIN IMPROVEMENT INITIATIVES

Figure 9.29 summarizes the characteristics of the "To-Be" supply-chain vision/business model.

Based on the assessment findings from all segments, Planning, Manufacturing, Quality, and Procurement, the following improvement initiatives were undertaken:

1. Establishing a formal A-B-C stratification of all purchased items, manufactured items, and finished-goods items, and differentiating the processes throughout the supply chain based on each item's A-B-C classification.

Overall Supply Chain Vision / Business Model

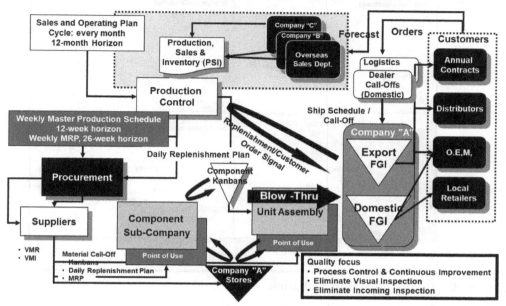

Figure 9.29 Supply-Chain Vision/Business Model.

2. Implementing a robust pull replenishment system for "A"-classified items throughout the supply chain (raw material until point-of-sales).
3. Sales & Operations Plan/Production. Sales & Inventory Plan for mid-/long-term capacity and resource planning.
4. Utilize max–min kanbans where possible for "A, B, and/or C" items, a simple trigger for replenishment.
5. Differentiated purchasing by commodity (see Figure 9.30):
   - Repetitive sequenced shipment/deliveries of high-volume regularly consumed items.
   - Blanket Purchase Orders with daily/weekly Material Call-Offs.
   - Purchase Cards and/or Small-Value Purchase Orders for trivial items.
   - Vendor-Managed Inventory and/or Vendor-Managed Replenishment will be deployed with selective strategic partners
6. Cellular manufacturing to improve manufacturing efficiencies throughout the manufacturing execution processes, and rhythm-based production sequencing (see Figure 9.31).
   - Reduced lot sizes, minimized non-value-added activities, and thus reduced Work-in-Process by 35%.
7. Reduce inspection costs.
   - Improved operator training (standard work) and certification process.
   - Improvement in supplier quality by external supplier development activities, e.g., critical-to-quality awareness, standard work, waste elimination.

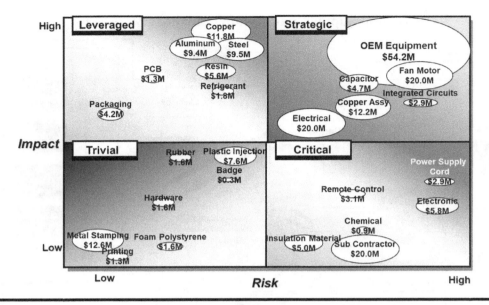

Figure 9.30 Commodity Differentiation.

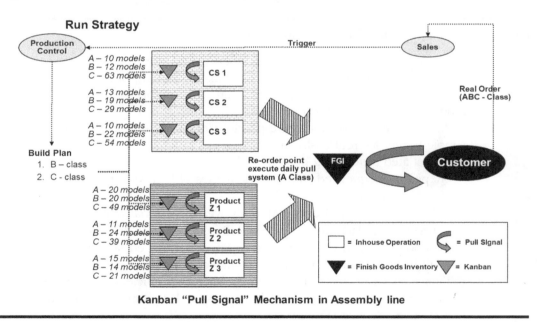

Figure 9.31 Manufacturing Run Strategy Model.

8. Reduced Cost-of-Quality (internal failures).
   - Process FMEAs to identify and implement mistake-proofing applications.
   - Implemented Statistical-Process-Control where applicable.
   - Improved supplier quality.

   – Minimize (eliminate) inventory obsolescence, partly through
     product portfolio rationalization.
 9. Finished-Goods Inventory reductions.
   – A-B-C differentiated stocking levels (see Figure 9.31).
   – Replenishment versus producing-to-forecast.
   – Product Portfolio rationalization.

Improvement Initiative #5: Differentiated Procurement Strategy
   One of the key findings from the procurement assessment was the lack of
differentiated purchasing strategy based on business impact and supply-chain
risk. And we utilized the Kraljic Model approach to devise a strategy for each
quadrant of the model, i.e., Leveraged, Strategic, Trivial, and Critical.
   Figure 9.30 reflects the commodity groupings plotted according to their
perceived business impact and supply-chain risk. The size of the ovals in
the matrix is roughly proportional to the amount of annual spend.
   The details of the Kraljic approach to differentiation is covered in detail
in Chapter 4, and *Case-in-Point 4-3* provides a detailed list of the differentiated procurement strategy for this company.
   Improvement Initiative #6: Manufacturing Run Strategy
   The "To-Be" manufacturing execution scheme will be designed around:

■ Cellular manufacturing.
■ Rhythm-based production sequencing.
■ Customer pull.

See Figure 9.31 for an illustration of the "To-Be" manufacturing run strategy
model.
   The rhythm-production pattern will be:

■ The top 5% SKUs based on demand will be slotted to run daily.
■ The remaining "A"s will be manufactured daily but will give slot prior-
  ity to the top 5%.
■ The "B"s will be slotted to run weekly.
■ The "C"s will be run monthly.

Improvement Initiative #9: Finished-Goods Inventory Strategy
   The finished-goods inventory model will be differentiated by A-B-C stratification based on annual demand. And the inventory levels will be aligned
with the manufacturing run strategy and the frequency that each category
(A-B-C) is manufactured.
   Figure 9.32 displays the "To-Be" inventory strategy.
   The impact on FGI inventory from establishing an inventory model,
based on flexible capacity, statistical sizing, and an ABC manufacturing run
strategy is the following:

SKU's ABC Stratification	Inventory Strategy
A items, 47 SKU's & ~50% of demand	Zero Inventory
A items, ~110 SKU's & ~30% of demand	1-week
B items	Safety stock per statistical analysis of demand history
C Items	Cycle stock + Safety stock per statistical analysis of demand history

Figure 9.32 "To-Be" Inventory Strategy.

- FGI's Inventory turns would be increased from 1.5 to 3.3.
- This would reduce Finished-Goods inventory by 55%, from $164.8M to $74.2M, with annual savings from carrying cost reduction of $7.1M.

The combination of finished-goods inventory-management and the manufacturing run strategy will impact the demand-production-inventory synchronization, which is graphically displayed by the Triple-Play charts. A robust pull-replenishment scheme is the main driver of synchronization of these three elements.

Figure 9.33 reflects the Triple-Play results for an "A"-classified (i.e., top 5%) finished-goods SKU after implementation of the improvement initiatives. This is a "fast-runner" part; we optimized the efficiency of its manufacturing process and reduced its manufacturing lead time to less than a day. Through the manufacturing rhythm sequencing, we dedicate slots of manufacturing-time for "A" SKUs to be built on demand. Thus, in Figure 9.32 you see NO finished-goods inventory – none! And you see perfectly synchronized demand-production quantities.

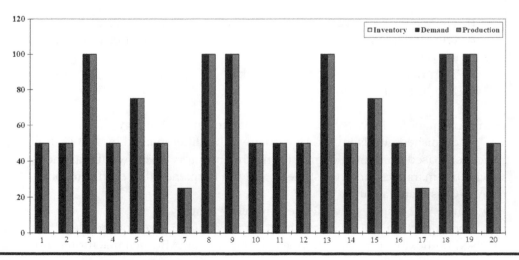

Figure 9.33 "To-Be" Triple-Play – "A"-Part.

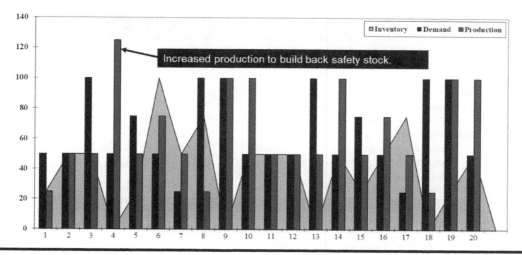

Figure 9.34 "To-Be" Triple-Play – "B"-Part.

Figure 9.34 reflects the Triple-Play results for a "B"-classified Finished-Goods SKU after implementation of the improvement initiatives. This is another SKU that historically has a significant amount of demand volatility throughout the year, and thus we must keep a strategic amount of safety stock. In the graph, you'll see variations in the demand quantities versus production quantities, as we've replenished the finished-goods inventory based on the consumption while maintaining strategically established safety-stock levels.

Figure 9.35 reflects the Triple-Play (demand, production, and inventory) results for a "C"-classified Finished-Goods SKU after implementation of the improvement initiatives. The chart shows an almost perfect synchronization

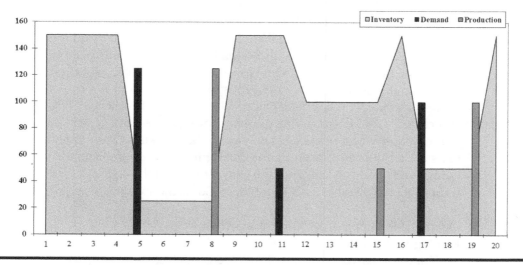

Figure 9.35 "To-Be" Triple-Play – "C"-Part.

Improvement Opportunities	Baseline	Projected Savings (%)	Annualized Savings	Cash Flow Impact
Procurement Optimization				
Procurement Cost	$3.3M	61%	$2.0M	n.a.
Raw Materials Inventory	$29.5M	40%	$1.0M	$11.8M
Manufacturing Efficiency				
Assembly Labor Cost	$11.7M	36%	$4.2M	n.a.
WIP Reduction	$6.0M	58%	$3.5M	$2.1M
Quality Improvement				
External Inspection Cost	$3.2M	28%	$0.9M	n.a.
Cost-of-Quality (Internal Failure)	$15.1M	15%	$2.3M	n.a.
Planning Simplification				
Finished Goods Inventory	$164.8M	55%	$7.1M	$90.6M
Savings*			**$21.0M**	**$104.5M**

*Savings are estimate as full implementation and verification had not been fully completed before this summary was compiled.

Figure 9.36 "To-Be" Financial Summary.

of production quantities to replenish demand quantities (i.e., shipments), a strategic amount of inventory is maintained, as this SKU has a large amount of demand variation throughout the year, and the risk of obsolescence is minimal.

In conclusion, Figure 9.36 summarizes the projected financial benefits from the "To-Be" improvement initiatives.

Case-in-Point 9.2: Supply-Chain Transformation

Company: An Asian privately owned pharmaceutical manufacturer with approximately US $1 billion in annual revenue.

Objective: Company "A" was a consultancy client that requested a comprehensive fact-based, data-driven assessment of their supply-chain operations. The assessment was conducted based on the Oliver Wight Business Excellence Checklist (a.k.a. MRP II Assessment) and complemented by a proven set of qualitative and quantifiable tools and methodologies. The company was also initiating an ERP implementation, and wanted to ensure that its processes, etc., would be reengineered to maximize the benefit of the new ERP system.

Baseline-Assessment: I utilized the Oliver Wight Business Excellence Checklist as a checklist for benchmarking the company's current ways of working against industry best practices as defined in the checklist. Oliver Wight's Class A checklists have been accepted as a proven/successful manufacturing excellence standard since the early 1970s. And the checklist was complemented by other assessment tools and methodologies, including:

■ Quantifiable Supply-Chain Inventory Analysis.
■ Routing-By-Walking-Around (process analysis).
  – Value-Added versus Non-Value-Added activities.
  – Cycle-time drivers.

- WIP drivers.
- Application of Lean-Manufacturing concepts.
■ Quantifiable Supply-Management Analysis.
■ Supply-Chain Synchronization.
■ Expanded range of Key Performance Indicators.

The objective of our approach is to identify gaps in the current ways-of-working versus supply-chain best practices and to identify opportunities for operational improvements. High-level recommendations were provided; implementation is out of scope. Figure 9.37 reflects the approach taken for the assessment.

The approach assesses the total supply chain at a high level, but I drilled down on a few representative products to:

■ Identify representative products for detailed operational analysis.
■ Detailed process-step/process-time analysis.
■ Focus extends to specific details.

For this case-example, I reference Product "X," which is a high-demand over-the-counter pharmaceutical product that's a nutritional supplement to help promote increased energy and enhance the immune system. Product "X" is classified as an "AA" product, which denotes it as one of the top 50 highest customer-demand products.

For reference, "AA"s are the top 50 SKUs based on customer demand, "A"s are the next 141 SKUs, "B"s are predictable medium-volume and the next 190 SKUs, "C"s, are somewhat predictable low-volume and the next 289 SKUs, and finally "D"s are a high supply-chain risk with sporadic non-predictable low-volume customer demand.

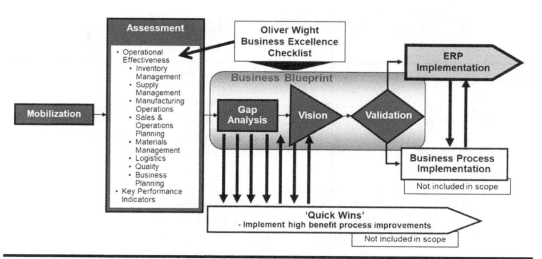

Figure 9.37 Assessment Approach.

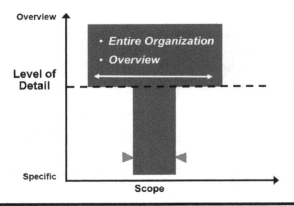

Figure 9.38   Drill-Down Approach.

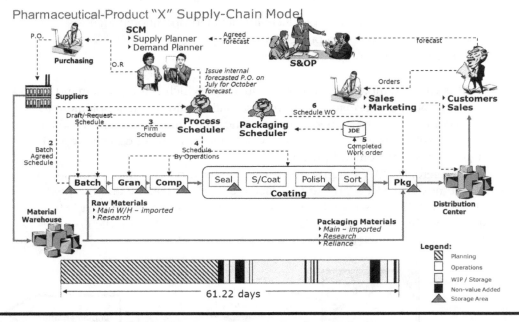

Figure 9.39   Supply-Chain Process Mapping – Product "X".

Figure 9.38 is the current-state supply-chain model for product "X," the drill-down focus of this case-example (see Figure 9.39).

The first area of focus for the assessment is the overall supply chain's processes' effectiveness. The following are three key metrics:

■ *Customer Service.* It should be measured as On-Time-In-Full (OTIF) with a target of >99.5%. Company "A" performance for the five (5) representative products (class AA/A) was 68.4%.
  – Product "X" has an OTIF of 69.7%, which is a very poor performance for an "AA" product. Figure 9.40 shows the formula used by Company "A" to calculate OTIF.

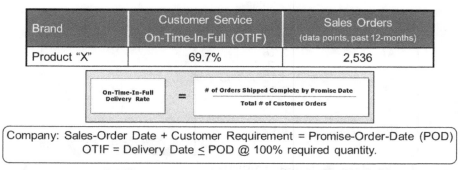

Brand	Customer Service On-Time-In-Full (OTIF)	Sales Orders (data points, past 12-months)
Product "X"	69.7%	2,536

$$\text{On-Time-In-Full Delivery Rate} = \frac{\text{\# of Orders Shipped Complete by Promise Date}}{\text{Total \# of Customer Orders}}$$

Company: Sales-Order Date + Customer Requirement = Promise-Order-Date (POD)
OTIF = Delivery Date ≤ POD @ 100% required quantity.

Figure 9.40   On-Time-In-Full As-Is for Product "X".

- *Schedule Adherence (OTIF):* Self-manufacturing = 47.2% and Toll-Manufacturing* = 50.5%. (OW: Suppliers (internal/external) must meet supply time, quantity, and quality of >99.5%.)
  - Toll Manufacturing: Company "A" provides all raw materials, packaging, recipes, etc. Company "A" owns and supplies all required equipment, the toll manufacturer provides labor and management as well as blending and packaging services.
- *Inventory Turns.* Should be monitored and continuously improved. Benchmarking pharmaceutical companies reveals supply chain turns to average 2.5 (circa 2007). Company "A"'s current supply-chain inventory target is 9.5 months, or 1.3 turns.

A further assessment (snapshot) of the inventory reveals that Company "A"'s current FGI, i.e., 2.9 months SOH (approximately $100 million) and shows that:

- Finished-Goods Inventory (Stock-on-Hand) (SOH) ranges from 0 months to 3,895 months.
- 8.6% of the SKUs have zero SOH, including "AA" and "A."
- 4% of their highest-demand items ("AA" and "A"s) have zero SOH, although the FGI for the "AA" and "A" averages 2.9 months.

    Figure 9.41 shows the distribution of FGI by "AA-A-B-C-D" product stratification.

    Company "A" being a pharmaceutical manufacturer, shelf line of product is a critical factor. "Short-Dated" finished-goods are items with a shelf-life expiration of fewer than six months remaining. Retailers (pharmacies, etc.) will return items as they approach shelf-life expiration in six months or fewer, so basically any product with less than six months remaining shelf life will most likely be destroyed or sold at a substantial discount for immediate use.

The analysis (see Figure 9.42) revealed that there was Short-Dated Inventory (SDI) for all demand classifications of product. Our snapshot analysis showed:

Class	Avg. Inventory Months-on-Hand (MOH)	SKU's with forecast but ZERO inventory
AA	2.18	2
A	3.58	6
B	3.67	17
C	31.74	17
"other"[1]	3.87	6
	Total	48

1 – no class assigned, 10 SKUs

Figure 9.41   FGI by "AA-A-B-C-D" Product-Stratification.

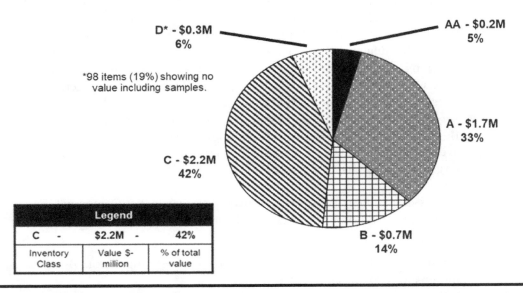

D* - $0.3M 6%

AA - $0.2M 5%

*98 items (19%) showing no value including samples.

A - $1.7M 33%

C - $2.2M 42%

B - $0.7M 14%

Legend		
C -	$2.2M -	42%
Inventory Class	Value $- million	% of total value

Figure 9.42   Short-Dated Inventory (SDI).

- Total SDI was US $5.1 million.
- "C"s equal 42% of the total, or $2.2 million.
- "A"s equal 33% of the total, or $1.7 million.
- "B"s equal 14% of the total, or $0.7 -million.
- "D"s equal 6% of the total, or $0.3 million.
- "AA"s equal 5% of the total, or $0.2 million.

The "A"s at $1.7 million is very alarming information and suggests major flaw(s) in their inventory-management system. The "A"s are characterized as predictable demand, so any SDI needed to be thoroughly evaluated and the root cause determined. And the "C"s at $2.2 million, which are again characterized as low-volume predictable demand, reflects a lack of proactive inventory-management.

Many of Company "A"'s supply-chain performance issues are due to their operating on a "Push" production system relying on forecasts. Their forecast accuracy is 65.4% and consists of a three-month rolling forecast scheme (see Figure 9.43).

A second major supply-chain issue uncovered by the assessment is their Supplier Reliability. Company "A"'s Supplier Delivery Reliability=50.5% (Oliver Wight's best-practice target=>99.5%).

Figure 9.44 shows an analysis of all Company "A" suppliers. The key analysis-results are:

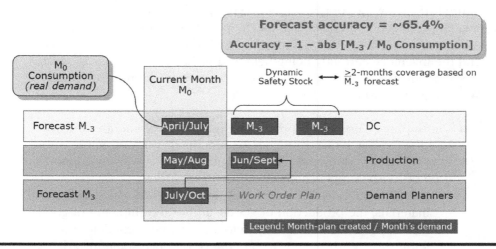

Figure 9.43   3-Month Forecasting Model.

All Suppliers			
	Order	Hit	OTIF
August	5269	2364	44.9%
September	5636	2588	45.9%
October	698	437	62.6%
November	598	368	61.5%
December	403	242	60.0%
January	525	378	72.0%
February	594	437	73.6%
March	555	395	71.2%
Total	**14278**	**7209**	**50.5%**

Finished Goods Suppliers			
	Order	Hit	OTIF
August	248	85	34.3%
September	266	88	33.1%
October	31	12	38.7%
November	40	20	50.0%
December	27	12	44.4%
January	15	8	53.3%
February	21	3	14.3%
March	34	12	35.3%
Total	**682**	**240**	**35.2%**

An acceptable measure would be 95%, but true excellence would require ≥99.5%

Packaging Material Suppliers			
	Order	Hit	OTIF
January	412	282	68.4%
February	466	341	73.2%
March	403	283	70.2%
Total	**1281**	**906**	**70.7%**

Raw Material Suppliers			
	Order	Hit	OTIF
January	98	88	89.8%
February	107	93	86.9%
March	118	100	84.7%
Total	**323**	**281**	**87.0%**

Figure 9.44   Supplier-Analysis.

■ OTIF for Toll Manufacturers for the studied eight months was a very poor 35.2%.
■ Packaging Material suppliers was 70.7% (eight months of data).
■ Raw Material suppliers was 87.0% (three months of data)

Company "A"'s monitoring of supplier delivery reliability was mainly an ad hoc activity, with no investigation into late, partial deliveries. Basically, there was very poor supplier management.

The deeper dive into Product "X," utilizing Triple-Play graphing (see Figure 9.45), shows a poor adherence to the production schedule (internally created production schedule), i.e., for the past 12 months, the aggregated adherence was 79.1%, and on a monthly basis the adherence is only 43.8%. And the inventory currently being held in distributors' warehouses equates to 3.3 months stock coverage. The forecast accuracy for Product "X" (an "AA" category item) is only 75%.

■ The supply chain pushes product based on a three-month forward-looking forecast which results in 3.3 months of stock-on-hand.
■ Supply-chain performance and strategies do not effectively support this type of "push" supply-chain model.
   – "Push" is typically defined as the model in which the delivery of materials, the production of goods, and/or the shipment of goods to customers is done according to a predefined schedule based on a forecast. "Push" means to procure or produce some material or product without an immediate demand to use it. As the material or product shows in inventory, there will be efforts to "push" it to

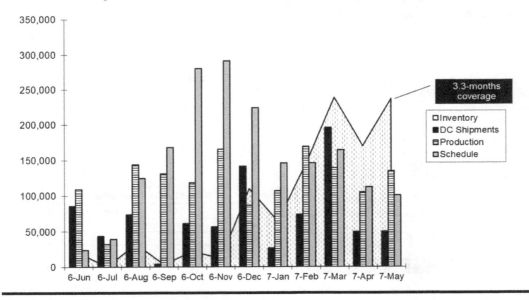

Figure 9.45 Product "X" Triple-Play Graphing.

the next stage of the supply chain and ultimately to the consumers. Poorly managed schedules tend to create many conditions like the following to push materials and products without a true demand for them:

- Schedules tend to accommodate "waste" (safety stock, safety lead time, lot-sizing, queues, setups, etc.), which makes schedules exceed the expected demands.
- The supply chain is often slow to react to true demand.
- Demand management and supply-chain management are not coordinated, leading to inefficiency and the failure to meet demands, which results in higher inventories. This further decouples the supply chain from the true demand.
- Personnel are not sufficiently trained and, combined with inaccurate data, produce inappropriate schedules. The mismatch between the formal schedules and the real execution erodes the credibility of the whole model.

    As a result, where these distortions happen, the schedule-driven model presents low efficiency, slow response, high inventories, and low customer-service levels.

■ Company "A"'s current ways of working and performance metric:
  - Forecast accuracy is approximately 75%.
  - Safety-stock sizing not statistically linked to supply-chain capabilities.
  - Supplier reliability is approximately 50.5% (average for all suppliers, all products).
  - Operations attainment of schedule approximately 43.8%.
  - Long planning and production cycle times and the arbitrary setting of safety stock lead to high risk of expiry/obsolete stock.

    Using roll-through yield, the probability of the customer receiving what they want is only 16.1 % (75% × 50.5% × 98.9% × 43.8% × 98%). See Figure 9.46.

    Company "A" compensates for poor supply-chain performance by amassing huge amounts of inventory (i.e., 3.3 months).

■ Other key observations of the "Push" scheme:
  - Finished-Goods destined to be consumed this month were planned and produced 3–5 months ago (i.e., two months safety -stock plus current month's demand requirement).
  - Raw material (dependent demand) was planned and procured four months ago, while maintaining safety stock. Safety-stock quantities are not linked to protection against fluctuations in demand and/or supply but to a budgeted value.
  - A long production planning cycle (1 month) and long production-processing time (1–2-months) compounds the situation, making it virtually impossible to respond to "true" demand, as this

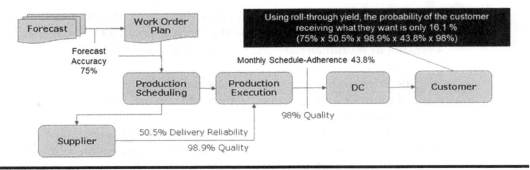

Figure 9.46   Order-Fulfillment Process's Roll-Through Yield.

planning cycle is three months removed from responding to actual consumption.

- This "push" supply chain accumulates a large amount of obsolete/ expired material:
  - Raw material: US $0.8 million
  - Packaging material: US $1.5 million
  - Finished-Goods: US $10.5 million

And this excludes "internal sales" of expired Finished-Goods.

SUPPLY-CHAIN ASSESSMENT FINDINGS

The summary of the key findings from the operational assessment of Company "A"'s supply-chain performance against key business measures is as follows:

- Forecast accuracy=65%. This is an extremely important measure, as it's the basis for Company "A"'s existing planning process. And it's not linked to "true" demand.
- Customer service (On-Time-In-Full) is not being measured, but when it was manually calculated for the five representative products it averaged about 65%, well below the Oliver Wight target of >99.5%.
- Production Schedule Attainment averaged 47.2%, again well below the Oliver Wight target of >99.5% for this measure.
- Supplier delivery (all purchased production material) averaged 50.5%.
- Inventory Turns (COGS/inventory value).
  - Supply Chain Target (9.5 months) = 1.3.
  - Raw Material/Packaging = <1.5.
  - Finished Goods = <2.5.
- Large amount of inventory leads to excessive obsolescence. Safety-stock targets are not aligned with supply chain capabilities.
  - Planning cycle time is one month, and production cycle time is planned at two months.

The Key improvement opportunities are:

- Improve overall factory efficiencies by implementing manufacturing run strategies that differentiate production planning and production execution between classes of product and is driven by a pull-replenishment process for high-volume products.
- Improve customer service by increasing responsiveness through continuous replenishment of high-volume products.
- Improve customer service by statistically and strategically establishing safety-stock levels (raw material and Finished Goods).
- Improve Production Schedule Attainment performance by reducing production cycle time, improving supply reliability, shortening planning cycle time, and minimizing non-value-added activities.
- Improve supplier reliability though differentiating supply strategies, supplier management, and supplier development.
- Reduce total cost of ownership through supply strategies, supplier management, and supplier development; e.g., 10–15% reduction in cost for strategic categories for pharmaceutical manufacturers.
- Substantially reduce supply-chain inventory by
  - Improving overall supply-chain performance/reliability.
  - Reducing cycle stock and safety stock through differentiated planning/production processes.
  - Statistically setting safety-stock levels.
  - Pulling inventory based on consumption rather than pushing based on inaccurate forecasts, while minimizing expired and obsolete materials/products.

PURCHASED-MATERIAL ANALYSIS

Potential Causes/Solutions

- Cause: Lack of stock because of forecast error, i.e., dependent demand.
  - Solution: Statistically calculated safety-stock smoothing demand variations
- Cause: Unreliable supply, delivery, and/or quality.
  - Solution: Statistically calculated safety-stock smoothing supply variations.
  - Solution: Supplier development and supplier relationship management.
- Cause: Expired Stock
  - Solution: Minimize stock of material with high unpredictable demand, e.g., "C"-items, constrained commodity, by aligning sourcing/procurement strategy to minimize risks.

After a thorough analysis of the overall supply-chain operations, we performed an assessment of their manufacturing-execution.

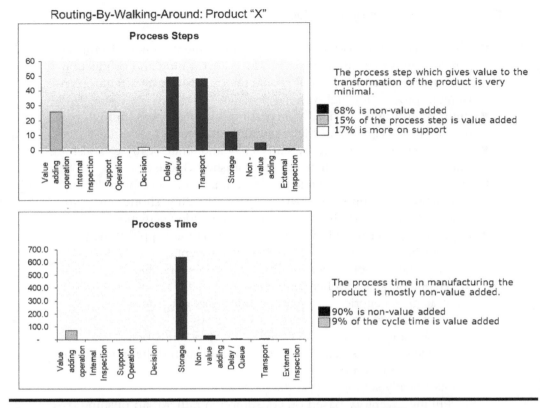

Figure 9.47   Routing-by-Walking-Around Analysis – Product "X".

Figure 9.47 is a graphical summary of an RBWA for Product "X." And Figure 9.48 provides a summary of the RBWA data.

Figure 9.49 is a spaghetti diagram of the manufacturing flow of Product "X." The largest inefficiency is that manufacturing lots are queued before each subsequent activity, and there is no continuous flow of any products.

The key gaps of the current-state manufacturing execution against operational excellence are:

■ Level Scheduling.
    – The scheduling process is fragmented. *That is, there is one scheduler for processing operations and another scheduler for packaging who schedules the work orders for packaging only after it is completed at all processing operations (i.e., batching, granulation).*
    – There is no run strategy of manufacturing a product.
■ Setup Time Reduction.
    – The line is not flexible to meet demand due to the long setup time.
    – The program of reducing setup time using the Single-Minute-Exchange-Die concept should be revived, as this is no longer practiced at the shop floor.

Product "X"	
Non-Added Value (% of total)	
Process Steps	68%
Process Time	90%
Key Waste / Non-Valued-Added Contributors	
Storage	
Process Steps	7%
Process Time	85%
Queue	
Process Steps	29%
Process Time	1%
Transport	
Process Steps	28%
Process Time	1%

Figure 9.48   Routing-by-Walking-Around Analysis Summary – Product "X".

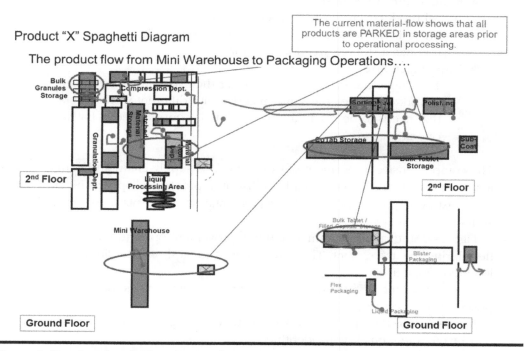

Figure 9.49   Spaghetti Diagram Product "X".

- The line is scheduled on campaign runs to optimize line loading and avoid long changeover downtime.
■ Quality at Source.
- There should be a continuous improvement to address the root cause of defects to control the process and prevent recurrence of

problems, i.e., there are some tablets stuck together that are sorted out as defects after coating. The possible root cause of the defect is the curvature of the tablet due to the worn-out tool at compression. Though the curvature is within spec, this causes some problems at the coating process.
- Sorting operations must be eliminated when process capability becomes robust.
■ Product Flow and Factory Layout,
- In every operation, the product is always kept at a storage area, contributing to longer cycle time.
- There are too many staging points of the product before it is completed, thus interrupting continuous product flow.
- The factory layout is not designed for smooth product flow.
■ Just-In-Time (JIT)
- The true philosophy of JIT is not practiced.
- Excess inventories are still seen, as no strategy is made on frequency of deliveries in small lot size to support operations.
■ Kanban/Pull Mechanism
- All products are pushed based on schedule.
- There is no linkage mechanism between operations, as each operation has a storage area for inventory.
■ Large Batch Size
- The bigger the batch size, the longer the cycle time to complete a work order, i.e., the same material with different work orders that needs to be batched per schedule is consolidated at batching operation.

The comprehensive assessment of Company "A"'s supply-chain and manufacturing operations uncovered a large list of improvement opportunities that must be improved prior to the implementation of the planned new ERP system.

Figures 9.50 thru 9.54 summarize the improvement opportunities identified during the assessment. They are categorized as short-, medium-, and long-term initiatives.

Figures 9.55 and 9.56 show projected improvement metrics for the proposed "To-Be" processes.

In addition to the opportunities summarized in Figures 9.50 thru 9.54, there were a few quick wins identified.

The quick wins identified were:

1. Improve Customer Service, statistically establish finished-goods safety-stock levels by SKU.
2. Eliminate the "excess inventory-check" process by establishing proper safety-stock/cycle-stock control.

3. Improve supplier reliability, statistically establish raw material safety-stock levels by SKU.
4. Reduce Finished-Goods Inventory, statistically establish safety-stock levels by SKU.
5. Reduce product changeover times within production.

Process Changes	Objectives
1. FGI Expired- / Obsolete-Material Management ♦ Proactive aging reporting of FGI (x-months before expiration) & required-action / deployment options. Establish clear ownership of inventory. ♦ Decision-matrix for disposal & "internal" sales ♦ Reconciliation of inventory-value & disposition action ♦ Create a Corrective-Action-Report for all instances over x-Php in disposal / internal sales	■ Proactively manage short-dated inventory within a timeline that allows for satisfactory redeployment ■ Establish root-cause of each occurrence. ■ Ensure accurate capturing of all occurrences & full-reconciliation
2. Raw Material / Packaging Excess- / Obsolete-/ Expired-Material Management ♦ Proactive aging- & excess-inventory reporting of material (x-months before expiration or amount in excess of x-DOH) & required-action / deployment options. Establish clear ownership of inventory. ♦ Create a Corrective-Action-Report for all instances of obsolescence or expiration ♦ Integrate "obsolescence" in engineering-change process & portfolio-management	■ Proactively manage excess inventory within a timeline that allows for satisfactory redeployment of product ■ Establish root-cause of each occurrence.
3. Optimize Raw Material / Packaging Inventory ♦ Statistically establish safety-stock for all purchased materials ♦ Make require adjustments to add or minimize stock ♦ On-going of monitoring of stock-levels ♦ Define continuous monitoring process & decision-matrix	■ Optimize inventory levels ■ Improve customer service ■ Reduce inventory levels by 10 ~ 50%

Figure 9.50 Key Improvement Opportunities: Short-/Medium-Term.

Process Changes	Objectives
4. Optimize Finished Goods Inventory ♦ Statistically establish safety-stock for all FGI SKUs based on supply-chain capability, and on product-class (AA-A-B-C-D) ♦ Define continuous monitoring process & decision-matrix	■ Optimize inventory levels ■ Improve customer service ■ Reduce inventory levels by 10 ~ 50%

5. Performance Measures
♦ Add key customer-centric performance measures, e.g.
  - Customer service (OTIF) vs. fill-rate
  - Production schedule attainment & adherence
  - Supply chain inventory turns (COGS/inventory-value)
  - Lead-time performance (across the supply chain)
  - Velocity (value-added time / total time), e.g. order fulfillment process, production cycle-times, etc.
  - Data integrity; e.g. transactional, inventory, customer / supplier master data, etc.
♦ Establish targets & required-actions when targets not met
	■ Align measures with customer value / satisfaction
	■ Promote continuous improvement of supply chain capabilities

6. Supplier Performance & Monitoring ♦ Enhance existing processes ♦ Proactive monitoring of suppliers' performance (scorecard) with targets, continuous-improvement actions and penalties / rewards. ♦ Evaluate suppliers by the following criteria: on-time delivery, quality, price, service, and multiple user-defined sub-criteria ♦ Define continuous monitoring process & decision-matrix	■ Improve supplier reliability ■ Improve customer service ■ Promote continuous improvement

Figure 9.51 Key Improvement Opportunities: Short-/Medium-Term.

Process Changes	Objectives
7. Define Manufacturing Strategy • Determine the production capabilities of each area; cycle-time, quality, cost, etc. • Establish differentiating production-planning / -execution strategies based on class of product (AA-A-B-C-D). Simplify processes. Replenishment. Self-scheduling / -planning. Make-to-Forecast. • Develop decision-matrix for strategic-decisions • Develop plans to reconcile identified deficiencies in production capabilities.	■ Reduce production & planning cycle-times ■ Optimize supply change inventory levels ■ Improve customer service ■ Promote continuous improvement of production's capabilities
8. Inter-plant / Toll-Manufacturing Raw Material Replenishment • Develop replenishment mechanics • Responsive replenishment vs. manual planning & scheduling • Develop replenishment processes to minimize administrative / non-value-added activities ; e.g. transactional, inventory, customer / supplier master data, etc.	■ Minimize non-value added planning / scheduling ■ Reduce overall inventory requirements
9. FGI Replenishment / Kanban Triggering • Develop continuous replenishment mechanics • Develop replenishment processes to minimize administrative / non-value-added • Develop process for "sizing" kanban, or establishing "trigger-points" • Develop monitoring / maintenance processes	■ Improve customer service by becoming responsive to "true-demand" ■ Minimize non-value added planning / scheduling ■ Reduce overall inventory requirements

Figure 9.52   Key Improvement Opportunities: Short-/Medium-Term.

Process Changes	Objectives
10. Raw Material Replenishment • Develop continuous replenishment mechanics • Develop replenishment processes to minimize administrative / non-value-added • Develop process for "sizing" kanban, or establishing "trigger-points" • Develop monitoring / maintenance processes	■ Minimize non-value added planning / scheduling ■ Reduce overall inventory requirements
11. Supply Chain / Production Planning • Based on the business strategy and defined financial and service level targets, develop an inventory plan that quantifies the levels of inventory carried for both finished goods and raw materials. • Develop short-, medium- & long-term planning processes • Identify appropriate fulfillment site(s) for production item and allocate production demand to the manufacturing facility or toll manufacturer capable of meeting capacity • Develop enterprise rough-cut capacity planning processes	■ Optimize supply chain inventory ■ Ensure supply availability ■ Plan enterprise capacity
12. Material Requirements Planning • Simplify MRP processes through differentiation; e.g. dependent-demand, rate-scheduling, kanbans, or true JIT • Link MRP-process with S&OP, empowering POs to be automatically generated and transmitted to suppliers • Develop requirement visibility for suppliers	■ Minimize non-value added activities ■ Shorten process-time
13. Sales & Operations Planning • Enhance existing processes • Develop an enterprise-wide integrated S&OP process • Ensure responsiveness to true-demand / consumption. • Develop enterprise-wide Integrated Reconciliation process, addressing gaps in S&OP plan with customer requirements, overall business strategies, supply plans, etc. • Close the Loop to Marketing, Planning, Manufacturing & Logistics	■ Enterprise-wide S&OP ■ Minimize conflicts

Figure 9.53   Key Improvement Opportunities: Short-/Medium-Term.

Process Changes	Objectives
14. Total-Cost-of-Ownership ◆ Develop processes & tools for defining the Total-Cost-of-Ownership objectives & mechanics ◆ Create total-cost-of-procurement template / model ◆ Integrate into decision-making processes, e.g. supplier selection, make-buy, outsourcing, etc.	■ Improve the decision-making process ■ Use total-cost-of-ownership to continuous reduce overall operating cost ■ Use total-cost-of-ownership for make / buy analysis
15. Develop Procurement Strategy ◆ Develop a process for establishing commodity- or material-groups ◆ Develop / align strategy for each commodity- or material-group ◆ Develop differentiated procurement processes for each commodity- or material-group	■ Reduce overall cost-of-ownership
16. Supplier Management / Development ◆ Develop processes for proactively managing supplier relationships and performance to ensure supply objectives are achieved ◆ Develop supplier certification processes ◆ Enhance existing program for developing suppliers' supply chain capability ◆ Develop processes for supplier-base rationalization & management ◆ Develop processes for supplier-tier management	■ Improve supplier reliability ■ Reduce overall cost-of-ownership ■ Ensure supply continuity
17. Monitor & Manage Supplier Contracts ◆ Enhance existing processes ◆ Develop processes for differentiating supplier contracts / supply-agreements with specific performance requirements, e.g. quality, delivery, cost, lead-time, etc.	■ Improve supplier reliability ■ Reduce overall cost-of-ownership
18. DC Warehouse Operations ◆ Develop internal replenishment processes / operations to reduce planning / scheduling at case-storage / picking, pick-to-light, etc.	■ Reduce response-time to customer ■ Simply process and eliminate non-value-added activities

Figure 9.54 Key Improvement Opportunities: Medium-/Long-Term.

Product "X"	
Planning Cycle (days)	
As-Is	30
To-Be	0
Production Cycle-Time (days)	
As-Is Plan	90
As-Is Process	31.2
To-Be	5.0
Total Replenishment Time (days)	
As-Is Plan	120
To-Be	5.0
Total Finished Goods Inventory (days) *Cycle-stock + Safety-stock*	
As-Is (May '07)	99
To-Be	10
Customer Service (OTIF)	
As-Is	70%
To-Be Target	>99.5%

Figure 9.55 "AS-Is" Metrics versus "To-Be" Metrics.

Class	AA	A	B	C	D
Planning Cycle (days)					
As-Is	30	30	30	30	30
To-Be	0	0	0	<14	<30
Production Cycle-Time (days)					
As Is Plan	Liquid= 30 Plain = 60 Coated = 90				
To-Be	Continuous	<7	14 ~ 28	<28	30 ~ 60
Total Replenishment Time (days)					
As-Is	Liquid= 60 Plain = 90 Coated = 120				
To-Be	1	<7	14 ~ 28	<42	60 ~ 90
Total Finished Goods Inventory (days) *Cycle-stock + Safety-stock*					
As Is Target	90	90	90	90	90
As-Is	44	131	122	207	2214
To-Be	<21	<35	<60	<60	strategic
Customer Service (OTIF)					
As-Is	*not measured*				
To-Be Target	>99.5%	>99.5%	>85%	>80%	negotiable

Figure 9.56   "AS-Is" Metrics versus "To-Be" Metrics by Product Class.

Case-in-Point 9.3: Comprehensive Supply-Chain Assessment and Optimization

Company: Pure-play Wafer Foundry in Asia. A pure-play foundry refers to an independent wafer-fabrication foundry that doesn't produce a semiconductor device but manufactures electronic circuitry in the form of a "wafer," with the "wafer" containing thousands of individual "dies" which constitute the intellectual property of an integrated circuit (a.k.a. semiconductor). This company primarily services design houses that design electronic circuitry that would be utilized in a wide array of end products such as computers, video games, telephones, automobiles, consumer electronics, and many more applications. The design houses are often referred to as "fabless" companies, as they create and own the design but have no means (i.e., capability) to convert the designs into a physical item, i.e., a wafer consisting of "dies." Figure 9.57 shows an overview of a typical electronics value chain.

Client: This was a consultancy project and the primary client was the Minister of Finance for an ASEAN country, as the country was the majority investor in the company (i.e., the wafer foundry) to be assessed.

Background: The majority shareholder (Ministry of Finance) in this company believed that the company was underperforming and wanted an

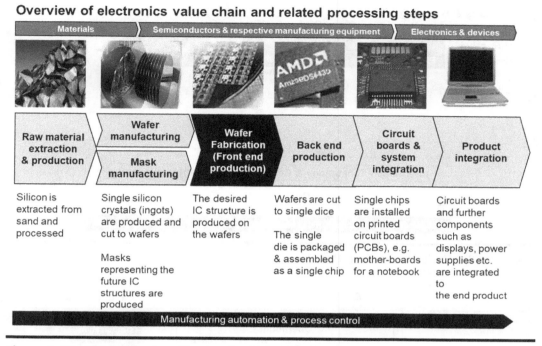

Figure 9.57 Example of an Electronics Value Chain.

independent party to assess the company's performance and assist in identifying opportunities for improvement. So this project was done under unreceptive conditions, as the other significant stakeholder was an American company, and the day-to-day operations of the wafer foundry were managed by a team of American expatriates. There was distrust by all parties.

Scope: The operational scope was the end-to-end order-fulfillment process and all associated sub-processes, etc. (see Figure 9.58). And a secondary scope was the assess the overall business and competitive health of the company and its strategies. Thus, the scope was to look at historical performance and the past business strategy along with current performance and effective executing of the present business strategy. Finally, the scope included making recommendations for operational and strategic improvements that would decrease operational expenses and increase revenues (see Figure 9.59).

Project Approach: The operational assessment follows our normal approach of establishing a data drive, a fact-based baseline of the current ways of working, and then establishing a gap from current ways and best practice and future ways of working (see Figure 9.60).

Figure 9.61 gives a more detailed breakdown of the internal and external elements of the assessment.

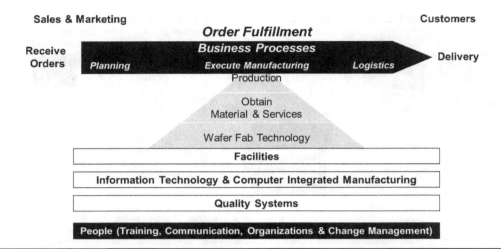

Figure 9.58   Order-Fulfillment Process.

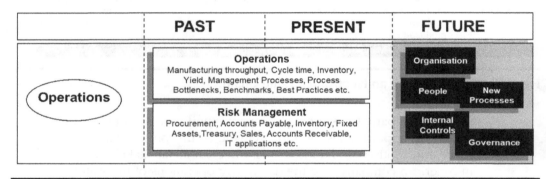

Figure 9.59   Objective.

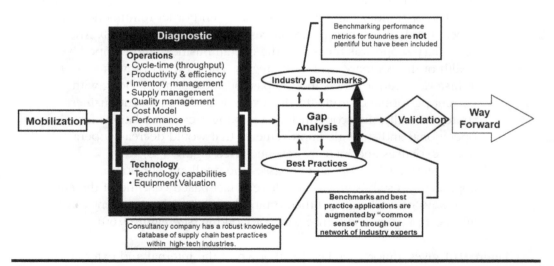

Figure 9.60   Approach.

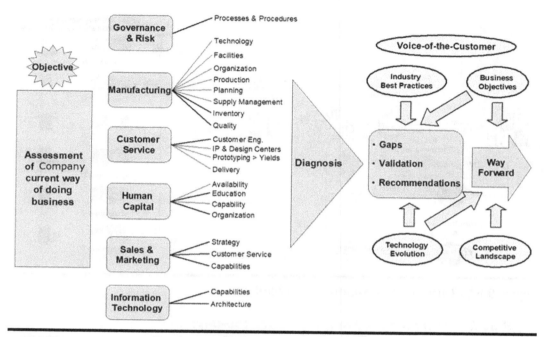

Figure 9.61   Internal- and External-Elements of the Assessment.

Figure 9.62 gives an overview of the major elements of the current-state supply-chain model.

ASSESSMENT FINDINGS

One of the first data points of our assessment was a snapshot of the current inventory levels along the supply chain, and its subsequent cash to cash cycle time (see Figure 9.63). So the initial inventory snapshot revealed:

- The company was holding 81 days of raw material inventory. (Industry benchmarking of wafer foundries showed an industry average for raw-material inventory of <30 days.)
- The fab (a.k.a. wafer foundry, a.k.a. foundry) cycle time is dependent on WIP (work-in-process) which "grows" due to customer holds/issues. The current WIP level is 60 days.
- Billing and collection cycle time of 84 days is contributing to negative cash flows and exceeds industry benchmarks (<30 days).

The supply chain had 164 days on inventory and an average collection-period of 84 days, so the cash to cash cycle is approximately 218 days (assuming they pay their suppliers in 30 days, which our analysis found).

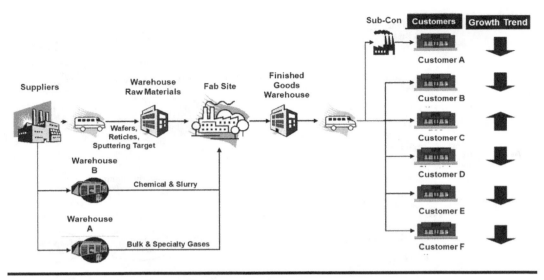

Figure 9.62   Current-State Supply-Chain Model.

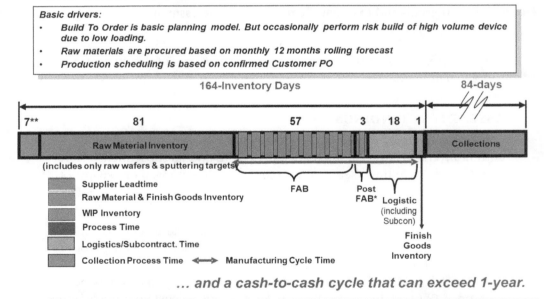

Figure 9.63   Supply-Chain Inventory Overview: Order-Fulfillment Process.

Regardless of their actual payment arrangement with their suppliers, they are looking at an extremely long period to have large sums of cash tied up in inventory and/or product.

Total inventory levels across the supply chain currently amount to $21.8 million (see Figure 9.64).

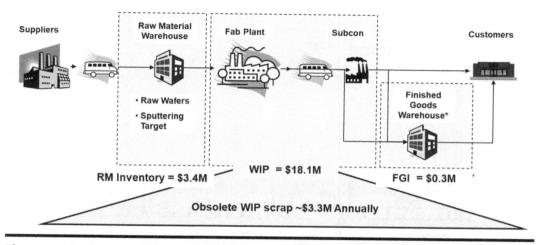

RM Inventory = $3.4M   **WIP = $18.1M**   FGI = $0.3M

Obsolete WIP scrap ~$3.3M Annually

Figure 9.64   Supply-Chain Inventory Overview: Supply-Chain Model.

- Raw Material inventory = $3.4-million.
- Work-in-Process inventory = $18.1-million.
  - Slow-moving WIP inventory as a percentage of total inventory and total revenue amounts to 4.2% and 1.1%, respectively. Relative to industry benchmarks, these percentages indicate an opportunity for improvement.
    - Company averages scrapping $3.3-million in obsolete WIP inventory annually due to obsolescence.
- Finished-Goods Inventory = $0.3-million.

A Triple-Play chart illustrates (see Figure 9.65) the synchronization between forecast, production, WIP, and shipments. The analysis reveals that:

- Shipments typically lag production starts by six weeks, which is in line with the company's quoted lead time (42 days).
- Shipments were erratic with the customer "B" products, but customer "L" shipments were more stable (at the time of the assessment, customer "L" was a significant minor shareholder in the foundry).
- Buildup of high WIP inventory levels was prevalent in all cases (60 days as noted above, which puts the average lead time at greater than 42 days)
- Forecast accuracy is 24–86%. Low forecast accuracy results in WIP obsolescence and buildup of raw material inventory (60% of the raw material was purchased for customer "B"'s products). And as noted earlier, obsolesce with WIP is a financial issue, plus having unneeded WIP cluttering the fabrication area creates inefficiencies and lean waste.

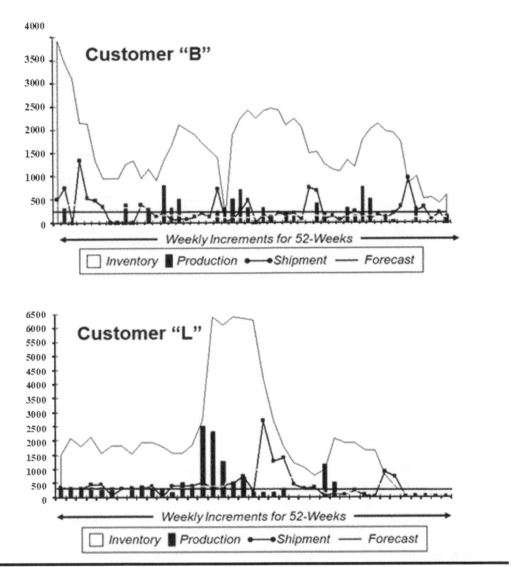

Figure 9.65 Triple-Play Analysis.

Summary of overall supply-chain findings:

■ Aggressive delivery dates are a feature of the industry, and this company has strived to accommodate original customer requests, resulting in an overall high level of satisfaction from the customers. But the company has further opportunities for delivery-performance improvement.
■ Total supply-chain process lead times and inventory levels are high.
■ Inventory levels, and WIP provisions, are high relative to the current revenue and represent room for improvement.

■ Low demand-forecast accuracy results in high WIP provisioning raw material inventory.

SUPPLY MANAGEMENT

Figure 9.66 shows a graphical breakdown of the company's annual spend; this particular figure doesn't highlight any significant improvement opportunities, but I wanted to share it as an example of a way to display a spend analysis.

But Figure 9.67 of "Control Material" reveals a lack of correlation between days of raw material on hand in relation to the supply lead time. "Control

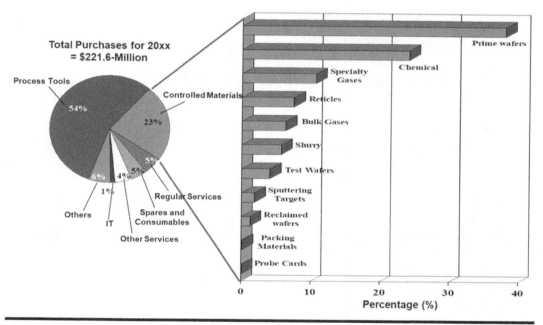

Figure 9.66   Example – Spend Analysis.

Major Control Materials	Suppliers		Number of Items	Inventory Days	Lead Time (Days)	Annual Value ($)
	Local	Imported (regional)				
Prime, Test & Reclaimed Wafers	76%	24%	8	78	42	22.1M (43%)
Chemical & Slurry	100%		34	55	7	15.2M (30%)
Specialty Gases	100%		27	90	1	5.5M (11%)
Bulk Gases	100%		6	Exp. Off	1	3.2M (6%)
Reticles	54%	46%	38	Exp. Off	3	3.8M (8%)
Sputtering Targets	100%		6	126	7	0.9M (2%)

Figure 9.67   Example – Supply-Management Analysis.

Material" are materials that have a high monetary value; thus they require more transactional and preservation control.

- "Prime, Test & Reclaimed Wafers" showed an average inventory of 78 days. The longest lead time item is 42-days which should result in a lower inventory, and since 62% of all spend for these items is local, that's too much inventory.
- "Chemicals & Slurry" showed an average inventory of 55 days. The longest lead time item is seven days, which should result in a lower inventory, and with all spend for these items from local sources, that's way too much inventory.
- "Specialty Gases" showed an average inventory of 90 days, which is excessive considering all sources are local with a one-day lead time.
- "Sputtering Targets" showed an average inventory of 126 days which is far excessive considering all sources are local with a seven-day lead time.
- "Bulk Gases" and "Reticles" are managed by distributors that are located within the same industrial park and provide daily deliveries; thus, no inventory required to be held by the wafer foundry.

The "Bulk Gases" are part of a best-practice inventory-management scheme where a third party manages a company's bulk industrial-gas needs, and the third party is basically establishing a consortium for manufacturers with similar needs in the area. This scheme is called Total Gas Management (TGM). And this third-party service provider is expanding its offerings to include chemicals, i.e., Total Chemical Management (TCM).

Key supply-management findings and opportunities:

- Excessive inventory days for raw wafers procured mainly from local suppliers.
- Long supply lead times for raw wafers resulting in lack of supply-chain flexibility and high risk.
- Company owns two months of "Chemicals & Slurry" stored locally at distributor and is liable for three months of "Specialty Gases" stored in supplier's warehouse locally, which had already been paid for by the company.
- Most of the TGM & TCM service costs are fixed and not based on volume. The company continues to pay a high price for these services while volume remains low.
- TGM & TCM service providers are not penalized for poor service, e.g., out-of-stock situations, delivery- or quality-performance, etc. Going forward, they must participate in the overall improvements in the company's supply chain.

- Long lead time for purchase-requisition to purchase-order conversion for raw materials due to multiple approval levels.
- Some spares and consumables are on consignment, but those stored in the warehouse have high inventory.

OPERATIONAL ANALYSIS

As is standard for my operational assessments, I conducted a routing-by-walking-around (RBWA) analysis for several products. I have included one in this example for reference.

The RBWA data revealed (see Figure 9.68):

- The estimated average process time to make a lot (a.k.a. batch) of wafers is 41.4 days from Fab start through to Outgoing Quality-Assurance, of which 22% is value-added operations.
  - Of the non-value-added time, 64% is storage/queues (i.e., work-in-process inventory). Based on Little's Law,[1] if the WIP were eliminated (i.e., one-lot flow), the process lead time could be reduced to 14.9 days.
- There were an estimated 2,419 steps carried out (281 major steps plus other manual activities and physical movements), of which only 12% classified as value-added.
  - Many of the "value-added" steps were inspections; typically, I would classify most inspections (unless by an operator of own work) as non-value-added.
  - Material transfers (a.k.a. transport) comprised 58% of the non-value-added activities.

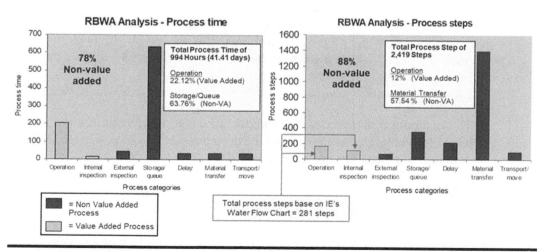

Figure 9.68 Graphical Representation of RBWA Data.

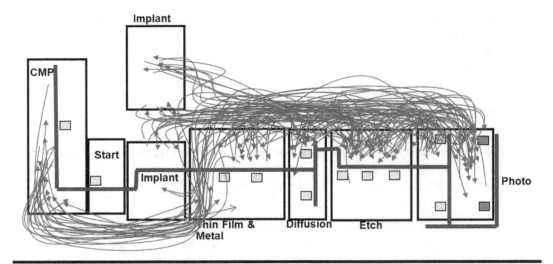

Figure 9.69   Spaghetti Diagram.

As usual with an RBWA, we were able to construct a spaghetti diagram from the RBWA data (see Figure 9.69). The spaghetti diagram exhibits a large number of physical movements between functional areas, which was highlighted by 58% of the total process steps being transport.

Overall Equipment Effectiveness (OEE) measures the true efficiency (a.k.a. effectiveness) of the equipment by considering all losses of potential productivity, including equipment downtime, losses occurring during utilization such as rework, scrap, etc., and suboptimal processing-rates.

This company's low OEE was attributed to low operational utilization and low performance efficiency, as a result of the current demand situation and suboptimum lot batching at equipment, respectively.

Figure 9.70 reflects the company's current OEE status.

One of the client's concerns about their investment was that the foundry's stated capacity, i.e., Wafer-Outs-Per-Month (WOPM) was below the budgeted capacity, on which their investment was based. Figure 9.71 reflects the capacity status at the time of our assessment.

The key findings and opportunities from the operational assessment were:

◼ The company's manufacturing is highly automated and is monitored by a fully integrated state-of-the-art information-technology system; as demand increases the overall efficiency of the factory should follow.
◼ Over-capitalization has greatly contributed to low Overall Equipment Efficiency (OEE).
◼ Large amount of WIP, even with low demand.
  – WIP is about 1.4 times of average WOPM.
◼ Large amount of non-value-added time and steps due to long queues and excess material transfers.

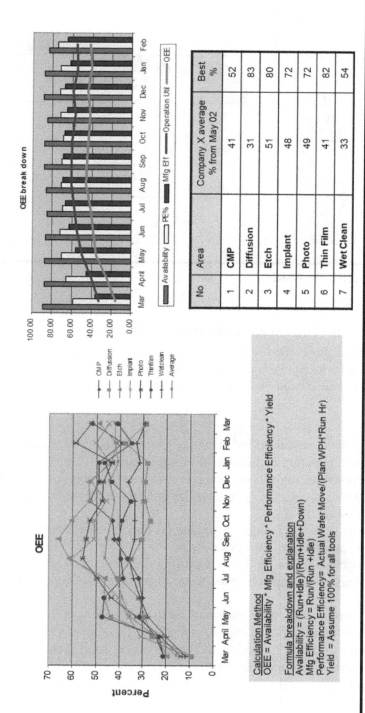

No	Area	Company X average % from May 02	Best %
1	CMP	41	52
2	Diffusion	31	83
3	Etch	51	80
4	Implant	48	72
5	Photo	49	72
6	Thin Film	41	82
7	Wet Clean	33	54

Calculation Method
OEE = Availability * Mfg Efficiency * Performance Efficiency * Yield

Formula breakdown and explanation
Availability = (Run+Idle)/(Run+Idle+Down)
Mfg Efficiency = Run/(Run +Idle)
Performance Efficiency= Actual Wafer Move/(Plan WPH*Run Hr)
Yield = Assume 100% for all tools

Figure 9.70 Overall Equipment Effectiveness (OEE).

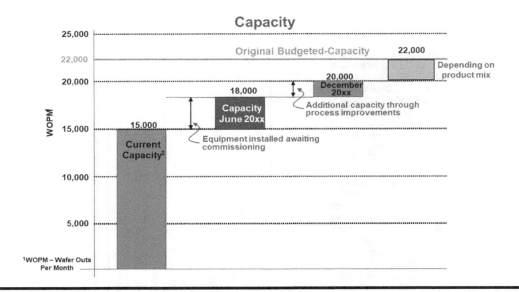

Figure 9.71 Capacity Analysis.

BUSINESS STRATEGY AND PERFORMANCE ASSESSMENT

To assess where the company is in relation to its competition and its strategy going-forward, we conducted Voice-of-Customer (VoC) interviews with many of their customers. And the general findings from the VoCs were:

- All interviewees praised the strong responsive and collaborative efforts from the company's technology and sales team.
- All interviewees praised the company success in "cloning" the industry leader's process, i.e., matching the industry leader's process compatibility.
- Price was stated as a huge advantage, as they are seemingly doing "almost" anything to gain business.
- There is considerable concern regarding the company's mid-/long-term technology road map, i.e., need to be aggressively seeking smaller line widths.
- Potential customers have expectations that their tier-one or tier-two level foundries have excess capacity and a defined plan for capacity expansion if needed, as the customers want their suppliers to be prepared if their (the customer's) demand rapidly grows.
- Concern was expressed over the lack of a staff succession plan and the existing vacancies.

Criteria	Importance to Customer	Comments
Pricing	1--------5--------10 (X)	Company X, was rated highly on this criteria, as they are aggressively providing pricing at-or-below market to fill-the-factory.
Industry's Leader Process Compatibility	1--------5--------X-10	Interviewed customers/partners see Company X's processes to be 90~100% compatible with TSMC. Given Company X business model, to be a 2nd source to TSMC's customers, this is an important criteria.
Technical Capability (staff's competency)	1--------5----X-X-10	Interviewees' response to Company X's technical capability varied. Most rated them highly but some were concerned with the recent lost of key technical staff and lack of pro-active successor development.
Technology Roadmap	1------X-5------X--10	Majority of the interviewees state very strongly that Company X must have a plan to develop 0.13μm technology, immediately. Most customer expect Company X to have 0.13μm capability in 8~12-months.

X – Criteria's importance to Interviewee   X - Where customer rates Company X

Criteria	Importance to Customer	Comments
Ease of Start-up	1--------5----XX--10	Implementing a product into a new foundry is a timely & costly process, so customers are seeking assistance in this process. Company X has been advance-funding Non Reoccurring Engineering (NRE) charges to attract new customers. A foundry's partnership with IP library providers and design service centers is, also, important in reducing start-up cost & time.
Capacity (excess & flexibility)	1--------5----X---10	Customers are purchasing a service from the foundry and they want insurance that the foundry has the capacity to fill their demand. Lower utilization rates are positive factor for customers. Most customers expect a foundry to have multiple-fabs. Company X's current low-utilization is seen as a positive.
Yield & Quality	1--------5X--X---10	Yield & quality are considered important by all, but they are considered a "given" so not an extremely important criteria in selecting a foundry

X – Criteria's importance to Interviewee   X - Where customer rates Company X

Figure 9.72 Voice-of-Customer (VoC) Analysis: Supplier Attributes.

Figure 9.72 shows a composite summary of all the VoCs in regard to key attributes, i.e., pricing, compatibility to industry leader, staff's technical capabilities, technology road map, new product introduction ease, capacity, and quality.

Figure 9.73 provides a simple summary of the VoC performance.

Category	Rating
Customer Expectations	Y
Pricing	**G** Y R
TSMC Process Capability	**G** Y R
Technical Capability	**G** Y R
Technology Roadmap	G Y **R**
Ease to Start-up	**G** Y R
Capacity	G **Y** R
Yield & Quality	G **Y** R

Key: **G** Good **Y** Acceptable **R** Of Concern

Figure 9.73   Voice-of-Customer (VoC) Analysis: Supplier Performance.

ASSESSMENT SUMMARY AND CONCLUSIONS

Figure 9.74 summarizes our assessment of key elements of the company's overall supply-chain operations.

Figure 9.75 reflects some of the key issues that the company must address to meet its full potential and meet its major shareholders' expectations.

Category	Rating			Category	Rating		
Business Model Overview	Y			Manufacturing	Y		
Market Position – Existing Technology	G **Y** R			Facility & Equipment	**G** Y R		
Product portfolio	G **Y** R			Value Added Operations	G Y **R**		
Logistics & Business Planning	R			WIP Inventory	G Y **R**		
Logistics Planning Hierarchy	G **Y** R			Factory Layout	G **Y** R		
Customer Service	G Y **R**			Manufacturing Cycle Time	G Y **R**		
Supply Chain Cycle Time	G Y **R**			Overall Equipment Effectiveness	G **Y** R		
Supply Chain Inventory	G Y **R**			Direct Labor Productivity	G **Y** R		
Supply Management	Y			Capacity	G **Y** R		
Controlled Materials	G Y **R**			Information Systems	**G** Y R		
Total Gas & Chemical Management	G **Y** R			Quality	R		
Spares & Consumables	G **Y** R			Yields	G Y **R**		
Key: **G** Good **Y** Acceptable **R** Of Concern				Cost of Quality	G Y **R**		

Figure 9.74   Supply-Chain Operations Analysis.

Operational Issues restricting the company from its Full-Potential
Poor Capital Management – Policies & Procedures
Long manufacturing cycle times due to high level of WIP and low Overall Equipment Efficiency
Low yields and large amount of scrap and/or inventory provisioning
Poor operator efficiency due to high level og production waste
Inefficient production planning and lot-prioritization processes.
Long new-process/production introduction time & multiple iterations

Figure 9.75   Operational Constraints.

High Impact Opportunities	P&L (annual)	Balance Sheet
Maximization of Manufacturing Throughput	20.6	11.1
Order Fulfillment Performance Management	5.4	15.0
Purchasing Best Practices	6.4	45.1
Improved Prototyping Execution	15.8	n.a.
Market Potential	tbd	n.a.
Estimated Savings ($-millions)	48.1	71.2

Figure 9.76   High-Impact Improvement Opportunities: Financial Impact.

Figure 9.76 summarizes our recommendation of high-impact improvement opportunities and estimated monetary impact of the company's Profit & Loss (P&L) and its financial Balance Sheet.

Figure 9.77 reflects the operational areas that will be impacted by the improvement initiatives (the size of the checkmark indicates a major or minor monetary impact).

Implementation of the identified high-impact opportunities will drive Cost of Goods Sold down by approximately 10% while lifting revenues by approximately 13%, resulting in a significant impact on the company's cash flow (see Figures 9.78).

Figures 9.79 and 9.80 reflect a high-level phase implementation plan.

High Impact Opportunities	Inventory Carrying Cost	Scrap (write-offs)	Material Cost	Labor	Revenue
Maximization of Manufacturing Throughput	✔	✔		✔	✔
Order Fulfillment Performance Management	✔				✔
Purchasing Best Practices	✔		✔		
Improved Prototyping Execution					✔
Market Potential					✔

Figure 9.77   High-Impact Improvement Opportunities: Impacted Areas.

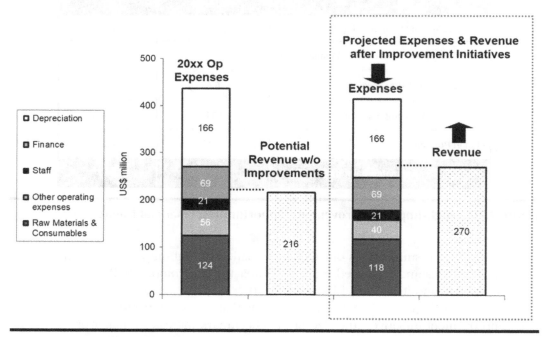

Figure 9.78   Expenses & Revenue Impact.

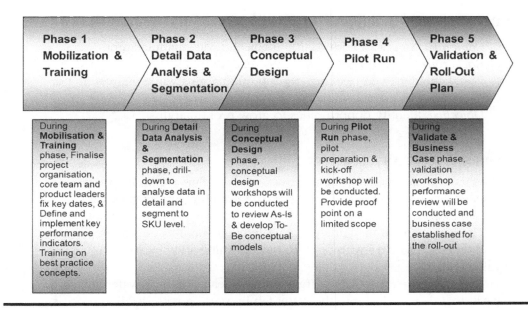

Figure 9.79   Implementation Plan: Phase Description.

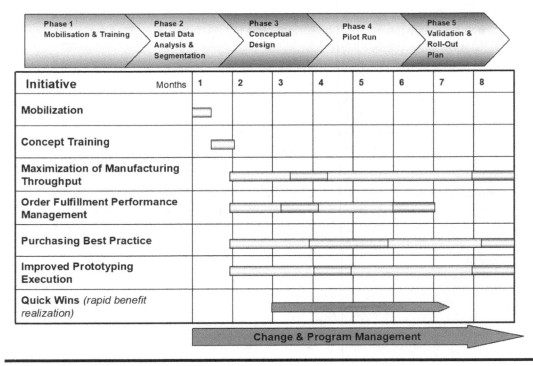

Figure 9.80   Implementation Plan: Timeline.

Case-in-Point 9.4: Supply-Chain Transformation – Medical Device

Company: American Fortune 100 medical-device manufacturer.
Background: The company was in a very competitive market space, but stakeholders were seeking larger profit margins while maintaining or growing its market share.
Objective: Identify opportunities to grow profit margins.

OPERATIONS-ASSESSMENT

The first operations-assessment activity was to value stream map a representative product. Figure 9.81 shows the resulting current-state value stream map.

The value stream map analysis revealed an overall value stream process lead time of 43.5 days with only 0.6 days of value-added activity (i.e., 1.4% value-added).

The value stream activity's largest process lead time was wafer-fab, so we'll do a deeper dive into the wafer-fab by starting with detailed process mapping utilizing the Routing-By-Walking-Around (RBWA) methodology. See Figure 9.82 for the wafer-fab process map.

- The wafer-fab process lead time (PLT) is 33.9 days (see Figure 9.83 shows the breakdown).
- 88.7% of the PLT is staging and queues.
  - There's staging/queueing between every activity.
  - Large lot sizes were used regardless of actual demand, i.e., same lot sizes for all A-B-C products.
- 6.6% of the PLT are necessary activities given the current technology and processes, but deemed non-value-added.

Through the RBWA analysis, we constructed a spaghetti diagram (see Figure 9.84), and the spaghetti diagram doesn't fully reflect the excessive movement. as there a large amount of back-and-forth movement, i.e., eight back-and-forth trips at one machine and four back-and-forth trips at another machine.

Using the process map and the value stream map, we brainstormed the following improvement opportunities (see Figure 9.85).

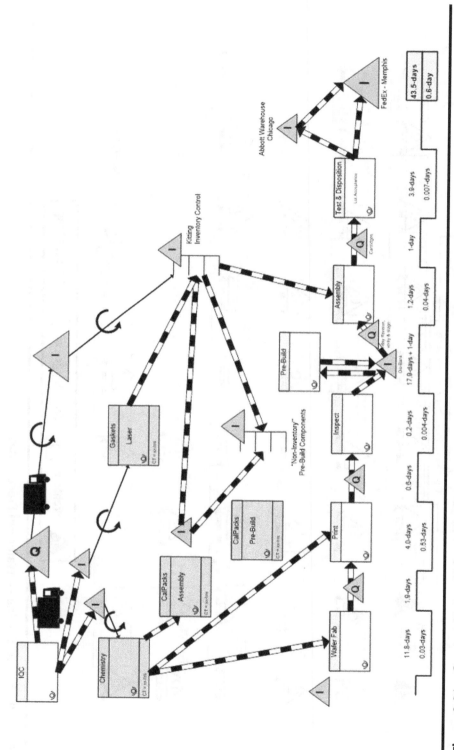

Figure 9.81   Current-State – Value Stream Map.

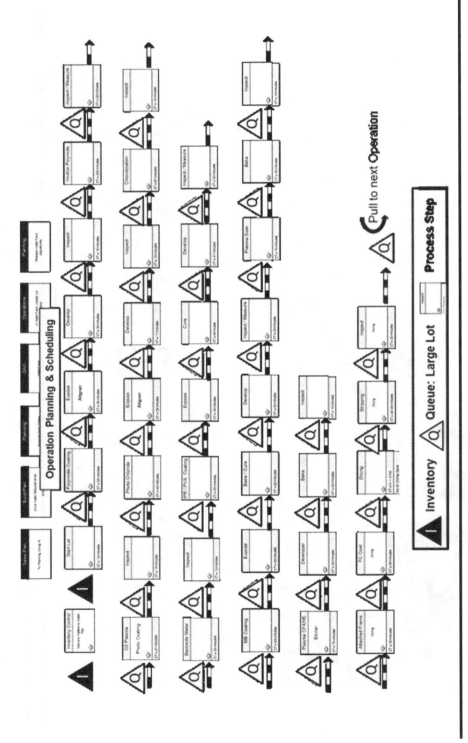

Figure 9.82 Current-State – Wafer-Fab Process Map.

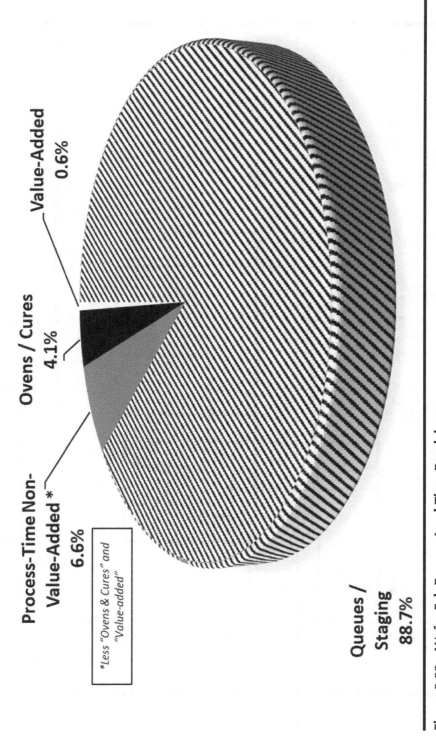

Value-Added
0.6%

Ovens / Cures
4.1%

Process-Time Non-
Value-Added *
6.6%

*Less "Ovens & Cures" and
"Value-added"

Queues /
Staging
88.7%

Figure 9.83   Wafer-Fab Process Lead Time Breakdown.

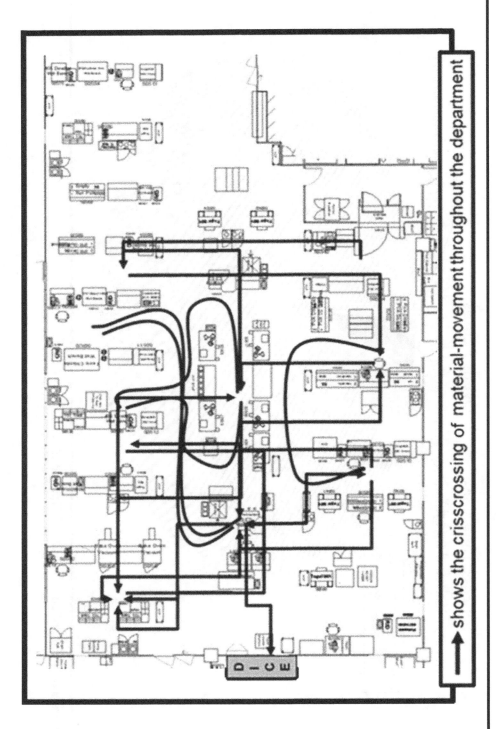

Figure 9.84 Current-State – Wafer-Fab Spaghetti Diagram.

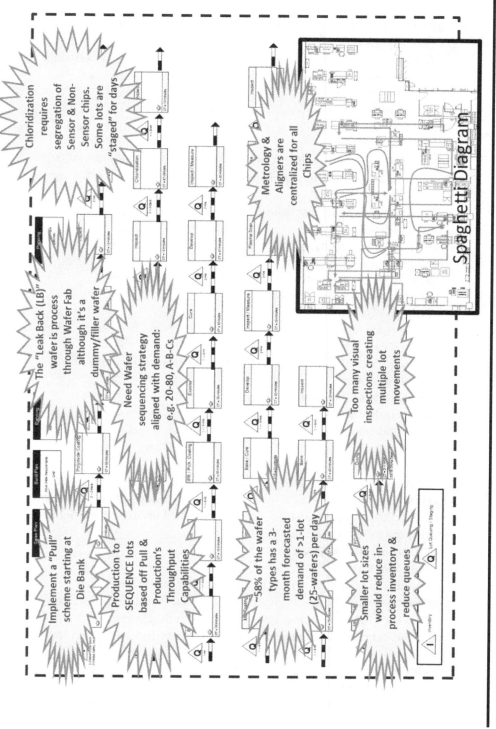

Figure 9.85 Improvement Opportunities Identified – Kaizen Bursts.

The improvement opportunities were summarized as:

1. Wafer-fab pull/lot-sequencing: Wafer-lot starts are not sequenced with process capability.
   - Implement Pull-Supermarkets to decouple functional-processing.
   - Sequence wafer-lot starts to balance equipment utilization.
   - Potential benefits:
     - Reduced Process Lead Time by 30–50%.
     - Improved Labor Efficiency, i.e., direct labor (DL), indirect labor (IDL).
     - WIP reduction, which equates to less time managing the WIP and less shrinkage/spoilage, which equates to about 10% of the value of the WIP.
     - Process Reliability (predictability), i.e., downstream confidence.
2. Inspection rationalization: Visual inspections are too frequent and require excessive movements of lots to/from centralized Metrology stations, e.g., Product-X chip has eight (8) visual inspections.
   - Minimize visual inspections.
   - Potential benefits:
     - Reduce movement of carriers to direct labor/from Inspection stations
     - Improve DL productivity. Each inspection takes approximately 10 minutes.
3. Lot size reduction @ post wafer-fab.
   - Reduce the "lot" sizes for wafers being processed post-fab.
   - Potential benefits:
     - Shorter lot cycle times at post-fab operations.
     - Less WIP.
4. Non-functional wafer outsourcing: The Leak Back (LB) is non-functional wafer that serves as a filler on some cartridges. It is currently processed through Wafer-Fab. And this adds additional movement and administrative effort for Fab.
   - Outsource the LB wafer.
   - Potential benefits:
     - Removes "noise" from the Wafer-Fab operations.
5. Optimize product flow – high runners: Layout is not optimized to process the highest-volume wafers. Centralized Aligners and Metrology stations created non-value-added lot movement and additional lot queueing.
   - Optimize layout for "A" wafers. Create a single cell for the "A"s.
   - Potential benefits:
     - Eliminate non-value-added activities: e.g., transportation, waiting, WIP.

6. Duplicate chloridization wet table: Sensor and un-sensor wafers must be segregated at the chloridization process, and this causes a large WIP buildup at the chloridization process.
   – Dedicate a chloridization wet table to Sensor and Non-Sensor wafers.
     • Smoother flow of wafer through Wafer-Fab. (Not required if "Wafer-Fab Pull/Lot-Sequencing" is implemented.)

Then a Benefit & Effort chart was created for these opportunities (see Figure 9.86).

The top three improvement opportunities are projected to save $200k annually.

1. Wafer-Fab Pull/Lot-Sequencing (see Figure 9.87)
   – Reduced Process Lead Time by 30–50%.
   – Improved Labor Efficiency, i.e., DL, IDL, and Planning (a cost savings of approximately 10% of the operating cost is seen as feasible but unconfirmed).
   – WIP reduction, which equates to less time managing the WIP and less shrinkage/spoilage.
   – Process Reliability (predictability), i.e., downstream confidence.
2. Inspection Rationalization
   – Reduce movement of carriers to/from Inspection stations. Improve spaghetti diagram.

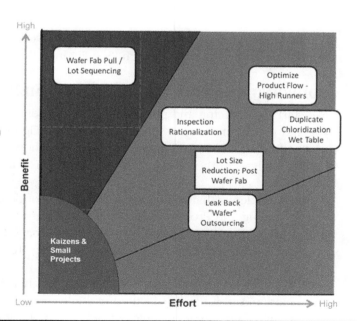

Figure 9.86   Improvement Opportunities Identified – Benefit & Effort.

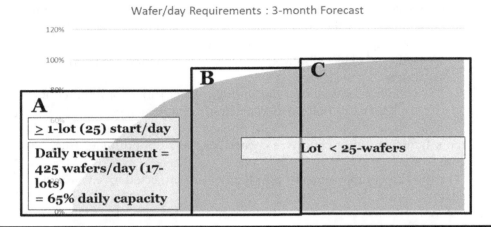

Figure 9.87   No A-B-C Differentiation for Lot-Sizing/-Sequencing.

- Improve DL productivity. Each inspection takes approximately 10 minutes.
3. Lot Size Reduction at Post Wafer-Fab
   - Wafers are processed through the Print/Inspect operations as single wafers, so the overall flow through the Print/Inspect operations would be improved by processing the low-volume wafers (e.g., Demand: <25-wafers/week) at lot sizes of less than 25 (processed based on actual demand, i.e., "pull" signal).

The wafer-fab pull/lot-sequencing initiative would be expanded beyond Wafer-Fab across the value stream. See Figure 9.88.

SOURCING AND PROCUREMENT ASSESSMENT

We start the sourcing and procurement assessment by populating the sourcing and procurement assessment template. See Figure 9.89.

The findings from the template analysis are shown in Figure 9.90.

The analysis of the procurement assessment is summarized below:

- No evidence that Industry (Life Sciences nor Semiconductor) Sourcing and Procurement Best Practices are being deployed, e.g., Commodity Management, Vendor-Managed Inventory/Replenishment, Low-Cost Country sourcing, Total Cost of Ownership assessments, etc.
- Purchased Parts inventory levels are far higher than industry benchmarks. And it has been stated multiple times that it's the company's point of view that "inventory levels" are not a focus (concern). But higher inventory levels do the following:

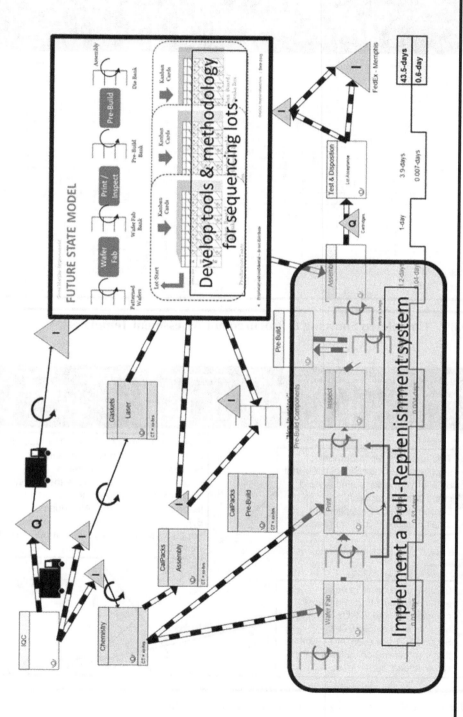

Figure 9.88 Future-State VSM with Pull-Replenishment & Lot-Sequencing.

Commodity	Annual Volume		Number of Articles (SKUs)	Average Inventory				Number of Suppliers		Purchase Orders	
	Value ($-thousands)	% of Total		Quantity (thousands)	Value ($-thousands)	Coverage (days)	Obsolescence ($-thousands)	North America	Overseas	No. of PO's	% of Total
Wafers	9.350	14.64%	44	31	1.409	55	93	4		74	1.39%
Base/Cover/Case	8.918	13.96%	63	35.712	2.221	91	71	4		144	2.71%
Chemicals - Other NORTH AMERICA	4.991	7.81%	330	2.164	2.053	150	268	50		651	12.23%
Consumables - Production	3.832	6.00%	1.400	120	3.533	337	77	130	4	1.677	31.52%
TG Adhesives	3.515	5.50%	7	3	642	67	31	3		23	0.43%
Bloodport Gasket	2.538	3.97%	2	2.317	103	15	7	1		16	0.30%
Packaging - Roll Stock (e.g. Pouch)	1.729	2.71%	27	28.870	716	151	56	1	1	11	0.21%
Diaphragm	1.134	1.78%	1	1.156	214	69	12	1		7	0.13%
Other direct materials	1.018	1.59%	54	9.431	534	191	17	7		58	1.09%
Desiccant	705	1.10%	5	5.992	273	141	0	1		12	0.23%
Labels (e.g. Cover Label)	638	1.00%	40	18.630	196	112	38	5		29	0.55%
Packaging - Paper/Boxes	621	0.97%	49	1.490	285	168	61	1		16	0.30%
Chemicals - Other IMPORT OVERSEAS	483	0.76%	9	68	73	55	2		5	29	0.55%
Barrier Film	295	0.46%	1	2.195	98	121	4	1		2	0.04%
Capture Antibody	235	0.37%	5	1	178	276	0	3	2	17	0.32%
Label Antibody	134	0.21%	3	0.3	123	335	12		2	6	0.11%
Packaging - Other	106	0.17%	2	2.179	31	107	4	1		3	0.06%
Gaskets - Other	29	0.05%	1	5.691	11	140	0	1		1	0.02%
Outside Services	5.329	8.34%	n/a	n/a	n/a	n/a	n/a	251	1	588	11.05%
Other	18.279	28.62%	n/a	n/a	n/a	n/a	n/a	395	9	1.957	36.78%
TOTAL	63,879	100.00%	2,043	116,051	12,693	143	752	860	24	5,321	100.00%

Figure 9.89   Completed Sourcing & Procurement Assessment Template.

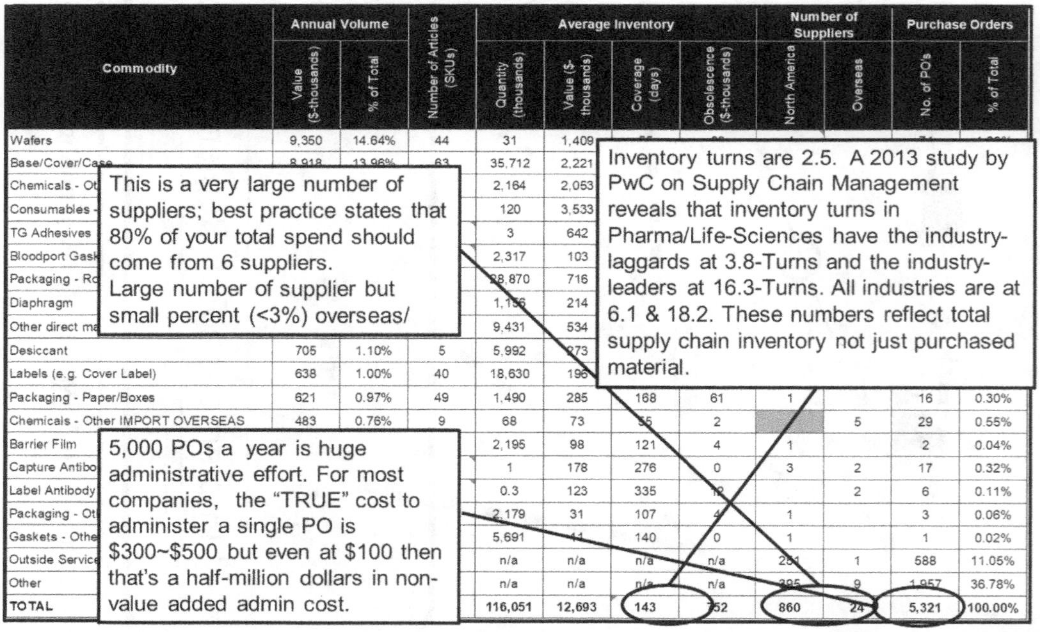

Commodity	Annual Volume		Number of Articles (SKUs)	Average Inventory				Number of Suppliers		Purchase Orders	
	Value ($-thousands)	% of Total		Quantity (thousands)	Value ($- thousands)	Coverage (days)	Obsolescence ($-thousands)	North America	Overseas	No. of PO's	% of Total
Wafers	9,350	14.64%	44	31	1,409						
Base/Cover/Case	8,918	13.96%	63	35,712	2,221						
Chemicals - Ot				2,164	2,053						
Consumables -				120	3,533						
TG Adhesives				3	642						
Bloodport Gask				2,317	103						
Packaging - Ro				28,870	716						
Diaphragm				1,156	214						
Other direct ma				9,431	534						
Desiccant	705	1.10%	5	5,992	273						
Labels (e.g. Cover Label)	638	1.00%	40	18,630	196						
Packaging - Paper/Boxes	621	0.97%	49	1,490	285	168	61	1		16	0.30%
Chemicals - Other IMPORT OVERSEAS	483	0.76%	9	68	73	55	2		5	29	0.55%
Barrier Film				2,195	98	121	4	1		2	0.04%
Capture Antibo				1	178	276	0	3	2	17	0.32%
Label Antibody				0.3	123	335			2	6	0.11%
Packaging - Ot				2,179	31	107	4	1		3	0.06%
Gaskets - Othe				5,691	11	140	0	1		1	0.02%
Outside Service				n/a	n/a	n/a	n/a	251	1	588	11.05%
Other				n/a	n/a	n/a	n/a	395	9	1,957	36.78%
TOTAL				116,051	12,693	143	752	860	24	5,321	100.00%

This is a very large number of suppliers; best practice states that 80% of your total spend should come from 6 suppliers.
Large number of supplier but small percent (<3%) overseas/

Inventory turns are 2.5. A 2013 study by PwC on Supply Chain Management reveals that inventory turns in Pharma/Life-Sciences have the industry-laggards at 3.8-Turns and the industry-leaders at 16.3-Turns. All industries are at 6.1 & 18.2. These numbers reflect total supply chain inventory not just purchased material.

5,000 POs a year is huge administrative effort. For most companies, the "TRUE" cost to administer a single PO is $300~$500 but even at $100 then that's a half-million dollars in non-value added admin cost.

Figure 9.90   Finding from Sourcing & Procurement Template.

- Consume valuable space which contributes to the need for a third-party warehouse which results in approximately $275k in outside services expenses plus additional non-value-added/"waste" activities (e.g., double and triple handling of material, added administrative efforts, added queues/staging, damaged material, etc.).
- Contribute to the scrap of >$750k in purchased material annually.
- Hide ineffective procurement processes and sourcing strategies (and hide high scrap rates).

■ Not leveraging some of the strong and very cost-competitive medical-device production capabilities in Southeast Asia (e.g., foil-packaging, plastics).

■ Overall high inventory levels of excess and obsolete material are "attributed" to the new product project.

- Ineffective Stage-Gate processes, Risk-Assessment analysis, accountability.

We have projected that a 5+% ($2 million) Purchased-Price-Variance (PPV) should be obtainable by a Strategic Sourcing/Procurement initiative. And this should be an ongoing annual PPV target.

■ Benchmarking data shows generically industries achieve an annual PPV of 3–4% but semiconductor >5% YOY PPV.

Figure 9.91 graphically shows the company's total spend.

Figures 9.92 through 9.96 graphically show the company's direct production spend.

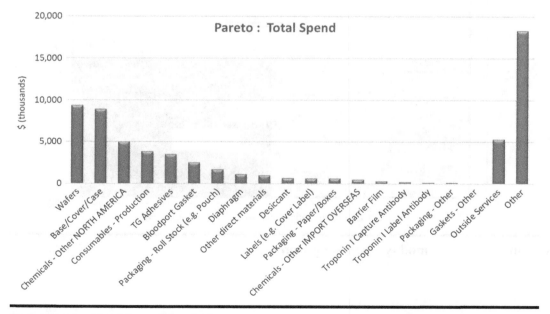

Figure 9.91 Total Spend Analysis.

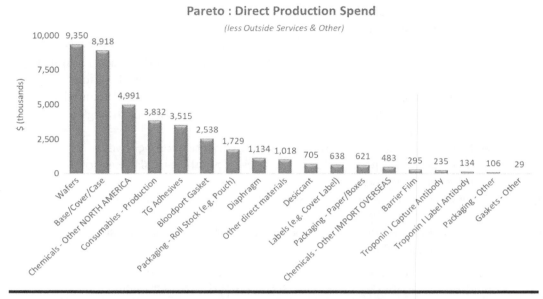

Figure 9.92   Deep-Dive Spend Analysis: Direct Production Spend.

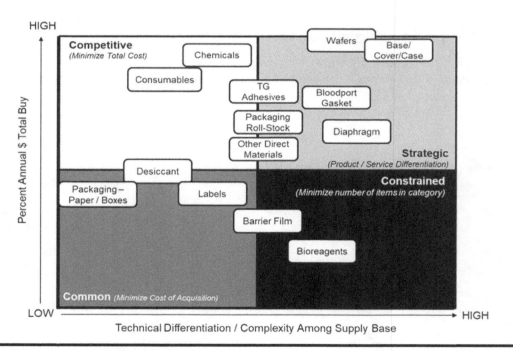

Figure 9.93   Commodity Positioning Matrix.

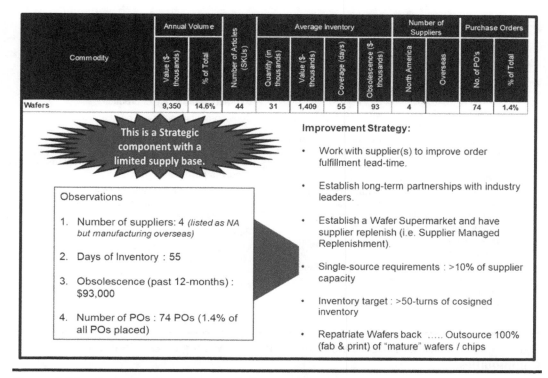

Figure 9.94   Example: Sourcing Analysis – Wafers.

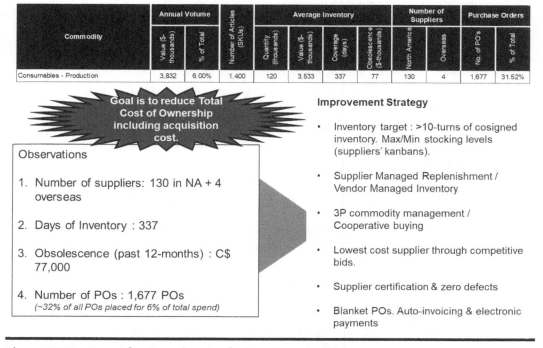

Figure 9.95   Example: Sourcing Analysis – Consumables.

Procurement Processes

STRATEGIC Commodities

- All logistic and commercial terms fixed in multi-year cooperative contracts
- Early involvement of suppliers in new product design for manufacturing / logistics
- Forecasts shared for capacity management purposes only, without commitment
- Manufacturing lead-times reduced to less than end-customer requirements
- Actual internal production schedule requirements communicated daily
- Mixed lots corresponding to daily requirements delivered directly to point of use; packaging and labeling include all information required to enable delivery to user without look-up
- Receipt of goods enables tracking of supplier delivery reliability
- "Back flush" increments consumption count and approves auto-invoice and electronic payment
- Suppliers and processes certified: No source or inbound inspection, no counting

COMMON Commodities

- The key principles: simplification and cost minimization
- All logistic and commercial terms fixed in contract covering "life of product"
- Consignment inventory at point of use
- Vendor managed replenishment based on "two bin" system
- Receiving increments consumption count and approves payment
- Consolidated monthly auto-invoice and electronic payment covering all shipments during the period
- Reusable packaging
- Items are not entered in materials planning system. There are no inventory transactions related to these items. For financial valuation purposes, the inventory is fixed at the average level.

Figure 9.96 Example: Procurement Strategies for "Strategic" & "Common" Commodities.

Final observations and opportunities to apply best practices (i.e., current gaps against best practices):

1. Operational-Excellence deployment gaps:
   - Balanced scorecard: cascading key performance indicators.
   - Focus: Vital (critical) few versus trivial many.
   - Cross-training/cross-functional (flexible and responsive workforce)/ job rotation.
   - "Project-Based" mentality: Once a project (or initiative) is complete, everyone moves on; no sustainment/control measures.
2. New Product Development: Design-for-Six-Sigma (DFSS)
   - Voice-of-Business/Voice-of-Customer/Voice-of-Process.
   - Effective stage-gate process. Add structure and ensure deliverables are complete.
   - Identify Critical-to-Quality (CTQ) upfront: Quality-Functional-Deployment (QFD)/CTQ correlation matrix.
   - Failure-Mode-Effect-Analysis (mistake-proofing)/risk-analysis.
3. Oliver Wight (OW) Business Excellence – Class A "Gaps"
   - "Heart and Soul" of OW is Sales and Operations Planning.
   - Strong reliance on Operational Excellence (a.k.a. Business Excellence).
   - Driving business-improvement (e.g., velocity throughout all business processes, pull).

Measurement	Worst	Average	Best	Company A
Wafer Starts Per Month / 1000 Sq.Ft. Gross	5	265	810	1,470
Cycle-Time / Mask-Layers (days)	3.7	2.75	1.5	2.9
Mask-Layers/Day to DL Headcount	18.4	42.6	71.7	40
Mask-Layers/Day to Total Headcount	8.8	32.5	57.3	22
Operators to Supervisors	6.0	11.0	15.0	24
Fab OEE (bottleneck)	64%	69%	85%	Not Measured
No. of Inspection Steps to Avg. Total Steps	40%	24.5%	10%	20%
Sales (US$) per Employee		$425k		$365k

Figure 9.97 Semiconductor Measurements Benchmarking.

- Managing the supply chain (e.g., inventory, data, and effectiveness).
- Managing the internal supply (e.g., velocity, lead time performance, and inventory).
- Managing the external sourcing (e.g., Total Cost of Ownership).

With semiconductor processes being the most critical portion of the value stream, we benchmarked this company's performance measurements against industry performance (see Figure 9.97).

Company A, in Figure 9.97, is the company that we were assessing. Figure 9.97 shows that they out-performed their industry counterparts in wafer-starts and operator-to-supervisor ratio; and in most of the other areas, they performed adequately near the average levels.

But one key metric, Overall Equipment Effectiveness (OEE), was not measured; but measuring OEE at bottlenecks is required to optimize performance and flow.

Case-in-Point 9.5: Optimizing a Supply Chain in Heavy Industry

Company: An Asian heavy-industry (a.k.a. engineer-to-order) manufacturer/ builder, a subsidiary of a Fortune Global 500 conglomerate.

Background: The company has a highly diversified business portfolio of manufacturing and construction projects such as nuclear power plants, thermal power stations, turbines, and generators.

Project Objective: The company was planning to implement an enterprise-wide information-technology system to support its order-fulfillment processes, but prior to its implementation, they wanted to assess and subsequently improve/optimize all of its order-fulfillment processes.

The company faced many challenges, as highlighted in Figure 9.98, and the biggest challenge is the nature of its business, i.e., complex customized engineering projects and products with process lead times of multiple years.

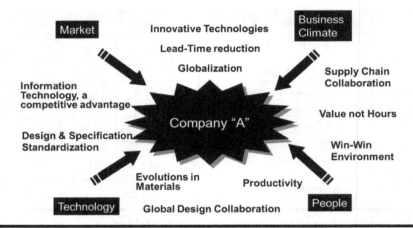

Figure 9.98 Challenges: Business Landscape.

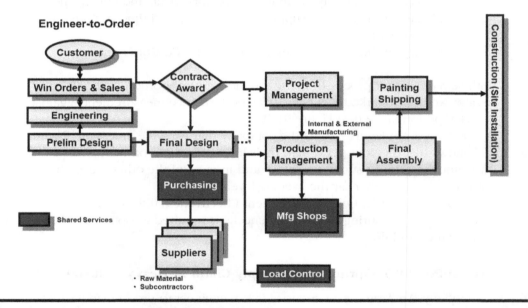

Figure 9.99 Win & Fulfill Orders Model.

Figure 9.99 is a very high level of the company's "win and fulfill orders" model. The company had several business units; each business unit had its own sales, engineering, production management, project management, and final assembly groups, but they shared purchasing and manufacturing operations.

Figure 9.100 shows the generic flow and elements of the "Win and Fulfill Orders" process.

Figure 9.101 reflects the complex and highly fragmented project-based planning and scheduling activities.

For this case-in-point example, I'll share information on our deep dive into one of the company's more traditional products, a "turbine."

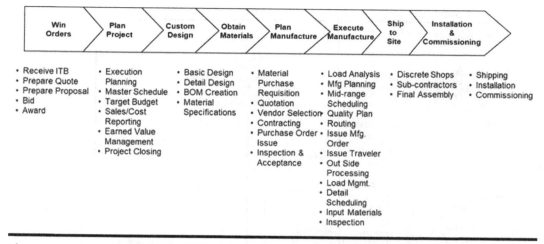

Figure 9.100   Win & Fulfill Orders Process.

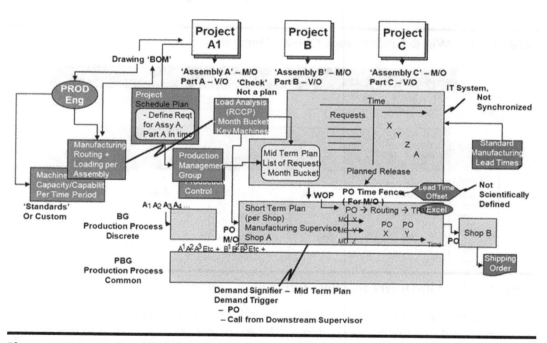

Figure 9.101   Project Planning & Scheduling Model.

This company produces a large range of customized and proprietary turbines primarily used in power generation, with steam turbines being the most common type produced. Figure 9.102 gives an overview of the "win and fulfill orders" model and timeline for turbines, which averages four years.

Figure 9.103 shows a more detailed breakdown of the "win-orders" elements and time line for the turbines, which averages 10 months.

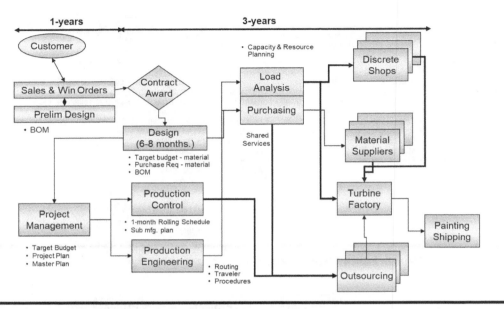

Figure 9.102   Win & Fulfill Orders Overall Timeline.

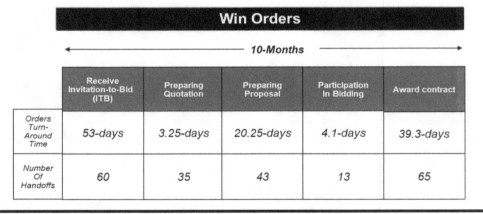

	Receive Invitation-to-Bid (ITB)	Preparing Quotation	Preparing Proposal	Participation In Bidding	Award contract
Orders Turn-Around Time	53-days	3.25-days	20.25-days	4.1-days	39.3-days
Number Of Handoffs	60	35	43	13	65

Figure 9.103   Win-Orders Timeline: Turbines.

Figure 9.104 shows a more detailed breakdown of the "plan project" elements and timeline for the turbines. The elemental timeline is broken down for a 36-day cycle time, but the process's cycle-time range is 36 to 120 days. The element "Earned Value Management," a project management technique for measuring project performance and progress against objectives, has a cycle time of 15.6 days, with 165 hand-offs (a.k.a. transfers between departments).

Figure 9.105 shows a more detailed breakdown of the "obtain material" elements and timeline for the turbines. The elemental timeline is broken down for a cycle-time range of one to four weeks, but the process's cycle-time range is one to seven months.

Plan Project						
	Project Execution Planning	Master Schedule	Target Budgeting	Sales/Cost Reporting	Earned Value Management	Project Financial Closing
Orders Turn-Around Time	5.73-days	1.57-days	8.93-days	2.68-days	15.52-days	1.28-days
Number Of Handoffs	36	52	11	25	165	17

36- ~ 120-days

Figure 9.104 Plan Project Timeline: Turbines.

Obtain Material						
	Material Purchase Requisition	Quotation for Purchasing	Vendor Selection	Contracting	Purchase Order Issue	Inspection And acceptance
Orders Turn-Around Time			1-4 Weeks			Domestic: 0.18-'day Import: 0.39-day
Number Of Handoffs	10	15	3	11	PRP: 16 Other: 13	Domestic: 25 Import: 46

1- ~ 7-months*

* Supplier lead-time 2-6 months

Figure 9.105 Obtain Materials Timeline: Turbines.

"Obtain Materials" observations (observations relevant to all business units):

■ The request-for-pricing process is fragmented and lengthy, and the design team often bypasses the procurement team and goes directly to potential suppliers.
■ Supplier selection is not based on total cost of ownership, nor the supplier's technical capabilities, etc.; the selection is based solely on the lowest purchased price.
■ There's no differentiating in the request-for-quote, supplier selection, or procurement processes; the same process is used for all items regardless of value, including over 50 million MRO (maintenance, repair, and operations) items with an average cost of US $0.001/each.
■ MRO items' requirements are determined by individuals based on personal-expectations (not substantiated by calculations or bill-of-materials, etc.) and submitted via Excel.

- Inventory is not managed systematically, and no A-B-C stratification exists.
- They don't maintain an Item-Master for item specifications, supplier info, etc. Individual business units keep some data on Excel spreadsheets.

Figure 9.106 shows the planning cycle for all self-manufactured items; the average planning cycle takes 35 days, but for a turbine "plan manufacture" that we tracked (via historical transactions, i.e., paperwork), the cycle time was 76.5 days. The incoming quality inspection of the material took 26.8 days with a total of 267 hand-offs.

Figure 9.107 shows the manufacturing supply chain for turbines.

	Plan Manufacture											
	Load Analysis	Mfg Planning	Mid-range Scheduling	Preparing Quality Plan	Routing	Issuing Mfg Order	Issuing Traveller	O S P	Load Mgt.	Detail Scheduling	Input Materials	Quality Inspection
Orders Turn-Around Time	7.70-days	1.87-days	25.48-days	0.68 day	1.43-days	0.17-days	4.75-days	2.98-days	2.30-days	1.40-days	1.17-days	26.79-days
Number Of Handoffs	28	32	98	7	10	18	38	49	29	26	17	267

35-days

Figure 9.106   Plan Manufacture Timeline: Turbines.

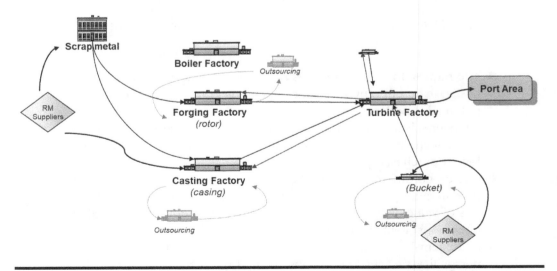

Figure 9.107   Manufacturing Supply-Chain: Turbines.

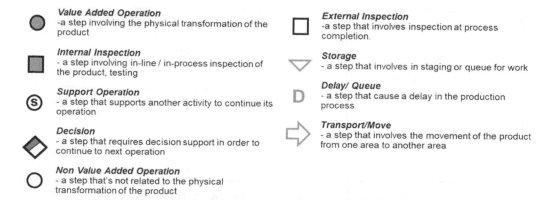

Value Added Operation
-a step involving the physical transformation of the product

Internal Inspection
- a step involving in-line / in-process inspection of the product, testing

Support Operation
- a step that supports another activity to continue its operation

Decision
- a step that requires decision support in order to continue to next operation

Non Value Added Operation
- a step that's not related to the physical transformation of the product

External Inspection
-a step that involves inspection at process completion.

Storage
- a step that involves in staging or queue for work

Delay/ Queue
- a step that cause a delay in the production process

Transport/Move
- a step that involves the movement of the product from one area to another area

Figure 9.108   Current-State Manufacturing Process Map: Turbines.

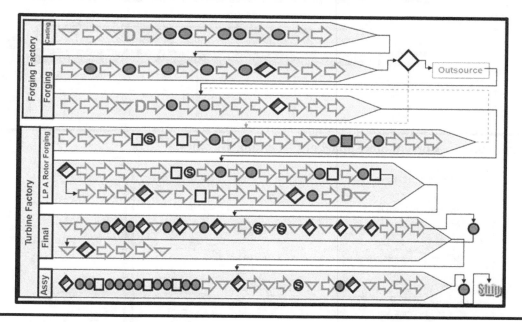

Figure 9.109   Process-Mapping Symbols.

Figure 9.108 shows the process map that was created from the Routing-By-Walking-Around (RBWA). Figure 9.109 is a legend of the symbols utilized in the process mapping.

The RBWA was not fully developed by our traditional means due to the very long cycle time, but we did walk the process, observing every activity and collecting transaction data (i.e., paperwork) to construct a representative timeline.

Figure 9.110 shows the process time obtained by the RBWA. The total manufacture cycle time totaled 885 days, with 55% of the process time being non-value-added. Storage or queues between manufacturing departments is over 250 days.

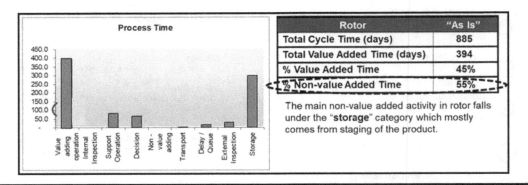

Figure 9.110   Current-State Manufacturing Process Map: Turbines.

	Casting	Forging	Turbine Factory	Forging	Turbine Factory	Turbine Factory	Turbine Factory	Total
Orders Turn-Around Time (days)	9	150	110	83	168	267	98	885
Number Of Handoffs	4	2	2	2	6	4	8	30

Figure 9.111   Current-State Spaghetti Diagram: Turbines.

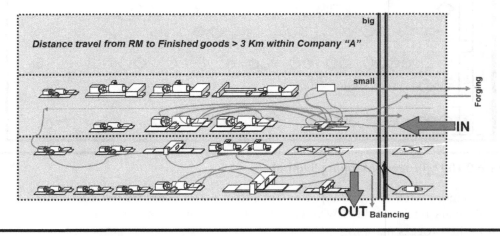

Figure 9.112   Current-State Manufacturing Process Breakdown: Turbines.

Figure 9.111 shows the flow of the turbine through the manufacturing functions and the breakdown of the 885 days of manufacturing cycle time.

Figure 9.112 shows a spaghetti diagram created from the RBWA data. The turbine travels over three kilometers (>1.86-miles) between manufacturing departments (buildings).

"Manufacturing Execution" observations (observations relevant to all business units):

- Long manufacturing cycle times:
  - Travel between multiple locations.
  - Large number of hand-offs and endorsements between functions within an organization (but far fewer than most other order-fulfillment processes).
  - Excessive (days) storage to stage the part for the next operation in a different factory site.
  - Lack of visibility of product flow for an effective pull mechanism, which results in excessive manual scheduling to transport the parts from one operation to another.
- Quality Assurance:
  - Heavily relies on visual inspection.
  - Lack of a robust quality-management system.
  - Inadequate process controls; relies on detection rather than prevention.
  - Excessive levels of visual inspection and redundant tests because of "Band-Aid" solutions, i.e., a huge example of over-processing waste.
- Indirect costs resulting from fragmented subcontracting activities:
  - Fragmented subcontracting operational processes disrupting flow, e.g., company "A" incoming material inspection → staging → outsourcing operations → staging → subsequent company "A" operations.
  - Subcontracting projects with at least two different contractors (everything based on lowest price, not highest value).
- Planning
  - No visibility of what product will be arriving on different site (functions are completed in "silos," i.e., "throwing-it-over-the-wall."
  - Some parts are outsourced due to unscheduled workload (a.k.a. unplanned demand) on different factory sites (i.e., there's no enterprise-wide integrated planning).
- Process Technology:
  - Casting and forging processes are not the leading-edge technology but rather basic standards of the industry.
  - Manufacturing process would benefit from implementing lean building blocks across all operations.

Summary of issues and opportunities across all functions (enterprise-wide and the end-to-end order-fulfillment processes):

- Project management methodologies are used across all processes, e.g., obtain materials, plan manufacture, execute manufacture, etc., i.e., not following best practices for manufacturing a product. Planning is by Microsoft Project and Excel.

Impact: Excessively long lead times and manufacturing inefficiencies, which stymie process innovations.

■ Mid-term schedule is a list of product requirements ignoring resource constraints.
  - No planning controls.
  - No linkage to production routers.
■ No production synchronization.
  Impact: Scheduling conflicts have to be resolved by manufacturing supervisor.
■ Lack of standardized business processes.
  Impact: Process inefficiencies and long lead times.
■ Minimal linkages of any master data across projects, but in most cases no master data exists.
  Impact: Process inefficiencies and long lead times, continuously "re-inventing" on every project.
■ No integration and poor utilization of existing information. Fragmented information system, with minimum linkage of data and information.
  - No Bill-of-Materials (BOM) standardization. Different BOMs for quotations, project targets, and production.
  - No baseline/standardization for product design.
  - No easily assessable design rules, etc., to drive standardization and reuse engineering. Need to establish commonalities, modularity, and configurability.
  - *Impact: Excessively long lead times for design, estimating, planning, etc. And continuously "reinventing" items.*
■ Engineering change process is poorly structured. Poor communication to affected parties. Process needs to be streamlined.
  Impact: Unnecessary rework.
■ Inefficient purchasing process and practices, i.e., poor utilization of preliminary purchasing process; supplier selection based on cost, not cost-of-ownership; minimal contract-based purchases, etc. Lack of supply-management strategies.
  Impact: High cost-of-ownership.
■ Lack of collaboration in bidding process. No historical database. Personal experiences are the driving factor.
  Impact: Process inefficiencies, long process times, inaccurate bids.
■ No data or system to support or validate project management decisions, i.e., cost data, KPIs, procedure monitoring system, etc.
  Impact: Process inefficiencies and uniformed decisions.
■ Duplicated efforts: routings, travelers, quality inspection plans, etc.
  Impact: Non-value-added activities.
■ Poor communication between business groups.
  Impact: No leveraging of efforts. No economies of scale.

- Processes and roles/responsibilities restructuring needed in design and project management, production control and technology, and quality control to reduce lead times and improve efficiency. of operations and overall effectiveness of project management.

    Impact: Non-value-added activities. Long lead time and process inefficiencies.

- Need to reduce pre-production activities and lead time of activities such as target budgeting and other non-value-added supporting activities.

    Impact: Non-value-added activities and long lead times.

- General issues related to scheduling:
    - Lack of integration between production control, production and equipment load analysis, and shop floor's load analysis. Upstream activities are unconsciously assuming infinite downstream capacity.
    - Manual coordination between shop-management department and shop floor to inform progress of WIP, information for scheduling. No visual management.
    - No roll-up of individual functional detailed schedules.
    - Lack of effective planning integration.
    - Overall lack of collaboration by key functions.

Case-in-Point 9.6: Optimizing a Fast-Moving Consumer-Goods (FMCG) Supply Chain

Company: Japanese FMCG manufacturer.

Background: One of the company's Asian manufacturing and distribution networks was performing at an unacceptable 60% customer-service level, as they were failing to have the right items at the right quantity at the right time at the right place, which was projected to result in about $20 million in lost sales per year.

The company's current situation was characterized by:

- Having four "central" warehouses that resulted in unnecessary complexity and therefore delays in shipping of products.
- There were large variations in performance, including service levels, inventory turns, space utilization and costs, across company "A"'s 18 sales offices.
- There are significant differences in costs and service levels among the nine third-party distribution service companies that company "A" used.
- There was a lot of manual intervention in the planning process that erroneously affected inventory balances across warehouses.

■ All of the company "A"'s major competitors were moving to structures where they used intermediaries to serve the traditional trade, and the competitors are moving away from third-party distribution companies.

Project Objectives:

■ Develop an understanding of the overall structure of the supply chain:
  – Product flows.
  – Costs.
  – Cycle times/lead times.
  – Service levels.
■ Carry out assessments of key components of the supply chain and its associated planning processes:
  – Central Warehouses.
  – Sales Offices.
  – Transportation.
  – Sales and Operations Planning.
■ Develop descriptions of the supply-chain structure of competing firms for comparative purposes.

Project Approach:

■ The *SCOR®* (Supply Chain Operations Research model) methodology was used as the basic framework for information collection and analysis.
■ Interviews were carried out with company "A" employees, both in management and operations, to understand current processes (e.g., sales operations, order processing, logistics planning, and sales and operations planning).
■ Data collection (through interviews, site visits, and self-assessment questionnaires) and analysis were carried out in the following areas:
  – Inventory levels.
  – Productivity and utilization of resources.
  – Product portfolio.
  – Supply-chain networking.
  – Cost of supply chain.
  – Structure of supply chain.
■ Sampling assessments were carried out to measure performance since company "A" does not currently capture performance measures such as order fill rate, shipping accuracy, truck utilization, lost sales, etc.

The company's supply chain was overly complex, with multiple factories, multiple central warehouses (4), and 18 sales offices, which led to an average 75-day order-fulfillment process lead time for its domestic market, in a country that's only about 20% larger in area (square feet) than California. And the company's manufacturing sites and "central" warehouses were centrally located, geographically and demographically, within the country, which should have resulted in shorter lead times. See Figure 9.113 for an overview of the current-state supply-chain model.

Figure 9.114 is a snapshot of the Finished-Goods inventory levels at the time of the assessment. The snapshot shows a very high level of inventory, especially for the "A"s, which should be your fast-moving, high-demand products; but the "A"s make up 68% of the total.

Figure 9.115 has a breakdown of the total cost associated with the existing supply-chain model.

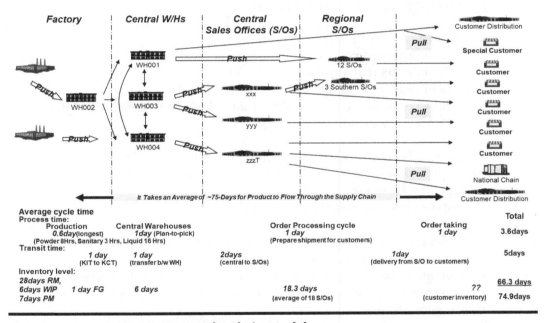

Figure 9.113   Current-State Supply-Chain Model.

Current Inventory	**US$ 11.4-million**
Annual Carrying Cost	**US$1.7-million**
Current Inventory-$ by Classification	
A	$7.7M
B	$1.97M
C	$1.71M
Total	$11.4M

Figure 9.114   Current-State Finished-Goods Inventory.

Figure 9.115   Current-State Supply-Chain Cost-Breakdown.

And the fragmented supply chain and excessive process lead time led to poor supply-chain performance, particularly the customer-service level of 60%.

The 60% OTIF can be broken down as:

■ *% On-Time-In-Full (OTIF) = 60%*
  – % of orders completed in full = 89%
  – % of orders partially completed = 10%
  – % of orders not fulfilled = 1%
  – % Delivered as promised = 67% (delivered within approximately 3 days)
  – % Accuracy of shipment = 97%

And the above breakdown shows that they only have the right product at the right quantity 89% of the time, which is poor, but the delivery on-time percentage was far worse, at 67%.

The supply-chain assessment has revealed:

■ Having four central warehouses results in complexity and therefore delays in shipping out products (see Figure 9.116).
■ There are large variations in performance levels – including service levels, inventory turns, space utilization and costs – across company "A"'s sales offices.
■ There are significant differences in costs and service levels among the nine third-party transport companies company "A" currently uses.
■ There are some differences in company "A"'s own fleet-utilization levels across sales offices.
■ There were a lot of manual interventions in the planning process that affected inventory balances across warehouses.

The issues related to the current-state central warehouse configuration are:

■ Insufficient number of loading bays, resulting in trucks having excessive queues.
■ Shortage of staff to prepare, pick, load, and unload products.

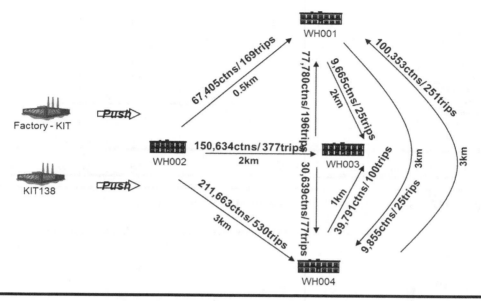

Figure 9.116   Central Warehouse Complexity.

- Warehouse #1: Limited space for shipment preparation (creates inefficiencies).
- Warehouse #1: Insufficient support for handling equipment.
- Warehouse #3: Accessibility problem; no space for truck to turn or pick up products.
- Warehouse #3: Sloping storage space (wasted vertical) and located in a subsided (a.k.a. underdeveloped) area of the greater capital area.
- Warehouse #4: Located in a subsided and flood-prone area (high-risk area to be isolated by floods).
- Warehouse #4: Had no shelter for trucks while loading or unloading (which were a high risk in the tropical climate).

Company "A" had 18 sales offices that processed 70% of total sales. The sales offices hold and distribute inventory (i.e., small distribution centers). None of the sales offices' customer-service levels were at acceptable levels; the highest On-Time-In-Full was 79%, and the lowest was 38% (see Figure 9.117).

The inventory levels at the sales office were poorly managed (particularly based on the poor customer-service levels); the inventory turns are about two (see Figure 9.118).

And the average utilization of the sales offices was a lowly 61%, which suggests that there was an opportunity for consolidation (see Figure 9.119).

Some of the inventory and service performance issues were attributable to poor communication between sales, distribution, and production, as they

%orders completed in full	87	83	89	90	100	93	86	99	99	85	73	82	71	86	91	94	79	95
%orders partially completed	13	17	11	10	0	7	13	1	0	15	19	18	29	14	8	6	19	4
%orders not fulfilled	0	0	0	0	0	0	1	0	1	0	9	0	0	0	1	0	2	1
%delivered as promised	67	65	68	72	65	69	44	80	68	63	57	63	79	66	62	77	71	72
%Accuracy of shipment	98	99	98	97	98	96	99	99	99	96	98	97	93	96	95	95	97	97
%OTIF	58	54	61	65	65	64	38	79	67	54	42	52	56	57	56	72	56	68

Figure 9.117   Sales Offices' Customer Service Performance.

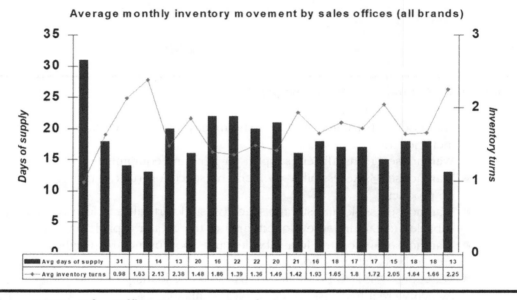

Figure 9.118   Sales Offices' Inventory Levels.

didn't have a Sales and Operations Planning process. They had two major monthly planning processes (see Figure 9.120):

■ Monthly sales target planning at the beginning of the month, and a review at month end.
■ Monthly production forecast mid-month after acknowledging sales target, and reviewed at month end.

And there were obvious issues with the planning and forecasting-processes:

■ Forecast frequently adjusted – no commitment and no information prior to adjustment (forecasting info of little use to supply management, inventory-management, or manufacturing):
  – Forecast accuracy was adjusted at the month-end period.

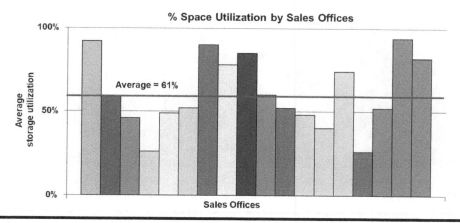

Figure 9.119   Sales Offices' Space Utilization.

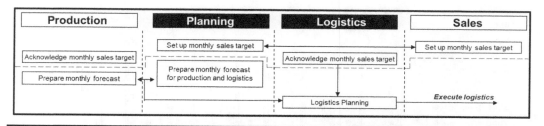

Figure 9.120   Overview of Sales-Planning Process.

- Current first-cut forecast accuracy 55–60% (by comparing first esti-
  mation against actual sales for the past 12 months).
- Adjusted forecast accuracy approximately 86% at closing period.
■ Different level of information from the whole planning processes:
- Production drives requirement items/week.
- Sales drive requirement brand/month.
- Planning drives brand/region.
- Logistics drives items/day.
■ Poor information flow when there were any changes in planning, pro-
motion, etc.

As discussed in Chapter 8. We use the Triple-Play chart to show the synchronization between sales, inventory, and production.
  See Figures 9.121 and 9.122.

■ These charts illustrate the weekly relationship between sales, inven-
tory, and production over a 12-month period.
■ Overall, the inventory levels seem acceptable.
■ However, the inventory profile, especially for the fast-moving
SKU (Figure 9.121), shows periods of stockout and long buildup
periods

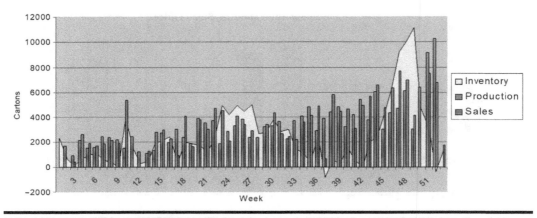

Figure 9.121   Triple-Play Chart – an "A" Product: Example #1.

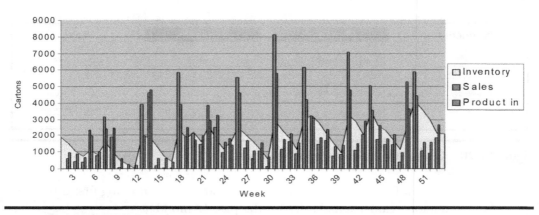

Figure 9.122   Triple-Play Chart – an "A" Product: Example #2.

Figure 9.123 and 9.124 show the inventory fluctuations across all sales offices for two separate "A" products. All of the offices show periods of very low stock levels and many periods of stockouts, and with these being "A" products, that is a very concerning situation. This is especially the case since we already stated that 68% of the current overall inventory holdings are "A" products.

Further, from the charts, we note that:

- The pattern of stock-balances (and stockouts) is consistent at most offices, especially the product charted in Figure 9.123.
- Some sales offices received a daily allocation/delivery of stock, which should prevent any stockouts at those locations.
- And the lack of stock allocations to some locations results in a higher probability of stockouts.

The causes of these stock-level variations and the stockouts at the sales offices were attributable to:

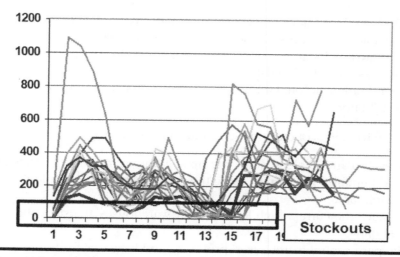

Figure 9.123   Sales Offices' Inventory Levels for an "A" Product: Example #1.

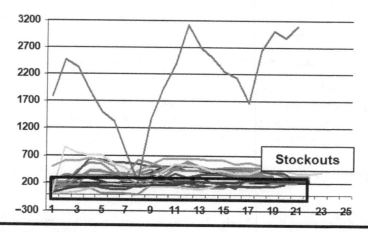

Figure 9.124   Sales Offices' Inventory Levels for an "A" Product: Example #2.

- Transport delays from the central warehouses.
- Unpredictable customer demand.
- Misallocation of stock (i.e., poor planning and/or a lack of responsiveness in replenishing stock).

This initial assessment and analysis led to a secondary "Consolidate Warehouse Project." The earlier assessment identified the following opportunities:

- Too much material handling between (and within) warehouses.
- Poor utilization of space (e.g., vertical space).
- Obsolete materials stored everywhere (not segregated and quarantined).
- Damaged inventory.
- FIFO schemes were difficult to follow.

- Dedicated inventory and space for prime customer were inefficient.
- Multiple warehouses and storage locations, i.e., four central warehouses plus two regional warehouses (in addition to the 18 sales offices that process 70% of all sales).
- Trend of key account customers moving to receiving through their distribution centers.

The objective and scope of this secondary project were:

- Develop and implement an interim solution to maximize service levels and minimize lead times, using the current structure of multiple central warehouses.
- Reduce the current high level of inter-warehouses' transfers and handling.
- Prepare central warehouses' processes and locations for future demand-pull implementation.
- Warehouses in scope of development and implementation of this project were three of the central warehouses (No. 1, 2, and 3) and both regional warehouses.

The current warehouse network had the following key problems:

- Duplicate handling of products.
- Inappropriate racking and warehouse facilities.
- Poor stock-management, e.g., FIFO was not practiced.
- Excessive inventory (especially the "A" products).

The proposed future state of the warehouse network should be characterized by:

- One directional flow (both physical and information); current flows are erratic, without structure or purpose
- Replenishment scheme for "A" products primarily routed through central warehouses No. 1 and 2.
- Substantial reduction in inventory through production synchronization and demand replenishment.
- Improve current infrastructure for better utilization and control of stock.
- Reengineer processes for better control of transfer schedules and transportation performance.
- Better inventory-management to reduce transfers between warehouses to result in less cost and elimination of in-transit damage.
- Seventeen of the sales offices would be put on a milk-run schedule to ensure repetitive and efficient deliveries and transfers.
- Products are clearly stored in specific locations; visual management of stock levels and preservation activities.

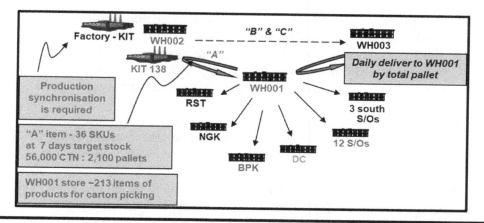

Figure 9.125   Future-State Warehouse Network.

Figure 9.125 reflects the future-state warehouse network.

Figure 9.126 reflects the future-state milk run to serve 17 of the sales offices. Milk runs are routine, scheduled deliveries and pick-ups. Milk runs are consistent and therefore easier to plan and control than random deliveries.

The challenges (a.k.a. barriers) to the transformation of the warehouse network were:

- The current goals of manufacturing are high machine utilization, long runtimes, etc. (i.e., anti-Lean), which conflict with the objectives of reducing "A" product days-on-hand (e.g., shorter lead times, production

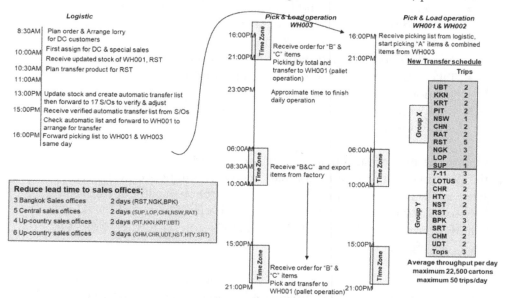

Figure 9.126   Sales-Office Milk-Run Scheme

equal demand (no overproduction), single-piece flow (small lots), etc.). Ideally, all goals should be integrated and consistent.

■ Similarly, sales goals and measurement points were obstacles as "month-end spiking" was occurring, which reduced the total number of "A" SKUs that can go directly from the factory to warehouse #1.

■ On-time service levels of transport companies must be consistently measured, as on-time performance would be critical to achieving the new warehouse-network design. Currently, performance levels are randomly monitored.

■ Export products in warehouse #2 were consuming valuable warehouse space, and the proposed new warehouse-network transformation includes shifting their stocking locations to warehouse #3. There was internal disagreement with this portion of the proposal.

The benefits to be obtained by the warehouse-network transformation were:

■ More efficient warehouse operations:
  – Improved racking (better use of vertical space).
  – Elimination of an inefficient warehouse which did not promote best-practice warehousing processes:
    • Poor aisle-ways (FIFO was difficult).
    • Poor lighting.
    • Loading and unloading unprotected from weather.
    • Dusty environment.
■ Reduction in transfers and improved overall customer service:
  – Move product directly from factory to central warehouses.
■ All warehousing resources centrally located.
■ Ability to optimize carton-picking operations.
■ Take actions to mitigate negative impact from flooding at warehouse locations.
■ Improved truck loading and unloading with installation of new loading docks, etc.

One of the major issues that was uncovered during the assessment was the poor material flow at the primary "central" warehouse. A-B-C items were, collectively, randomly stored in the warehouse without regard to the frequency of pulls/putaways, resulting in excessive travel by "A" items. The new layout, see Figure 9.127, has all "A"s stored together, closest to the receiving-shipping docks, i.e., minimizing their travel distance and travel time.

After most of the aforementioned issues had been addressed and improvement opportunities implemented, the projected composite savings were:

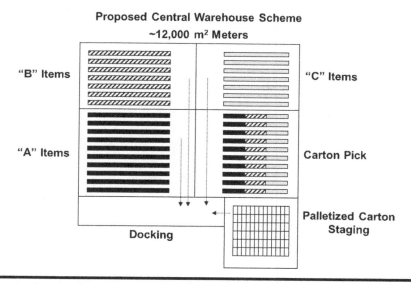

Figure 9.127   Proposed Central Warehouse Scheme.

- One-time reduction inventory = US $2.4 million.
- Annualized operating savings = US $0.6 million.
- Further consolidation of the sales offices will result in an additional annualized savings of US $2.0 million.

Conclusion

This concludes the case-in-point examples, as well as the end of the book.

I hope that these case-in-point examples give you a structure for undergoing your own supply-chain optimization/improvement initiatives, and I hope that the results achieved by the various companies in these examples (and the more than 30 other examples in this book) inspire you and your organization to improve your supply chain's performance and thus improve your overall competitiveness.

And finally, I hope this book has taken you from the theoretical aspects of optimizing your supply chain to understanding the practical steps to assess and improve your company's supply-chain strategy and execution capabilities

End Note

1. Little's Law states that your process lead time is equal to your work-in-process inventory divided by the process's exits rate (or takt-rate).

Index

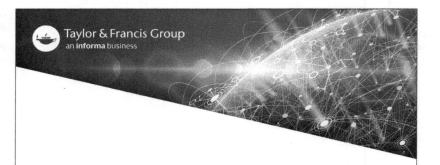